GERMAN IS FUN

BOOK 2

Lively Lessons for Advancing Students

Margrit Diehl

German Language Educator
Syracuse, NY

AMSCO

Amsco School Publications, Inc.,
a division of Perfection Learning®

Cover and Text Design: Merrill Haber

Compositor: Initial Graphics Systems Inc.

Cover Photo from; Westlight® / Neuschwanstein Castle, Germany

Part Opening Photos: Stock Market / Toy Store

Stock Market / Bicycle Rider

Image Bank / Family Group

Comstock / Teacher in Classroom

Please visit our Web sites at: *www.amscopub.com* and *www.perfectionlearning.com*

When ordering this book, please specify;
either **13750** *or*
GERMAN IS FUN, BOOK 2

ISBN 978-1-56765-403-5
NYC Item 56765-403-6

Copyright © 1999 by Amsco School Publications, Inc.,
a division of Perfection Learning®
No part of this book may be reproduced in any form
without written permission from the publisher.

Printed in the United States of America

7 8 9 10 11 PP 26 25 24 23 22

Preface

GERMAN IS FUN, BOOK 2 provides a lively, communicative course for the study of German. Topics such as family and friends, sports, hobbies, vacations, pets, school, snack foods, and clothes are useful and interesting to young people, motivating them to talk about their own lives and experiences, tastes and interests. The activities are varied, fun, and communicative and often require students to use critical thinking skills such as categorizing, sequencing, deducing, analyzing, and interpreting. There are many opportunities for students to work in pairs and in groups, to play games, do projects, and participate in hands-on activities that will help them to really internalize vocabulary and structure.

GERMAN IS FUN, BOOK 2 consists of four parts. Each part has five chapters followed by a review chapter. In the review chapter there is a summary of structure introduced in the preceding five chapters, games, activities, and exercises to review both vocabulary and structure; and proficiency activities for each of the four skills: speaking, listening, reading, and writing.

Structure and vocabulary introduced in GERMAN IS FUN, BOOK I are systematically reviewed in the first chapters of BOOK 2. They are reintroduced throughout the book and integrated with new structure and vocabulary so that students are constantly reinforcing and building on what they have already learned.

GERMAN IS FUN, BOOK 2 has several new elements:

- Vocabulary is introduced in a real context, for example a menu, a travel poster, an excerpt from a TV schedule.

- Exercises and activities are presented in context and many activities are communicative, providing opportunities for partner and group work.

- Each chapter includes suggestions for individual and/or group projects.

- Each chapter has a listening activity.

- Each chapter has a vocabulary list with words and expressions students need to know, followed by vocabulary-building activities and games to practice new vocabulary in fun and meaningful ways.

- Each of the four review chapters includes a section with proficiency activities in each of the four skills.

The chapters in GERMAN IS FUN, BOOK 2 introduce vocabulary and structure in context. The write-in format of the book enables students to "think along." Through illustrations, appealing examples in context, and activities, students are carefully guided and led to observe, analyze, and come to conclusions. They are not just presented with English translations and grammar rules but are required to actively participate in their own learning. Engaging students in this way sparks their interest and makes them much more likely to remember what they are learning. The chapters contain the following elements:

Vocabulary

New vocabulary is introduced in a real context with illustrations and activities to establish meaning. Topics have been chosen that young people can relate to, and these topics yield a vocabulary that is useful and high-frequency. To be proficient in another language, students must learn vocabulary. GERMAN IS FUN, BOOK 2 provides many exercises, activities, games, and projects to practice vocabulary in various ways that are fun and interesting. It is hoped that students will enjoy participating and be motivated to learn and use German.

Structure

In GERMAN IS FUN, BOOK 2, students learn the structure they need to communicate. The topics have been carefully matched with the structure so that students practice in natural situations, often not even realizing that they are practicing "grammar." New structure is presented in context and students are guided in observing and discovering the structure for themselves, a process that results in better understanding and real learning.

Exercises and Activities

Students are provided with a variety of exercises and activities to practice listening, speaking, reading, and writing. Most exercises are in a context and many have visual cues. As students begin their practice, they will find that the exercises are structured and directed. Then they gradually become freer and more open-ended as students gain the confidence and facility that comes with practice.

Conversation

There are many opportunities for conversation. The students progress from directed pair work to free conversation. The personalized questions in each chapter guide the students in relating the topic to their own experiences. They work together to prepare and present dialogs and little scenes. They do interviews and present information about themselves and their classmates. The book contains many suggestions for oral presentations as well.

Reading

GERMAN IS FUN, BOOK 2, exposes students to many kinds of reading. They read dialogues and stories, fables and proverbs, jokes and advertisements, newspaper articles and recipes, excuse notes and TV schedules, maps and menus. They learn to recognize cognates and use reading strategies to help their comprehension.

Writing

Writing practice in GERMAN IS FUN, BOOK 2 ranges from patterned responses and cloze activities where students are required to fill in a word or phrase to compositions, letters, invitations, and thank-you notes. Personalized questions require them to write about their own interests, experiences, and opinions; games require them to make vocabulary cards and write out structural cues; class projects suggest writing articles for a class newspaper, designing a travel poster, drawing and labeling a map of one's neighborhood or writing a children's book in German, among other things.

Culture

Each chapter ends with a culture page that gives information about life in the German-speaking countries. Culture pages include recipes, songs, proverbs, and maps. Many pages have questions and activities to encourage students to think about how German culture compares with their own.

Teacher's Manual

The *Teacher's Manual and Answer Key* includes Quizzes for all lessons, Unit Tests for all parts, and two Achievement Tests.

Contents

Dritter Teil

Vierter Teil

1
Erster Teil

1

Die Schule beginnt

Reviewing:
Definite and Indefinite Articles;
Noun Plurals; *kein*;
Nominative and Accusative Cases

1 Wortschatz

Alles für die Schule!

1. Bleistifte DM 1, - -
2. Kulis DM 4, - -
3. Hefte DM 1, - -
4. Taschenrechner DM 20, - -
5. Lineale DM 2, - -
6. Schultaschen DM 24, - -
7. Wörterbücher in Deutsch-Englisch, Englisch-Deutsch DM 14, - -

Unsere Top-Hits—jetzt im Angebot!

1. Turnhosen DM 10,50
2. Sweatshirts DM 25, - -
3. T-Shirts DM 8,90
4. Turnschuhe DM 39,95

2 The phrase **es gibt** means *there is* or *there are*. Look at the store window on the preceding page and write all the things there are to buy.

Was gibt es alles zu kaufen? Es gibt Bleistifte, _____

_____

_____

_____

3 Do you remember how to read prices in German? When you see **DM 1,50** you say **eine Mark fünfzig**; DM 9,95 is expressed **neun Mark fünfundneunzig**; DM 0,50 is **fünfzig Pfennig**. Work with a partner and ask each other what the items pictured in the store window on pages 4 and 5 cost.

BEISPIEL: Du   Was kosten die Bleistifte?
            Partner   Die Bleistifte kosten eine Mark.

4 Look at the following list of nouns. What do the words that precede the nouns mean? What do they tell you about the noun?

der Bleistift, -e	der Taschenrechner
das Heft, -e	das T-Shirt, -s
der Kuli, -s	die Turnhose, -n
das Lineal, -e	der Turnschuh, -e
die Schultasche, -n	das Wörterbuch, ¨er
das Sweatshirt, -s	

You have learned that German nouns are grouped into three classes or genders: masculine, feminine, and neuter. The words **der, die,** or **das** preceding the noun tell you its class or gender. **Der** is _____, **die** is _____, and **das** is _____. They are called definite articles and they all mean *the*. In English there is just one definite article. In German there are three.

Remember that the term gender used in this way is grammatical. Although male persons are usually masculine (**der Vater, der Junge**) and female persons are usually feminine (**die Mutter, die Lehrerin**), some female persons are grammatically neuter (**das Mädchen, das Fräulein**)—and all the many inanimate objects and abstract ideas referred to as "it" in English may be masculine, feminine, or neuter in German. It is therefore very important to learn the definite article along with each noun as you study vocabulary.

Fill in the definite article and the English meaning for each noun.

MASCULINE	FEMININE	NEUTER
____ Vater _____	____ Mutter _____	____ Mädchen _____
____ Bleistift _____	____ Schultasche _____	____ Buch _____
____ Lehrer _____	____ Turnhose _____	____ Kind _____
____ Kuli _____	____ Lehrerin _____	____ Heft _____

Now see if you can remember what the following things are called in German. Don't forget to write the definite article.

1. _____

2. _____

3. _____

4. _____

5. _____

6. _____

7. _____

8. _____

9. _____

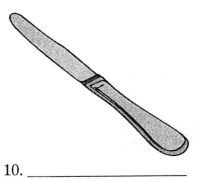

10. _____

5 The words listed on page 5 appear the way they do in the dictionary section at the back of this book. Each entry tells you the gender of the noun and how the plural is formed. You must learn the plural form of each noun along with the definite article.

The plural definite article for all three genders is **die**.

Here is a chart to help you remember how German nouns form their plurals. Most German nouns form their plurals in one of five ways. As you can see, some nouns add endings in the plural, some add endings and/or an umlaut. (Only the vowels **a, o, u**, and the diphthong **au** can take an umlaut. If a noun has an umlaut in the singular, it keeps it in the plural.) Continue the chart by filling in the rest of the words listed on page 5.

	1	2	3	4	5
ENDING	——	-e	¨er	-(e)n	-s
UMLAUT	sometimes	sometimes	always (if possible)	never	never
	der Lehrer die Lehrer	der Bleistift die Bleistifte	das Buch die Bücher	die Schule die Schulen	der Kuli die Kulis

6 Other words can precede a noun instead of the definite article. These words, called determiners, make things clearer. For example, they indicate or determine whether you are referring to *this* book or *that* book, to *my* book or to *your* book, or maybe just to *any* book.

Another one of these determiners you have learned is the indefinite article **ein**, *a, an.* The masculine and neuter form is **ein**, the feminine form is **eine**. There is no plural form of **ein**. You have to use words like **einige**, *some,* and **mehrere**, *several.*

Turn back to the picture of the store window on pages 3 and 4. Work with a partner. You ask what each item costs, your partner answers. Use indefinite articles.

> BEISPIEL: Du   Was kostet ein Bleistift?
> Partner   Ein Bleistift kostet eine Mark.

Was brauchst du noch für die Schule?

The fall term is about to begin. Two friends are discussing what they will still need to buy for school.

SILVIA: Du, Nikki, hast du schon alles für die Schule?

NIKKI: Nein, ich brauche noch ein paar Sachen.

SILVIA: Was brauchst du noch?

NIKKI: Hm, ich brauche einen Taschenrechner für Mathe, ein Wörterbuch für Englisch und—was noch? Tja, meine Turnhose ist zu klein. Für Sport brauche ich eine Turnhose und auch Turnschuhe.

SILVIA: Das Kaufhaus in der Albrechtstrasse hat Schulsachen im Angebot. Ich brauche eine Schultasche. Gehen wir heute einkaufen!

NIKKI: Gute Idee. Ich kann den Taschenerchner, das Wörterbuch und die Turnhose im Kaufhaus kaufen, aber ich kaufe die Turnschuhe lieber im Sportgeschäft. Wann gehen wir? Heute Nachmittag, so um 14 Uhr?

SILVIA: Ja, prima! Also, bis dann!

ein paar Sachen *a few things*
im Angebot *on sale*
im Sportgeschäft *in the sporting goods store*
heute Nachmittag *this afternoon*

Hast du verstanden? Draw lines matching the questions and the answers.

1. Wer?   heute Nachmittag um 14 Uhr
2. Was?   Nikki und Silvia
3. Wann?   Sie brauchen Schulsachen
4. Warum?   einkaufen

Fragen zum Inhalt. Answer the questions.

1. Was braucht Nikki? _____

2. Was braucht Silvia? _____

3. Warum braucht Nikki eine Turnhose? _____

   _____

4. Warum gehen Nikki und Silvia zum Kaufhaus? _____

   _____

5. Wann gehen die Mädchen einkaufen? _____

7 Determiners such as the definite and indefinite articles give you information about the noun. Read the following two pairs of sentences:

> *Ein Taschenrechner* ist nicht teuer.
> Ich brauche *einen Taschenrechner* für die Schule.

> *Der Taschenrechner* kostet nur DM 20, - -.
> Ich nehme *den Taschenrechner* für DM 20, - -.

Name the determiner in each sentence. Why do you think the endings on the determiners in each pair of sentences are different?

In the first sentence of each pair, the noun phrase—the determiner plus the noun—is the <u>subject</u> of the sentence and is in the <u>nominative</u> case.

In the second sentence of each pair, the noun phrase is the <u>direct object</u> and in the <u>accusative</u> case.

Look at the following chart. Which articles are different in the nominative and accusative cases and which ones are the same?

	MASCULINE	FEMININE	NEUTER	PLURAL
NOMINATIVE (SUBJECT)	der ein	die eine	das ein	die ————
ACCUSATIVE (DIRECT OBJECT)	den einen			

Note that the nominative and accusative-case articles are only different when the noun is _____ singular.

Do you know how to recognize the subject and direct object in a sentence? The subject is usually what the sentence is about. If the verb indicates an action, the subject does that action. The direct object receives the action of the verb. Read the following sentences.

Der Schüler kauft das Wörterbuch.
Den Taschenrechner kauft der Schüler nicht.

In the first sentence, **der Schüler** is the _____ and **das Wörterbuch** is the _____. In the second sentence, **der Schüler** is again the _____ and **den Taschenrechner** is the _____. You see that the position in the sentence does not always tell you which is which!

Read the following sentences and write whether the italicized noun phrase is the subject of the sentence (the nominative case) or the direct object (in the accusative case).

1. **Das Sweatshirt ist teuer.** _____

2. **Kaufst du den Taschenrechner?** _____

3. **Ich brauche ein Heft.** _____

4. **Hat der Lehrer ein Wörterbuch?** _____

5. **Sabine kauft die Schultasche.** _____

6. **Das T-Shirt kauft sie nicht.** _____

ÜBUNG A

Here is Nikki's schoolbag. Write what she has in it. Don't forget to identify the indefinite article.

Was hat Nikki in der Schultasche? Sie hat…

1. _____ 4. _____

2. _____ 5. _____

3. _____ 6. _____

ÜBUNG B

In school Nikki is unpacking her school bag. Look again at the picture in Übung A and write all the items she takes out of her bag. Use definite articles.

Nikki packt die Schultasche aus. Aus der Schultasche nimmt sie…

1. _____   4. _____

2. _____   5. _____

3. _____   6. _____

8 The negative determiner **kein** means *no*, *none*, or *not any*. It has the same endings as **ein**.

	MASCULINE	FEMININE	NEUTER	PLURAL
NOMINATIVE	ein kein	eine keine	ein kein	——— keine
ACCUSATIVE	einen keinen			

Here are some more items you often need for school.

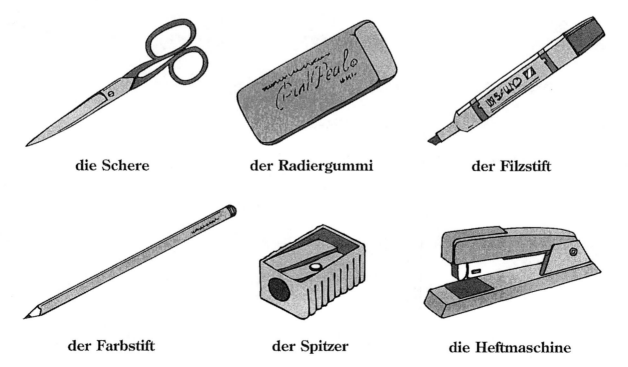

| die Schere | der Radiergummi | der Filzstift |
| der Farbstift | der Spitzer | die Heftmaschine |

Tell your teacher that you don't have the articles pictured above and ask if he or she has each one.

BEISPIEL: **Ich habe keine Schere. Haben Sie eine Schere?**

1. _____

_____

2. _____

_____

3. _____

_____

4. _____

_____

5. _____

_____

PERSÖNLICHE FRAGEN ?

1. Wo kaufst du deine Schulsachen?

_____

2. Was für Schulsachen brauchst du?

_____

3. Hat deine Schule einen Laden, wo du Schulsachen kaufen kannst? Was gibt es alles dort zu kaufen?

_____

_____

GESPRÄCH

Im Kaufhaus

Was kostet der Taschenrechner, bitte?

Der Taschenrechner kostet zwanzig Mark.

Danke.

Bitte.

Und was kostet das Wörterbuch?

Das Wörterbuch kostet vierzehn Mark.

Hm, das ist nicht zu teuer. Ich nehme den Taschenrechner und das Wörterbuch.

Schön. Du hast einen Taschenrechner für zwanzig Mark und ein Wörterbuch für vierzehn Mark. Das macht zusammen 34 Mark.

Hier sind vierzig Mark.

Vierzig Mark und sechs Mark zurück. Danke schön und auf Wiedersehen!

Bitte schön. Auf Wiedersehen.

PARTNERARBEIT

Read the dialog in the store. With a partner, write a similar dialog. Choose two different items to buy. Practice your dialog and present it to the class.

ÜBUNG C

Hör gut zu! You have been asked to put prices on the items pictured. Listen to what each item costs and draw a line matching the picture of the item with the price.

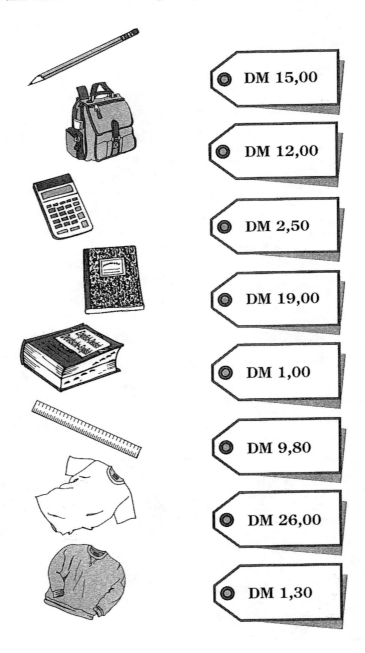

DM 15,00

DM 12,00

DM 2,50

DM 19,00

DM 1,00

DM 9,80

DM 26,00

DM 1,30

KLASSENPROJEKT

Set up a store in part of the classroom. Spread out school supplies and price them in German marks. One student is the salesperson. Take turns going into the store, asking about prices, and buying a few items.

WORTSCHATZ A-Z

die Schulsachen (pl.) *school supplies*

der Farbstift, -e *colored pencil*
der Filzstift, -e *marker*
die Heftmaschine, -n *stapler*
die Schere, -n *scissors*
die Schultasche, -n *schoolbag*
der Spitzer *pencil sharpener*

das Sweatshirt, -s *sweatshirt*
der Taschenrechner *calculator*
das T-Shirt, -s *T-shirt*
die Turnhose, -n *gym shorts*
der Turnschuh, -e *sneaker*

Diese Wörter kennst du schon

der Bleistift, -e *pencil*
das Heft, -e *notebook*
der Kuli, -s *ballpoint pen*

das Lineal, -e *ruler*
der Radiergummi, -s *eraser*
das Wörterbuch, -er *dictionary*

Gehen wir einkaufen *let's go shopping*

im Angebot *on sale*
das Kaufhaus, -er *department store*

das Sportgeschäft, -e *sporting goods store*
die Mark *mark* (German monetary unit)

Noch einige Wörter

alles *everything*
ein paar *a few*

heute *today*
heute nachmittag *this afternoon*

Und so sagst du das *Here's how to...*

say what's there, what's available

es gibt *there is, there are*

ask how much something costs

Was kostet... ? *How much does . . . cost? How much is . . . ?*
Was kosten... ? *How much do . . . cost? How much are . . . ?*

express need

Ich brauche... *I need . . .*
Ich habe schon... *I already have . . .*
Ich brauche noch... *I still need . . .*

say please, thank you, and you are welcome

Bitte *Please*
Danke or Danke schön *Thank you* or *Thanks.*
Bitte or Bitte schön *You're welcome.*

Building your vocabulary

Write the compound words you can form. What do they mean in English?

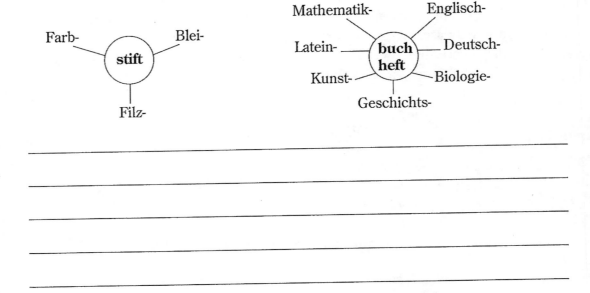

_____

_____

_____

_____

_____

ÜBUNG **D**

Memory-Spiel: Was hast du in der Schultasche?

How long can you and your classmates keep this game going?

In meiner Schultasche habe ich... ein Deutschbuch.
In meiner Schultasche habe ich... ein Deutschbuch und einen Kuli.
In meiner Schultasche habe ich... ein Deutschbuch, einen Kuli und . . .

KULTURECKE

Das deutsche Geld

German money has bills and coins.

Die Scheine	**Die Münzen**
5-Mark-Schein	ein-Pfennig-Stück
10-Mark-Schein	zwei-Pfennig-Stück
20-Mark-Schein	fünf-Pfennig-Stück
50-Mark-Schein	zehn-Pfennig-Stück
100-Mark-Schein	fünfzig-Pfennig-Stück
500-Mark-Schein	eine-Mark-Stück
1000-Mark-Schein	fünf-Mark-Stück
	(100 Pfennig = eine Mark)

You have 150 marks. Look at the ads. What would you like to buy?

CDs   DM 25,00

Toni Braxton
Peter Andre
Dune
Spice Girls
No Mercy
Backstreet Boys
'N Sync

CD-Rack
DM 52,00

Inline-Skates
DM 149,50

Schüler-Rucksack
DM 14,99

Leder-Fussball
DM 39,00

2

In der Freizeit

Reviewing:
Verbs, Present Tense;
Verbs with Stem Vowel Changes:
gern, nicht gern

1 Wortschatz

Umfrage: Was machst du in der Freizeit?

Was machen junge Leute in der Freizeit? Lies die Umfrage und kreuze an (x), was du alles machst!

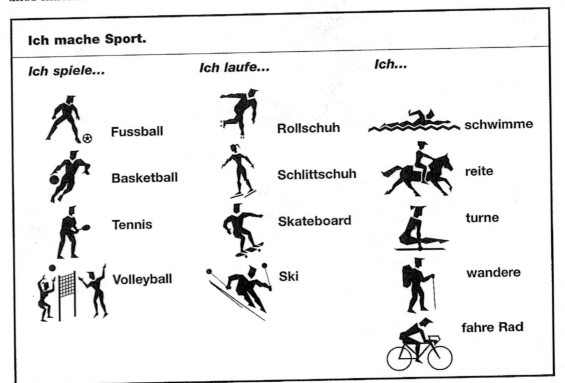

Ich mache Sport.		
Ich spiele...	*Ich laufe...*	*Ich...*
Fussball	Rollschuh	schwimme
Basketball	Schlittschuh	reite
Tennis	Skateboard	turne
Volleyball	Ski	wandere
		fahre Rad

Ich habe Hobbys.

Ich sammle...

 Briefmarken

 Comic-Hefte

 Münzen

 CDs

Ich...

 zeichne

 höre Musik

 bastle

 sehe fern

 lese

 spiele Videospeile

 fotografiere

 spiele Computerspiele

Ich spiele ein Instrument. Ich spiele...

 Klavier

 Gitarre

 in einem Orchester

 Geige

 Keyboard

 in einer Band

 Flöte

 Schlagzeug

 Trompete

 Bass

Und was noch? Ich spiele...

 Schach

 Karten

 Monopoly

2 In sports and music, German has taken over many words from English. On the survey you just filled out you can find many examples. Words that are the same or almost the same in German and English are called cognates. Some are spelled exactly the same way, some are spelled a little differently. List all the cognates that are in the survey.

_____

_____

_____

What do you think a false cognate is? There is one in the survey. A false cognate is a word that looks the same in both languages but does not have the same meaning. The word **wandern** can mean _to wander_ or _to roam_, but that's not what it means as it is used here on the survey. Here _wandern_ means _____.

ÜBUNG A

Erzähle, was du alles machst! Look at the survey and write all the things you checked off.

Ich _____

_____

_____

ÜBUNG B

What goes together? Choose the appropriate verb and complete the phrases.

laufen   sammeln   spielen

1. Briefmarken _____

2. Gitarre _____

3. Rollschuh _____

4. Fussball _____

5. Schach _____

6. Ski _____

ÜBUNG C

All the sports and hobbies got mixed together. Sort them out and write them on the appropriate list.

Basketball	Geige	Schach	Tennis
basteln	Gitarre	Schlagzeug	Trompete
Briefmarken sammeln	Karten	schwimmen	turnen
fotografieren	Klavier	Skateboard laufen	Videospiele
Fussball	Monopoly	Ski laufen	zeichnen

Sport

_____

_____

_____

_____

_____

Spiel

_____

_____

_____

_____

Hobby

_____

_____

_____

_____

Instrument

_____

_____

_____

_____

ÜBUNG D

Which sports do you usually do in each season? Write the sports in the appropriate space.

Frühling

_____

_____

_____

Sommer

_____

_____

_____

Winter

_____

_____

_____

Herbst

_____

_____

_____

3 Write sentences telling what you do in each season. Remember, if a word or phrase other than the subject begins the sentence, you must use inverted word order.

Regular word order: *Ich spiele* im Frühling Tennis.
Inverted word order: **Im Frühling** *spiele ich Tennis.*

In the first sentence the subject comes _____ the verb. In the second sentence the subject comes _____ the verb. In both sentences, the verb is in second position.

Im Frühling spiele ich…

_____

Im Sommer spiele ich…

_____

Im Herbst spiele ich…

_____

Im Winter spiele ich…

_____

DIALOG

At the beginning of the school year you catch up with people you haven't seen all summer. What are Karin and Robert talking about?

ROBERT: Du, Karin, spielst du immer noch so viel Tennis?
KARIN: Ja, ich spiele sehr viel. Spielst du auch?
ROBERT: Ab und zu. Meine Freundin, die Julia, spielt gern. Wir spielen manchmal zusammen.
KARIN: Wo spielt ihr?
ROBERT: In der Parkstrasse. Dort gibt es einen schönen Tennisplatz.
KARIN: Kennst du Felix und Peter? Sie spielen immer in der Parkstrasse.
ROBERT: Ja, ich weiss. Wir spielen manchmal zu viert.

immer noch *still*
ab und zu *now and then*
zusammen *together*
zu viert *the four of us*

Robert and Karin are talking about _____. What verb do they use?
_____ Reread the dialog and underline the verb **spielen** each time it appears. What do you notice about the endings? Why are they different?

_____

Which two are the same? _____

4 The endings on German verbs change to match the subject, or you could say to agree with the subject. Fill in the forms of **spielen** that are used with each subject pronoun. Do you remember what the pronouns mean?

spielen   *to play*

ich _____   wir _____

du _____   ihr _____

er ⎱
Robert ⎰ _____   sie ⎱
                                     Robert und Karin ⎰ _____

sie ⎱
Karin ⎰ _____

das Kind ⎱
es ⎰ _____   Sie _____

All verbs have a base form called an _____: **spielen,** *to play;* **machen,** *to do, to make;* **schwimmen,** *to swim.* The infinitive, or the *to*-form of the verb, is the form that is used on vocabulary lists and in dictionaries.

Verbs in German have a stem and an ending. The infinitive ending is **-en** or sometimes just **-n.** Complete the chart, filling in the verb stem and infinitive ending for each verb.

INFINITIVE	STEM	ENDING
spielen	spiel-	-en
basteln	bastel-	-n
hören		
schwimmen		
reiten		
laufen		
sammeln		
fotografieren		
wandern		

When you use a verb in a sentence, you take off the infinitive ending and add the ending that matches the subject. Complete the following paragraph by adding the correct ending to each verb stem.

Die Lehrerin frag_____ die Schüler: «Was mach_____ ihr gern in der Freizeit?» «Ich spiel_____ gern Fussball», sag_____ Michael. «Ich auch», sag_____ Jenny. «Spiel_____ ihr mit den Jungen zusammen?» «Nein, wir hab_____ ein Team mit nur Mädchen. Wir spiel_____ gut, und wir gewinn_____ oft das Spiel!»

ÜBUNG E

Write what everyone does. Be sure the verb ending matches the subject!

BEISPIEL:　　**Michael spielt Fussball.**

1. Ich _____.

2. Wir _____.

3. Alle Schüler _____.

4. Du _____.

5. Ihr _____.

6. Julia _____.

7. Susanne und Thomas _____.

8. Du _____.

5 Look at the following verb forms. What can you observe about the endings?

finden *to find; to think*	**reiten** *to ride* (a horse)
du findest er/sie findet ihr findet	du reitest er/sie reitet ihr reitet

When the verb stem ends in **-d** or **-t**, the **du**-form ends in _____; the **er-**, **sie-**, **es-**form and the **ihr**-form end in _____.

Now look at these verbs that end in an s-sound.

heissen *to be called*	**tanzen** *to dance*
du heisst	du tanzt

The **du**-form only adds _____, not **-st**.

And here is one more thing to take note of.

basteln *to do crafts*	**sammeln** *to collect*
ich bastle *but* du bastelst	ich sammle *but* du sammelst

Verbs ending in **-eln** drop the stem's **-e-** in the **ich**-form — but only in the **ich**-form.

Now write the infinitive and fill in the missing forms in the chart.

INFINITIVE				
ich	arbeite			
du				
er/Robert sie/Karin		sammelt		
wir				heissen
ihr				
sie/Robert und Karin				
Sie			finden	

ÜBUNG F

Karin is talking about her sports and hobbies.

This is what she says: *This is what she does:*

BEISPIEL: (turnen)   **Ich turne.**   **Sie turnt.**

(basteln)   **Ich** _____   Sie _____

(wandern)   _____   _____

(fotografieren)   _____   _____

(reiten)   _____   _____

When Peter and Stefan talk about their sports and hobbies,

This is what they say: *This is what they do:*

(zeichnen)   **Wir** _____   Sie _____

(Videospiele spielen)   _____   _____

(Comic-Hefte sammeln)   _____   _____

(Ski laufen)   _____   _____

(schwimmen)   _____   _____

6 Here are some verbs you have seen before. Read the sentences. Do you remember
what the verbs mean?

Ich *laufe* gern Ski.
Meine Freundin *läuft* auch gern Ski.

Wir *fahren* immer Rad.
Fährst du auch immer Rad?

Ich *lese* viel.
Mein Bruder *liest* nicht viel.

Ich *sehe* zu viel fern.
Du *siehst* auch zu viel fern.

Ich *esse* gern Pizza.
Du *isst* Pizza nicht gern?

There are a number of verbs in German that have a stem vowel change. Draw a slash
between the stem and the ending in the above example. Now underline the stem
vowel(s) in each verb.

Verbs that have stem vowel changes follow specific patterns. The vowel change
occurs in the **du**-form and the **er/sie**-form. Fill in the forms below. Write the verbs
in the appropriate column.

	essen	geben	schlafen	tragen
	fahren	laufen	sehen	vergessen
	fallen	lesen	sprechen	waschen
	fressen	nehmen		

	e → i	e → ie	a → ä	au → äu
infinitive	**essen**	_____	_____	_____
du	_____	_____	_____	_____
er/sie	_____	_____	_____	_____
infinitive	_____	_____	_____	_____
du	_____	_____	_____	_____
er/sie	_____	_____	_____	_____
infinitive	_____	_____	_____	_____
du	_____	_____	_____	_____
er/sie	_____	_____	_____	_____
infinitive	_____	_____	_____	_____
du	_____	_____	_____	_____
er/sie	_____	_____	_____	_____
infinitive	_____	_____	_____	_____
du	_____	_____	_____	_____
er/sie	_____	_____	_____	_____

What can you observe about the verb **nehmen**? — The verb **nehmen** also has a consonant change: in the **du**-form and in the **er/sie**-form, the _____ is dropped and an _____ is added.

ÜBUNG G

Ja oder nein? Write questions with the following phrases. Then write an answer. Follow the example.

BEISPIEL: **gut Deutsch sprechen**

Sprichst du gut Deutsch?　　　**Ja, ich spreche gut Deutsch.**
OR
Nein, ich spreche nicht gut Deutsch.

1. viel lesen

_____

_____

2. Ski laufen

_____

_____

3. gut schlafen

_____

_____

4. die Hausaufgaben manchmal vergessen

_____

_____

5. oft Pizza essen

_____

_____

ÜBUNG **H**

Use the phrases in the preceding activity and write questions addressing two people. Also write an answer.

BEISPIEL: **gut Deutsch sprechen**

Sprecht ihr gut Deutsch?   **Ja, wir sprechen gut Deutsch.**
OR
Nein, wir sprechen nicht gut Deutsch.

1. _____

   _____

2. _____

   _____

3. _____

   _____

4. _____

   _____

5. _____

   _____

7 Do you remember how to say if you like something or not? You use the phrase **gern haben**. The forms of **haben** are regular except for the **du**-form and the **er/sie**-form, so it will be easy for you to supply the missing forms below. The verb **haben** means *to have*; the phrase **gern haben** means *to like*.

ich _____	wir _____
du hast	ihr _____
er/sie } es } hat	sie, Sie _____

Practice using the phrase **gern haben**. Read the following list and place a check mark (✓) next to what you like, an *X* next to what you don't like. Report to the class, adding items if you would like.

<table>
<tr><td>**Deutsch**</td><td>**Volleyball**</td><td>**Videospiele**</td></tr>
<tr><td>**Mathe**</td><td>**Tennis**</td><td>**Techno-Musik**</td></tr>
</table>

Ich habe... gern.
Ich habe... nicht gern.

8 You can also use **gern** and **nicht gern** with specific verbs.

Was machst du gern?	**Ich spiele gern Basketball.**
Und was machst du nicht gern?	**Ich laufe nicht gern Ski.**

Look at the sports and activities on pages 18 and 19. Fill in what you like and don't like.

Use words and phrases: **Schlittschuh laufen, Tennis, Musik hören.**

NICHT GERN	GERN	SEHR GERN

PARTNERARBEIT

Interview a classmate about his or her likes and dislikes. Draw a chart like the one above to take notes and report to the class.

ÜBUNG I

Hör gut zu! You will hear a German student talk about what he likes to do and doesn't like to do. Look at the pictures below as you listen to what the student says and circle the activities he likes to do.

PERSÖNLICHE FRAGEN ?

1. Was machst du in der Freizeit? Machst du Sport? Hast du Hobbys? Spielst du ein Instrument?

   _____

   _____

2. Was machst du gern?

   _____

   _____

3. Was machst du nicht gern?

   _____

   _____

ÜBUNG J

Aufsatz. Write a paragraph telling some of the things you do in your leisure time.

_____

_____

_____

_____

_____

KLASSENPROJEKT

Make a bulletin board display with the names of class members along with their interests and hobbies. Cut out pictures of activities mentioned to use as a background collage or to illustrate each text. Include photos of each student if possible.

WORTSCHATZ A-Z

der Sport *sport(s)*

radfahern *to bicycle*
  er/sie fährt Rad *he/she bicycles*
Rollschuh *to roller skate*
  er/sie läuft Rollschuh *he/she roller skates*
Schlittschuh laufen *to ice skate*
  er/sie läuft Schlittschuh *he/she ice skates*

das Spiel, -e *game*
Sport machen *to play (do) sports*
das Team, -s *team*

Diese Wörter kennst du schon

reiten *to ride (a horse)*
schwimmen *to swim*
Ski laufen *to ski*
  er/sie läuft Ski *he/she skis*

turnen *to do gymnastics*
wandern *to hike*

das Hobby, -s *hobby*

basteln *to do crafts*
Computerspiele spielen
  to play computer games
Musik hören *to listen to music*
Videospiele spielen *to play video games*
sammeln *to collect*
die Briefmarke, -n *stamp*
die CD, -s *CD (compact disc)*
das Comic-Heft, -e *comic book*

die Münze, -n *coin*
das Instrument, -e *instrument*
der Bass, -e *bass*
die Flöte, -n *flute*
die Geige, -n *violin*
das Keyboard, -s *keyboard*
das Schlagzeug, -e *drums*
in einem Orchester *in an orchestra*
in einer Band *in a band*

Diese Wörter kennst du schon

fernsehen *to watch television*
  er/sie sieht fern *he/she watches television*
fotografieren *to photograph*
lesen *to read*
  er/sie liest *he/she reads*

zeichnen *to draw*
die Gitarre, -n *guitar*
die Klarinette, -n *clarinet*
das Klavier, -e *piano*
die Trompete, -n *trumpet*

Noch einige Wörter

ad und zu *now and then*   was noch? *what else?*
immer noch *still*   zusammen *together*

Und so sagst du das *Here's how to...*

talk about sports and hobbies

Was machst du in der Freizeit?   *What do you do in your free time?*
Machst du Sport?   *Do you do sports?*
Hast du Hobbys?   *Do you have hobbies?*
Spielst du ein Instrument?   *Do you play an instrument?*
Ich spiele...   *I play . . .*
Ich sammle...   *I collect . . .*

express likes and dislikes

Hast du Musik gern?   *Do you like music?*
Ja, ich habe Musik sehr gern.   *Yes, I like music very much.*
Was machst du gern?   *What do you like to do?*
Ich spiele gern Basketball.   *I like to play basketball.*
Was machst du nicht gern?   *What don't you like to do?*
Ich spiele nicht gern Tennis.   *I don't like to play tennis.*

Building your vocabulary

Write the compound words you can form. What do they mean in English?

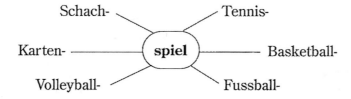

Schach-   Tennis-

Karten- ———— **spiel** ———— Basketball-

Volleyball-   Fussball-

ÜBUNG K

Detective-Spiel Try to find out the following information. Mingle with your classmates, asking questions in German. Jot down the information, then form a circle with your classmates and share your findings. You may ask your teacher also.

Finde...

    a. eine Person, die Schach spielt
    b. zwei Personen, die Basketball spielen
    c. eine Person, die nicht Tennis spielt
    d. eine Person, die Klavier spielt
    e. eine Person, die Briefmarken sammelt
    f. drei Personen, die gern tanzen

KULTURECKE

Young people in Germany participate in all kinds of sports and activities. They belong to clubs and have many different hobbies and interests. Sports are extremely popular—everything from soccer, volleyball, tennis, and skiing to more unusual sports such as hang gliding, windsurfing, and snowboarding. Many currently popular activities come from the USA: skateboarding, rollerblading, American football, baseball, and streetball or **Strassen-Basketball**.

In Germany many young people join clubs to pursue their interests. There are hunting and fishing clubs, rowing and sailing clubs, hiking clubs, computer clubs, and model railroading clubs, just to mention a few. Many young people are involved in music. They play in orchestras or community bands, they sing in choruses, and, of course, there are many who form their own rock groups.

Read the following newspaper article about a fast-growing sport in Germany. How many words can you recognize from English?

Streetball — ein neuer Trend

Hamburg — Der amerikanische Sporttrend Streetball wird in Deutschland immer mehr populär. Die Strassen-Basketball-Saison beginnt im April und endet im Oktober mit den Deutschen Streetball-Meisterschaften. Es gibt in Deutschland schon eine Million Fans. Man braucht nicht viel, um Streetball zu spielen: drei Spieler pro Team, einen Ball und einen Korb. Ganz einfach! Am 24./25. September machte in Hamburg die amerikanische Profiliga NBA die «3-gegen-3-Welttournee» mit mehr als 700 Teams und 2800 Spieler. Es ist eine richtige Massenbewegung! NBA-Manager David Stern erklärte dazu:«Wir fühlen uns verpflichtet, den Basketball in Europa zu fördern».

3

Familie und Freunde

Reviewing:
Possessive Adjectives;
Interrogatives;
Countries, Nationalities, and Languages

1 Wortschatz

Stefan zeigt sein Fotoalbum

meine Eltern

meine Geschwister:
mein Bruder Matthias
und meine Schwester Gabi

Gabi und ihr Pferd Micki

unser Hund,
der Schnappsi

unser Haus
unser Garten

unser Wagen

meine Grosseltern
auf ihrem Bauernhof
in Österreich

ihre Katze,
die Mietze

mein Onkel Karl und
meine Tante Ilse
mein Vetter Franz und
meine Kusine Isabel

meine Freunde:
Susi, Beatrice, Philipp,
Milo

Philipp mit seinem
Skateboard

12. Mai
Milos Geburtstagsparty

ÜBUNG A

Look at the pictures from Stefan's photo album and answer the questions.

1. Wie heisst Stefans Bruder?

_____

2. Wie heisst seine Schwester?

_____

3. Was macht seine Schwester gern?

_____

4. Wer ist Schnappsi?

_____

5. Wer ist Philipp?

_____

6. Was macht er gern?

_____

7. Wo wohnen Stefans Grosseltern?

_____

8. Wie heisst ihre Katze?

_____

9. Wer ist Schnappsi?

_____

10. Wann hat Milo Geburtstag?

_____

2 Etwas mehr über meine Familie und Freunde

Das sind meine Eltern. Meine Mutter heisst Erika. Sie arbeitet immer viel im Garten. Meine Mutter liebt ihre Blumen. Sie ist auch sehr musikalisch. Sie spielt Geige in einem Orchester. Mein Vater heisst Paul. Er ist sehr sportlich. Er spielt Golf, Tennis und Squash.

Hier siehst du meinen Bruder Matthias. Er ist sechzehn Jahre alt. Er spielt Gitarre. Das ist er mit seiner Rock-Band.

Das ist meine Schwester, die Gabi. Sie ist zwölf Jahre alt. Sie reitet gern. Du siehst sie hier auf ihrem Pferd.

Meine Grosseltern heissen Gustav und Maria Heinemann. Das sind die Eltern von meiner Mutter. Sie haben einen Bauernhof in Österreich. Wir besuchen sie immer im Sommer. Dort ist es sehr schön.

Mein Onkel Karl und meine Tante Ilse haben auch einen Bauernhof ganz in der Nähe. Wenn wir im Sommer kommen, sind wir oft bei ihnen. Sie haben eine Tochter, unsere Kusine Isabel, und einen Sohn, unser Vetter Franz.

Und das sind meine Freunde. Milo kommt aus Italien, aber er spricht echt gut Deutsch! Eine tolle Clique! Alle sind ganz nett und lustig.

etwas meher über *something more about*
ganz in der Nähe *very near by*
bei ihnen *at their house*
lustig *funny, fun*

3 The words **mein, dein, sein, ihr, unser, euer,** and **ihr** show possession or relationship. They are called possessive adjectives. Do you remember what they mean? Match the German and the English and write the pairs.

mein _____	sein _____		
ihr _____	ihr _____		
euer _____	dein _____		
unser _____	Ihr _____		

your (sing.)	*our*
my	*his*
your (pl.)	*their*
her	*your* (formal)

Go back to the reading in which Stefan tells about his family and friends. Underline the possessive adjectives.

Why do the possessive adjectives you underlined have different endings?

Possessive adjectives are determiners and give you information about the noun—whether it is masculine, feminine, or neuter, singular or plural, and if it is in the nominative, accusative, or dative case.

Here is a chart summarizing the endings for all possessive adjectives. These determiners take the same endings as **ein** and **kein** and are therefore often called **ein-words**.

	MASCULINE	FEMININE	NEUTER	PLURAL
NOMINATIVE	mein	meine	mein	meine
ACCUSATIVE	meinen	meine	mein	meine
DATIVE*	meinem	meiner	meinem	meinen

ÜBUNG B

There is an event at school. Who is coming? Fill in the possessive adjective that corresponds to the personal pronoun.

Wer kommt alles?
Ich und *meine* Eltern,

du und _____ Eltern,

er (Matthias) und _____ Eltern,

sie (Susi) und _____ Eltern,

wir und _____ Eltern,**

ihr und _____ Eltern,**

sie (Stefan und Gabi) und _____ Eltern,

Sie (formal) und _____ Eltern.

*You learned about the dative case in Book I. You will review it and learn more about it later in this book.

The words **unsere and **euere** can also be written **unsre** and **eure**.

ÜBUNG **C**

Here is a chart and a few more vocabulary words to help you see the relationships in Stefan's family. Look back at the pictures and fill in the names in the space provided.

Die Verwandten

Grosseltern

Grossmutter   **Grossvater**

_____   _____

Tante   **Onkel**

_____   _____

Eltern

Mutter/Frau   **Vater/Mann**

_____   _____

Kusine   **Vetter**

_____   _____

Kinder

Enkelin

_____

Tochter

_____

Schwester

_____

Nichte

_____

Enkel

_____

Sohn

_____

Bruder

_____

Neffe

_____

ÜBUNG D

Now describe how the following people are related.

BEISPIEL: **to Gabi:**

 Erika ist *ihre Mutter*.

1. to Gabi:

 Paul ist _____.

 Gustav und Maria sind _____.

 Matthias ist _____.

 Franz ist _____.

 Isabel ist _____.

2. to Karl:

 Erika ist seine _____.

 Gustav ist _____.

 Franz ist _____.

 Isabel ist _____.

 Gabi ist _____.

 Stefan ist _____.

3. to Franz und Isabel:

 Ilse ist ihre_____.

 Erika ist _____.

 Paul ist _____.

 Gabi ist _____.

 Gustav und Maria sind _____.

 Stefan ist _____.

ÜBUNG E

You are asking Stefan about the pictures in his album. Use **unser, euer, mein,** and **dein**. Write the question and Stefan's answer based on the picture.

BEISPIEL:

Ist das euer Wagen?
Ja, das ist *unser* Wagen.

1. _____

_____

2. _____

_____

3. _____

_____

4. _____

_____

Sind das deine Eltern?
Nein, das sind nicht *meine* Eltern.

5. _____

6. _____

7. _____

8. _____

4 There are two other ways in German to show possession or relationship:

> Erika ist *Gabis Mutter.*
> Erika ist die *Mutter von Gabi.*

Note that the possessive does not have an apostrophe as it does in English.

ÜBUNG F

Look at the chart again in Übung C on page 40. Write how the following people are related, expressing the relationships as they are shown in the above examples.

1. Matthias und Gabi
   Matthias ist _____.

2. Stefan und Franz _____.

3. Gustav und Isabel _____.

4. Paul und Erika _____.

5. Stefan und Erika _____.

5 As you have been looking at Stefan's album, you have asked questions about the pictures. There are different ways to ask questions in German, as there are in English. You can simply make a question out of a statement by putting a question mark at the end of the sentence instead of a period. Read the following statement and the question.

Das ist deine Schwester.   **Das ist deine Schwester?**

Notice how in the question, your voice goes up at the end.

Another way to ask a question is to invert the word order—put the verb in first position. You practiced this type of question in Übung E.

Das *ist* euer Haus.   ***Ist* das euer Haus?**

These two types of questions ask for a yes or no answer. Sometimes such questions seem to require a little more explanation beyond a simple yes or no.

Heisst dein Hund Waldi?   **Nein, er heisst Schnappsi.**

To get more specific information, you use question words, or interrogatives.

> *Wer* ist das? —Das ist mein Freund.
> *Wie* heisst er? —Milo.
> *Woher* kommt er? —Aus Italien.
> *Wie* alt ist er? —14 Jahre alt.

Make a list of question words in English, then write the German equivalents. Compare your list with the one below. Did you get them all?

wer? *who?*	**wann?** *when?*	**wohin?** *to where?*	**wie alt?** *how old?*
wen? *whom?*	**wo?** *where?*	**woher?** *from where?*	**wie viel?** *how much?*
was? *what?*	**warum?** *why?*	**wie?** *how?*	**wie viele?** *how many?*

ÜBUNG G

Match each question with the appropriate answer.

1. Wie heisst dein Bruder?   _____ Aus New York.

2. Wie alt ist er?   _____ Das ist mein Lehrer.

3. Wer ist das?   _____ Er heisst Matthias.

4. Wie viele Geschwister hast du?   _____ Es kostet zu viel Geld.

5. Wo wohnt ihr?   _____ Ich habe zwei Geschwister, eine Schwester und einen Bruder.

6. Woher kommen deine Eltern?   _____ Um 8 Uhr.

7. Wann beginnt die Schule?   _____ Vierzehn Jahre alt.

8. Wen besucht ihr diesen Sommer?   _____ Wir wohnen in der Blumenstrasse.

9. Warum fliegst du nicht nach Deutschland?   _____ Wir besuchen die Grosseltern.

ÜBUNG H

Read the following paragraph and make up five questions that can be answered by information given in the paragraph. Exchange questions with a classmate and answer each other's questions.

Hallo! Ich heisse Sabine Sahlmann. Ich bin dreizehn Jahre alt und komme aus Deutschland, aus Hamburg. Ich besuche im Sommer meine Tante in den USA. Meine Tante wohnt in New Jersey. Ich möchte New York sehen, und ich möchte Englisch lernen!

1. _____

2. _____

3. _____

4. _____

5. _____

ÜBUNG I

Here are some more pictures from Stefan's album. Write questions you could ask Stefan about them.

ÜBUNG J

Bring in pictures of your friends and family. Show them to the class. Your classmates will ask you questions and you answer.

ÜBUNG K

Hör gut zu! You will hear an interview with a student. For each question the interviewer asks, you will hear two responses. Listen carefully and determine which response answers the question. Mark the appropriate box.

Frage	1	2	3	4	5	6
Antwort A						
Antwort B						

GESPRÄCH

Stefan's friend Milo is from Italy. Stefan introduces him to another friend, Uwe. What is Uwe's connection with Italy?

STEFAN: Uwe, das ist mein Freund Milo.

UWE: Tag, Milo!

MILO: Hallo, Uwe!

UWE: Du kommst aus Italien, nicht wahr? Meine Tante ist Italienerin. Sie kommt aus Florenz.

MILO: Ja, wirklich? Meine Grosseltern wohnen in Florenz. Wir besuchen sie jeden Sommer.

UWE: Toll! Ich war noch nie in Italien. Sag mal, du sprichst sehr gut Deutsch. Wie lange bist du schon in Deutschland?

MILO: Ich bin seit vier Jahren hier.

ÜBUNG L

Woher kommen sie? Was sprechen sie? Can you complete the chart?

Land	Er ist...	Sie ist...	Sprache
1. China	Chinese	Chinesin	Chinesisch
2. _____	Deutscher	Deutsche	_____
3. England	Engländer	Engländerin	_____
4. Frankreich	Franzose	Französin	_____
5. Italien	Italiener	_____	_____
6. Japan	Japaner	_____	Japanisch
7. Mexiko	_____	Mexikanerin	_____
8. Österreich	Österreicher	_____	_____
9. die Schweiz*	Schweizer	_____	Französisch _____ Romansch*
10. Spanien	_____	Spanierin	_____
11. Vietnam	Vietnamese	Vietnamesin	Vietnamesisch

*In Switzerland there are four official languages: German, French, Italian, and Romansh, a dialect spoken in a small part of Switzerland. Romansh became the fourth official language in 1938.

ÜBUNG **M**

Do you know someone from another country? Write who that person is and where he or she comes from.

Stefan sagt: **Mein Freund Milo kommt aus Italien.**
Uwe sagt: **Meine Tante kommt auch aus Italien.**

Was sagst du?

_____

_____

PERSÖNLICHE FRAGEN ?

1. Wie heisst du?

_____

2. Wie alt bist du?

_____

3. Woher kommst du?

_____

4. Woher kommen deine Eltern?

_____

5. Woher kommen deine Grosseltern?

_____

6. Welche Sprache(n) sprecht ihr zu Hause?

_____

7. Hast du Geschwister? Wenn ja, erzähle darüber: wie heissen sie? wie alt sind sie?

_____

_____

8. Hast du ein Haustier? Was für eins und wie heisst es?

_____

9. Was machst du gern? Was sind deine Hobbys?

_____

_____

ÜBUNG N

Aufsatz. Using the questions above as a guide, write a paragraph about your best friend.

_____

_____

_____

_____

_____

_____

_____

_____

_____

KLASSENPROJEKT

1. Collect your essays and make either a bulletin board or a class scrapbook. Include pictures, if possible.

2. Draw your family tree, using the diagram on page 40 as a model. Label your family tree in German and explain it to the class. Display the family trees on the bulletin board.

WORTSCHATZ A-Z

der Verwandte, -n* *relative*

die Geschwister (pl.) *brothers and sisters*
die Frau, -en *wife; woman*
die Mann, ̈er *husband; man*
die Nichte, -n *niece*

der Neffe, -n* *nephew*
der Enkel *grandson*
die Enkelin, -nen *granddaughter*

Noch einige Wörter

die Clique, -n *group of friends, clique*
der Wagen *car*
musikalisch *musical*
sportlich *athletic*

lustig *funny, fun*
ganz nett *really nice*
ganz in der Nähe *right near by*

Frage-Wörter

wer? *who?*
wen? *whom?*
was? *what?*

wann? *when?*
wo? *where?*
warum? *why?*

wohin? *where to?*
woher? *where from?*
wie? *how?*

wie alt? *how old?*
wie viel? *how much?*
wie viele? *how many?*

Diese Wörter kennst du schon

die Familie, -n *family*
der Freund, -e *friend*
die Freundin, -nen *girlfriend*
die Eltern (pl) *parents*
die Mutter, ̈ *mother*
der Vater, ̈ *father*
das Kind, -er *child*
die Schwester, -n *sister*
der Bruder, ̈ *brother*
die Grosseltern (pl.) *grandparents*
die Grossmutter, ̈ *grandmother*
der Grossvater, ̈ *grandfather*
die Tante, -n *aunt*
der Onkel *uncle*
die Kusine, -n *(female) cousin*

der Vetter, -n *(male) cousin*
die Tochter, ̈ *daughter*
der Sohn, ̈e *son*
das Haustier, -e *pet*
der Hund, -e *dog*
die Katze, -n *cat*
das Haus, ̈er *house*
der Garten, *garden*
der Bauernhof, ̈e *farm*
die Blume, -n *flower*
das Pferd, -e *horse*
arbeiten *to work*
besuchen *to visit*
kommen aus *to come from*
lieben *to love*

*Some nouns in German add an **-n** or **-en** in the accusative and dative case: **der Verwandte, den Verwandten, dem Verwandten; der Neffe, den Neffen, dem Neffen.**
   Nouns like this will be indicated on the vocabulary lists in this book. Here are the ones that were introduced in Book I: **der Junge, der Löwe, der Hase, der Affe, der Elefant.**

Und so sagst du das *Here's how to...*

express relationship

Das ist Stefans Mutter.	*That's Stefan's mother.*
Das ist die Mutter von Stefan.	*That's the mother of Stefan.*
Das ist seine Mutter.	*That's his mother.*

ask someone's name and give yours

Wie heisst du?	*What's your name?*
Ich heisse . . .	*My name is . . .*

ask someone's age and give yours

Wie alt bist du?	*How old are you?*
Ich bin 14 Jahre alt.	*I'm 14 years old.*

*ask where someone comes from
and say where you come from*

Woher kommst du?	*Where are you from?*
Ich komme aus USA.	*I come from the USA.*

identify who someone is

Wer ist das?	*Who is that?*
Das ist der Deutschlehrer.	*That's the German teacher.*

Building your vocabulary

In this lesson about family and friends there are many cognates. How many can you find? Which ones are spelled the same way in English and German? Which ones are slightly different? Point out any patterns you observe, for example, **t** or **tt** in German is often *th* in English. Can you find any false cognates?

_____

_____

_____

_____

ÜBUNG O

Spiel Divide the class into two teams. The first person on Team A gives information about his or her family — name, age, hobbies, etc.

The first person on Team B has to repeat the information accurately. If he or she does, the team gets a point. If he or she doesn't, the next person tries. The team with the most points wins.

Ich habe zwei Geschwister.
Mein Bruder heisst...
Meine Schwester heisst...

Daniel hat zwei Geschwister.
Sein Bruder heisst...
Seine Schwester heisst...

KULTURECKE

Many Americans can trace their ancestry back to Germany. In fact, in 1986 according to the census, about forty-four million Americans did—approximately eighteen percent of the population. Although the last decades have not seen many new immigrants from German-speaking countries, the presence of Germans in America from the time the first Germans landed and settled in Pennsylvania in 1683 to the present is evident in many ways. The Germans settled all over the country, but there were concentrations in certain areas such as New York, Pennsylvania, Ohio, Wisconsin, and Texas. Look at a map and you will find many towns and cities named after places in the German-speaking world where the new immigrants came from. If you look in the phone book, you will also find many German names. Some may have been changed—Schmidt became Smith, Müller became Miller—but they were originally German. Think, too, of all the words that come from the German that are a part of the English language today, for example, **kindergarten, wiener, sauerkraut, hausfrau, kuchen, delicatessen, pumpernickel,** and **noodle**.

1. Look at a map of your state or particular area. Can you find names of places that are also in Germany, Austria, or Switzerland?

2. Look in the phone book and make a list of the German names you find.

3. Make a list of famous Germans, for example, John Peter Zenger, Friedrich Wilhelm von Steuben, Carl Schurz, Levi Strauss, Albert Einstein, and Marlene Dietrich. Pick one and find out about that person. Report to the class. Make a display in your classroom featuring famous Germans and German Americans.

4

Wir haben Hunger!

Reviewing
Pronouns, Nominative, and
Accusative Cases;
The *möchte*-forms; The Verb *mögen*

1 Wortschatz

Schnell-Imbiss am Markt

Hamburger		4,00
Superburger		6,50
mit Mayonnaise Ketchup Gurken Zwiebeln Tomaten Salat Käse Senf		
Hähnchen vom Grill		8,00

Pizza		6,00
mit Paprika Oliven Wurst Pilzen Extra-Käse		8,00
Bratwurst		2,60
Currywurst		3,20
Fischbrot		3,80

Pommes frites	2,20
Eis	1,50
Apfelkuchen	2,40
	2,80
mit Schlagsahne	

Cola	1,80
Fanta	1,80
Apfelsaft	2,00
Mineralwasser	1,90
Kaffee	2,00

ÜBUNG **A**

Read the menu and answer the questions.

1. Wie heisst der Imbiss-Stand?

_____

2. Was gibt es zu essen?

_____

_____

3. Was gibt es zu trinken?

_____

_____

4. Was kostet ein Superburger?

_____

5. Was kostet ein Eis?

_____

2 A pronoun is a word that can take the place of a noun or a noun phrase. You use pronouns so you don't always have to repeat the noun or noun phrase in every sentence. Read the following dialogue taking place at a snack bar. How many pronouns can you find? Underline them.

Du, ich habe Hunger, und ich habe Durst!

Ich auch! Gehen wir zum Imbiss am Markt!

Was isst du?

Der Superburger sieht gut aus.

Ja, er sieht sehr gut aus.

Ich nehme den Superburger. Nimmst du ihn auch?

Ich esse das Hähnchen.

Es sieht auch ganz lecker aus.

Martin

Till

lecker *delicious*
bekommen *to get*
Was möchtest du draufhaben? *What would you like on it?*

übung **B**

Hast du verstanden? Answer the questions.

1. Was isst Martin?

_____

2. Was trinkt er?

_____

3. Was isst Till?

_____

4. Was trinkt er?

_____

5. Was bekommt Till alles auf seinem Superburger? Schreib alles auf!

_____

_____

6. Isst Martin seine Pommes frites mit oder ohne Ketchup?

_____

3 Did you recognize all the pronouns in the dialogue? Fill in the German equivalents of the personal pronouns below.

I _____   we _____

you (singular, familiar) _____   you (plural, familiar) _____

he _____   they _____

she _____   you (singular and plural, polite) _____

it _____

You notice that there are three ways of saying "you" in German: _____,

_____, and _____.

Supply the corresponding pronouns in English.

the father _____   the children _____

the mother _____   the cars _____

the girl _____   the table _____

the pizza _____   the book _____

Now supply the pronouns in German.

der Vater _____   die Kinder _____

die Mutter _____   die Autos _____

das Mädchen _____   der Tisch _____

die Pizza _____   das Buch _____

You notice that there are three pronouns in German which mean "it" in English:

_____, _____, and _____. Masculine nouns (**der Vater, der Tisch**) can be replaced by _____, feminine nouns (**die Mutter, die Pizza**) by _____, and neuter nouns (**das Mädchen, das Buch**) by _____. As you can see, inanimate objects that are referred to as "it" in English may be masculine, **er**, feminine, **sie**, or neuter, **es**, in German.

übung C

Look at the menu on page 53 and give the price of each item. Refer to the item using the appropriate pronoun, **er, sie,** or **es.**

BEISPIEL: **Was kostet der Hamburger einfach?   Er kostet DM 4,00.**

Was kostet…

1. der Superburger?   _____ kostet _____.

2. das Hähnchen?   _____ kostet _____.

3. die Pizza?   _____ kostet _____.

4. die Pizza mit Extra-Käse?   _____ kostet _____.

5. die Bratwurst   _____ kostet _____.

6. die Currywurst?   _____ kostet _____.

7. das Fischbrot?   _____ kostet _____.

8. die Pommes frites?   _____ kosten _____.

9. die Cola?   _____ kostet _____.

10. die Fanta?   _____ kostet _____.

11. der Apfelsaft?   _____ kostet _____.

12. das Mineralwasser?   _____ kostet _____.

13. der Kaffee?   _____ kostet _____.

14. das Eis?   _____ kostet _____.

15. der Apfelkuchen   _____ kostet _____.

ÜBUNG D

Your classmates have ordered different things to eat and drink. Ask them if it tastes good and complete their answers.

BEISPIEL:  **Schmeckt die Bratwurst gut?**

 Ja, sie schmeckt sehr gut.

OR

 Nein, sie schmeckt nicht.

1. 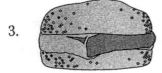   Schmeckt _____ gut?

 _____

2.   Schmeckt _____ gut?

_____

3.   Schmeckt _____ gut?

 _____

4.

Schmecken _____ gut?

_____

5.

Schmeckt _____ gut?

_____

4 Read the following conversation. What can you observe about the underlined nouns and pronouns?

—Was isst du?
—Ich esse den Superburger. Isst du ihn auch?
—Hm, ich weiss nicht.
—Isst du vielleicht das Hähnchen?
—Nein, ich esse es nicht. Ich nehme lieber die Pizza, aber ich möchte sie ohne Oliven.
—Gut. Ich bestelle auch die Pommes frites. Pommes frites esse ich zu gern!
—Ja, ich esse sie auch gern.

The underlined nouns and pronouns in the above conversation are in the _____ case. Complete the questions by supplying the accusative pronoun.

Ich esse den Superburger. Isst du _____ auch?

Ich esse die Pizza. Isst du _____ auch?

Ich esse das Hähnchen. Isst du _____ auch?

Ich esse die Pommes frites. Isst du _____ auch?

Here is a summary of third person pronouns in the nominative and accusative case.

	NOMINATIVE	ACCUSATIVE
MASCULINE	er	ihn
FEMININE	sie	sie
NEUTER	es	es
PLURAL	sie	sie

5 You have been using the verb phrases **gern haben** and **gern essen** to express liking. Another useful verb to know, especially when talking about food, is the verb **mögen**. Here are the forms.

mögen *to like*			
ich	mag	wir	mögen
du	magst	ihr	mögt
er, sie, es	mag	sie, Sie	mögen

To say you like something very much, use **gern mögen**: **Ich mag das gern!**

ÜBUNG E

Complete the puzzle with the correct forms of **mögen.**

↓ 1. Wir _____ Fleisch nicht.

→ 2. Was _____ ihr gern?

↓ Ich_____ Fisch nicht.

→ 3. Meine Eltern _____ Hamburger nicht.

↓ Meine Mutter _____ Pommes frites.

→ 4. Du _____ keine Oliven?

```
    ¹M Ö G E N
      ²
    ³
  ⁴
```

ÜBUNG F

Magst du das? You are eating at a friend's house. Respond politely when you are asked whether you like various foods. Use pronouns to refer to the foods.

BEISPIEL: Freund: **Magst du die Suppe?**
          Du: **Ja, sie schmeckt gut! Ich mag sie gern!**

Magst du...

1. die Wurst?

   2. den Käse?

_____

   3. das Fleisch?

_____

   4. den Fisch?

_____

   5. die Tomaten?

_____

   6. das Brot?

_____

   7. den Salat?

_____

   8. die Kartoffeln?

_____

ÜBUNG G

Give your personal opinion using a pronoun in your answer.

1. Wie magst du deinen Hamburger — mit oder ohne Zwiebeln?

_____

2. Wie magst du deine Pommes frites — mit oder ohne Ketchup?

_____

3. Wie magst du dein Fischbrot — mit oder ohne Mayonnaise?

_____

4. Wie magst du deine Pizza — mit oder ohne Oliven?

_____

5. Wie magst du deine Bratwurst — mit oder ohne Senf?

_____

6. Wie magst du deinen Apfelkuchen — mit oder ohne Schlagsahne?

_____

ÜBUNG H

You and several friends are at a food stand. One friend is hard to please. You make suggestions and urge your friend to try the various items. Practice these exchanges with a classmate. Be sure to use the correct pronoun. Here are some expressions your classmate might use:

zu fett	_too greasy_	**zu klein**	_too small_	**zu scharf**	_too spicy_
zu gross	_too big_	**zu salzig**	_too salty_	**zu süss**	_too sweet_

BEISPIEL: Du: **Die Currywurst sieht gut aus!**
          Freund: **Sie ist zu scharf!**
          Du: **Ach, probier sie doch mal!**

1.   Du: Die Pommes frites sehen gut aus!

    Freund: _____

    Du: _____

2.   Du: Die Pizza sieht gut aus!

    Freund: _____

    Du: _____

3.   Du: Der Superburger sieht gut aus!

    Freund: _____

    Du: _____

4.   Du: Das Fischbrot sieht gut aus!

    Freund: _____

    Du: _____

5.   Du: Der Apfelkuchen sieht gut aus!

Freund: _____

    Du: _____

6 In this lesson you have been reviewing the personal pronouns in the nominative and accusative cases. The following examples show you two ways of ordering something to eat or drink and also summarize the personal pronouns in both cases. Remember, the preposition **für**, *for*, is one of several prepositions that are always followed by the accusative case.

Ich möchte den Hamburger.

Für *mich* den Hamburger.

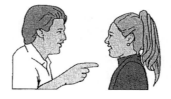

Du möchtest die Pizza.

Für *dich* die Pizza.

Robert, *er* möchte die Pommes frites.

Für den Robert, für *ihn* die Pommes frites.

Eva, *sie* möchte die Currywurst.

Für die Eva, für *sie* die Currywurst.

Wir möchten die Bratwurst.

Für *uns* die Bratwurst.

Ihr möchtet das Fischbrot.

Für *euch* das Fischbrot.

Ralf und Gabi, sie möchten den Superburger.

Für Ralf und Gabi, für *sie* sie den Superburger.

Take another look at the **möchte**-forms. Underline the endings. Which verb ending

does not follow the pattern for most verbs? _____ . The **er/sie**-form

ends in _____ , not in _____ .

ÜBUNG I

Ask what everyone would like using **möchte**. Answer using **für** and the personal pronoun.

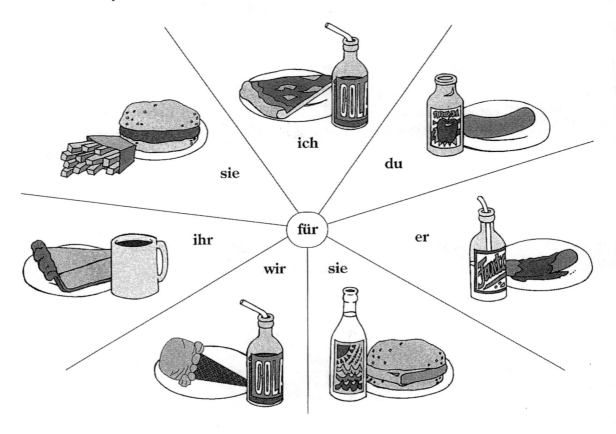

Was möchte ich? — Für mich die Pizza und...

1. _____

_____

2. _____

_____

3. _____

_____

4. _____

_____

5. _____

_____

6. _____

_____

7. _____

_____

ÜBUNG J

You and your friends have all placed your orders at the food stand and the food is eady. Who gets what? Follow the example, using the correct pronouns.

BEISPIEL: **Wer bekommt den Hamburger?**
Ich **bekomme den Hamburger. Er ist für** *mich***.**

1. Wer bekommt das Fischbrot?

Daniel _____.

2. Wer bekommt die Pommes frites?

Wir _____.

3. Wer bekommt den Apfelkuchen?

   Julia _____.

4. Wer bekommt die Cola?

   Du, Gabi, du _____.

5. Wer bekommt die Pizza?

   Uwe und Jochen, ihr _____.

6. Wer bekommt das Eis?

   Ralf, Oliver und Sandra, sie _____.

7. Und wer bekommt den Kaffee?

   Frau Schmidt, Sie _____.

ÜBUNG K

Hör gut zu! A group of friends are in a restaurant ordering something to eat and drink. Listen to what each one orders and write the number of that order under the corresponding picture.

PERSÖNLICHE FRAGEN ?

1. Was isst du gern auf deinem Hamburger?

_____

2. Was isst du gern auf deiner Pizza?

_____

3. Wie heisst ein Schnell-Imbiss, wo du mit deinen Freunden gern hingehst?

_____

4. Was bekommt ihr dort zu essen und zu trinken?

_____

ÜBUNG L

Work with two classmates to create a dialogue at a food stand. Use the phrases given as a guide. Practice your dialogue and present it to the class.

Was bekommt ihr denn?

Was möchtest du essen?

Magst du...?

Was isst du auf deiner Pizza?

Was möchtest du trinken?

Was nimmst du?

Probier doch mal...!

Ich esse kein(e)...

... sieht lecker aus!

Ich nehme...

Ich mag... nicht.

Was möchtest du alles auf deinem Hamburger?

Ich möchte den Hamburger mit... aber ohne...

Ich möchte mit... und ohne...

KLASSENPROJEKT

Set up a food stand in your classroom. Draw a large menu with prices. Take turns playing the role of the counter person as classmates come to buy something to eat and drink.

WORTSCHATZ A-Z

der Imbiss-Stand *snack stand*

der Hamburger *hamburger*
die Mayonnaise *mayonnaise*
die Zwiebel, -n *onion*
der Ketchup *ketchup*
das Hähnchen *chicken*
die Pizza, -s *pizza*
der Paprika *pepper* (vegetable)
der Pilz, -e *mushroom*

die Olive, -n *olive*
die Currywurst, -e *sausage with spicy curry sauce*
das Fischbrot, -e *fish sandwich*
der Apfelkuchen *apple cake*
die Schlagsahne *whipped cream*
die Fanta, -s *orange-flavored carbonated drink*
das Mineralwasser *mineral water*

Noch einige Wörter

alles *everything*
lecker *delicious*

ich auch *me too*
bestellen *to order*

mögen *to like*

Diese Wörter kennst du schon

die Bratwurst, ⁃e *fried sausage*
die Gurke, -n *pickle*
der Käse *cheese*
der Salat, -e *lettuce*
der Senf *mustard*
die Tomate, -n *tomato*
die Wurst, ⁃e *sausage*
die Pommes frites (pl.) *French fries*
das Eis *ice cream*
der Apfelsaft, ⁃e *apple juice*
die Cola, -s *cola*
der Kaffee, -s *coffee*

aussehen: das sieht gut aus *that looks good*
bekommen *to get, receive*
essen *to eat*
    er/sie isst *he/she eats*
trinken *to drink*
möchten *would like*
probieren *to try;*
    probier doch mal... *why don't you try . . .*
für *for*
mit *with*
ohne *without*

Und so sagst du das *Here's how to . . .*

say you are hungry and thirsty

Ich habe Hunger. *I'm hungry.*   Ich habe Durst. *I'm thirsty.*

ask what someone would like and say what you would like

Was möchtest du? *What would you like?*
Was bekommst du? *What are you having?*
    What will you have?

Ich möchte... *I would like . . .*
Ich bekomme... *I'll have . . .*
Ich nehme... *I'll take . . .*

express liking and disliking

Ich mag (gern)... *I like . . .*   Ich mag nicht (gern)... *I don't like . . .*

ask and tell how something tastes

Schmeckt das Hähnchen gut? *Does the chicken taste good?*
Ja, es schmeckt sehr gut! *Yes, it tastes very good!*
Nein, es schmeckt nicht. *No, it doesn't taste good.*

Building your vocabulary

Look for words you know in compounds to help you with meaning. If you remember that **Bratwurst** means a kind of sausage, you can probably figure out that **Currywurst** is also a kind of sausage and what **Wurst** on the pizza menu means.

Don't forget to look for cognates. How many can you find on this vocabulary list?

_____

_____

_____

_____

_____

_____

ÜBUNG **M**

Bingo-Spiel   Make a set of bingo cards with food and drink items you have learned in this lesson. Each student makes a bingo card with nine spaces, filling in each space with either the German words or with pictures. The teacher or a student reads off food items from the vocabulary list randomly. The first one to fill his or her bingo card is the winner.

The winner could also be the first one to get three items in a row horizontally, vertically, or diagonally.

Currywurst	Hähnchen	Zwiebel
Fischbrot	Apfelkuchen	Paprika
Pilze	Schlagsahne	Mineralwasser

GESPRÄCH

Snack stands can be found all over Germany and American-style fast food restaurants have become quite popular. Hamburgers, French fries, and pizza are favorite foods, especially for young people. There are also many traditionally German "fast foods." **Frankfurter-würstchen**, (frankfurters), and **Bratwürste**, (fried sausages), are sold everywhere, and many regions in Germany have their specialties. Many department stores have store-front counters where they sell ham, cheese, or cold cut sandwiches on rolls.

IMBISS

Currywurst mit Brot	4,00
Hamburger	3,50
Portion Pommes frites	3,00
Mini Pizza	4,50
Frühlingsrolle mit süsssaurer Sauce	5,00

Soft-Eis

Heisse Brezel

SANDWICH-BAR

Schinkenbrot	4,00
Käsebrot	3,00
Salamibrot	3,50
Veggi-Brot	3,50

DÖNERKEBAB
Der Hit aus der Türkei

5

Eine Party

Verbs with Separable and Inseparable Prefixes; Modals

1 Wortschatz

Julia möchte eine Party haben.

Julia bittet ihre
Eltern um Erlaubnis.

Sie räumt den
Keller auf.

Sie ruft ihre Freunde
an und lädt sie ein.

Sie plant die Party
und schreibt eine
Einkaufsliste.

Sie kauft die Party-
sachen ein.

Sie bereitet das
Essen vor.

Sie probiert ihre neue Bluse an.

Sie begrüsst die Gäste.

Sie feiert ganz toll!

ÜBUNG A

Julia would like to have a party. She has a lot to do but things got a little mixed up. Replace the italicized words with more appropriate ones from the box below and write the sentences in the space provided.

das Essen	eine Party	den Keller	feiert
eine Einkaufsliste	ihre Eltern	die Party	die Gäste
die Partysachen	die Freunde	zur Party	Bluse

1. Julia möchte *ein Fahrrad* haben.

   _____

2. Sie bittet *ihre Katze* um Erlaubnis.

   _____

3. Sie räumt *die Garage* auf.

   _____

4. Sie ruft *ihre Lehrer* an und lädt sie zum Konzert ein.

   _____

5. Sie plant *die Reise* und schreibt *einen Brief*.

   _____

6. Sie kauft *die Schulsachen* ein.

   _____

7. Sie bereitet *das Fotoalbum* vor.

   _____

8. Sie probiert ihre neue *Schultasche* an.

_____

9. Sie begrüsst *ihren Hund.*

_____

10. Sie *schläft* ganz toll.

_____

ÜBUNG B

Wer sagt was? Read what each person says and write it in the appropriate speech bubble below and on the next page.

«Hm, was brauchen wir alles zu essen und zu trinken? –Bratwurst, Kartoffelsalat, Cola,…»

«Ich möchte eine Party haben. Geht das?»

«Hallo Karin! Hallo Jens! Schön, dass ihr gekommen seid!»

«Ja, ich komme gern!»

«Soviel Kram!»

«Ich habe am Samstag eine Party. Kommst du?»

«He, super Party!»

«So, wie sehe ich aus? Gefällt dir meine neue Bluse?»

«Ja, das geht schon, aber räume bitte den Keller auf!»

ÜBUNG C

Which verb most appropriately completes the phrase? Draw lines matching the beginning of the phrase with the verb on the right. Write the complete phrases below.

die Eltern um Erlaubnis	anprobieren
den Keller	anrufen
ihre Freunde und sie	aufräumen
eine Einkaufsliste	begrüssen
die Partysachen	bitten
das Essen	einkaufen
die neue Bluse	einladen
die Gäste	feiern
ganz toll	schreiben
	vorbereiten

1. _____

2. _____

3. _____

4. _____

5. _____

6. _____

7. _____

8. _____

9. _____

2 Take a closer look at some of the verbs you have been using to talk about Julia's party. In the preceding activity you practiced verb phrases.

den Keller aufräumen

ihre Freunde anrufen

Look at how these verbs are used in sentences on page 71. What can you observe?

Julia räumt den Keller auf.

Sie ruft ihre Freunde an.

Verbs such as **aufräumen** and **anrufen** are called separable prefix verbs. The infinitive has a prefix that is sometimes separated from the verb. Separable prefixes are small words that have a meaning and can stand alone. Sometimes prefixes change meaning in combination with different infinitives; sometimes the meaning of the prefix remains the same. For example, the prefix **mit** can mean *along* or *along with*.

Knowing this, you can easily figure out the meaning of many verbs:

mitnehmen   *to take along*

mitbringen   _____

mitkommen   _____

mitgehen   _____

Here are some separable prefix verbs you came across in Book 1. Put a slash between the prefix and the main part of the verb. Note as you pronounce them that the prefix is stressed.

abfahren   *to depart, drive off*   **fernsehen**   *to watch TV*
ausgeben   *to spend (money)*   **vorbereiten** *to prepare*
aussehen   *to seem; to appear, look*   **vorschlagen** *to suggest*
einladen   *to invite*

On vocabulary lists and in the dictionary section at the back of this book, separable prefix verbs will be listed this way: **an•rufen**.

ÜBUNG **D**

Was bringen alle mit? Everyone is going to bring along something or someone to the party. Write sentences using the cues given.

BEISPIEL: **Jens / Kartoffelchips**
          Jens *bringt* Kartoffelchips *mit*.

1. ich / Musikkassetten

_____

2. wir / einen Freund

_____

3. du / Karten

_____

4. Benjamin / seine Schwester

_____

5. Tina / ein lustiges Video

_____

6. ihr / einen Kuchen

_____

7. Sandra und Jochen / Cola

_____

ÜBUNG E

Julia's mother is reminding Julia of all the things she has to do for her party. Write what Julia says in response. Follow the example.

BEISPIEL: Mutter: **Du musst den Keller aufräumen.**
           Julia: **Ja, ich räume den Keller auf.**

1. Mutter: Du musst deine Freunde anrufen.

   Julia: _____

2. Mutter: Du musst sie einladen.

   Julia: _____

3. Mutter: Du musst die Partysachen einkaufen.

   Julia: _____

4. Mutter: Du musst das Essen vorbereiten.

   Julia: _____

5. Mutter: Du musst deine neue Bluse anprobieren.

   Julia: _____

ÜBUNG F

Roleplay the situation in Activity E with a partner. You are having a party. Your partner plays the role of your mother or father. Practice and then switch roles.

3 The verb **einladen** (to invite) is a separable prefix verb and it is also a verb with a stem vowel change. The _____ in the **du-** and **er/sie-**form changes to _____.

einladen	
ich lade ein	wir laden ein
du lädst ein	ihr ladet ein
er/sie/es lädt ein	sie/Sie laden ein

Note that the **du-** and **er/sie** forms do not add -e, although the verb stem ends in **d.**

ÜBUNG G

Wer lädt wen zu was ein? Write sentences with **einladen** and the information in the chart.

BEISPIEL: **Meine Mutter lädt Frau Roth zum Kaffee ein.**

wer? meine Mutter	wen? Frau Roth	zu was? zum Kaffee
1. wir	unsere Grosseltern	zu einem Konzert
2. Barbara	ihre Freundin	zu einer Party
3. du	deinen Freund	zum Essen
4. die Kinder	ihre Lehrerin	zu einem Picknick
5. Paul	Angelika	zum Tennisspielen
6. ich	dich	ins Theater
7. ihr	uns	zum Kartenspielen

1. _____

2. _____

3. _____

4. _____

5. _____

6. _____

7. _____

4 You have been learning about verbs with separable prefixes, but there are also many verbs in German that have inseparable prefixes. Inseparable prefixes cannot stand alone as words and are never separated from the verb. They are unstressed.

besúchen **gefállen** **vergéssen**

5 Some of Julia's friends have come to help get ready for the party. Read what they say. What do you think the words in italics mean?

Wir *wollen* helfen!

Was *können* wir tun?

***Willst* du einkaufen gehen?**

***Soll* ich den Keller aufräumen?**

***Darf* ich einen Kuchen backen?**

***Kannst* du einen Kartoffelsalat machen?**

Du *musst* zuerst die Kartoffeln kochen.

Ich *kann* die Bowle machen.

The words in italics are examples of a group of verbs called *modal auxilaries*, or just *modals*. These verbs are extremely useful in both English and German. Here is a summary of the modals with their English equivalents. You will recognize some of them from Book 1.

sollen *to be supposed to; ought; should*
wollen *to want to*
müssen *to have to; must*
dürfen *to be permitted or allowed to; may*
können *to be able to; can*
mögen *to like* (and the related **möchte**-forms, meaning *would like*)

You can see that the modal used can be very important. How does the modal change the meaning of the following sentences? Write the English meaning for each one.

Wir wollen zu Hause bleiben.

_____

Wir sollen zu Hause bleiben.

_____

Wir können zu Hause bleiben.

_____

Wir müssen zu Hause bleiben.

_____

Wir dürfen zu Hause bleiben.

_____

Wir möchten zu Hause bleiben.

_____

Think of a little situation that would go with each sentence you have written and that would show the difference in meaning. For example:

—*We want to stay home. There is a good show on TV and we don't want to miss it.*

—*We should stay home. We have lots of homework and we really should stay home and do it.*

Take turns sharing your situations (in English) with the class.

Here are the forms of the modals. Look at them carefully, paying attention to spelling changes and endings. What patterns can you observe?

	sollen	wollen	können	müssen	dürfen	mögen
ich	soll	will	kann	muss	darf	mag
du	sollst	willst	kannst	musst	darfst	magst
er, sie, es	soll	will	kann	muss	darf	mag
wir	sollen	wollen	können	müssen	dürfen	mögen
ihr	sollt	wollt	könnt	müsst	dürft	mögt
sie, Sie	sollen	wollen	können	müssen	dürfen	mögen

1. What modals have stem vowel changes?

_____

2. Where do the vowel changes occur?

_____

3. How are the **ich-** and the **er-, sie-, es-**forms of the modals different from otherverbs?

_____

Look again at all the sentences with modals. You will notice that the modals are inflected—that is, the endings change to match the subject—and each sentence with a modal also has an infinitive at the end.

	1ST POSITION	2ND POSITION		LAST POSITION
STATEMENT	Ich	kann	die Bowle	machen.
QUESTION	Soll	ich	den Keller	aufräumen?

If the meaning of the final infinitive is clearly understood, it is sometimes omitted.

Kommst du zu Julias Party?   **Ich *kann* leider nicht. (kommen)**

ÜBUNG **H**

Practice the forms of the modals. Next to the singular forms write the corresponding plural forms and next to the plural, write the corresponding singular.

1. du darfst / ihr _____

2. wir wollen / ich _____

3. ihr sollt / du _____

4. er muss / sie (*pl.*) _____

5. wir können / ich _____

6. sie dürfen / sie (*sing.*) _____

7. ihr mögt / du _____

8. du willst / ihr _____

9. ich mag / wir _____

10. wir müssen / ich _____

ÜBUNG **I**

Julia wants to have a party. She asks her mother for permission. Her mother agrees to all her requests. What do they each say? Use **dürfen**.

BEISPIEL: **Julia möchte eine Party haben.**

JULIA: *Darf* ich eine Party haben?

MUTTER: **Ja, du *darfst* eine Party haben.**

1. Sie möchte ihre Freunde einladen.

_____

_____

2. Sie möchte eine Bowle machen.

_____

_____

3. Julia und ihre Freunde möchten im Keller tanzen.

_____

_____

4. Die Freunde möchten bis 23 Uhr feiern.

_____

_____

5. Julia möchte eine neue Bluse kaufen.

_____

_____

ÜBUNG J

Julia's mother has given Julia permission to have a party. Read what she says to Julia and then go back and underline the modals.

Julias Mutter sagt:—Julia, du darfst eine Party haben. Du kannst deine Freunde einladen und im Keller feiern. Du musst aber den Keller aufräumen. Du willst auch etwas zu essen und zu trinken haben. Du kannst Bratwurst und Kartoffelsalat haben. Du musst einkaufen gehen. Du sollst dann auch viel Cola und Saft kaufen. Du willst ja genug haben!

Julia and her friend Karin are giving the party together. What does Julia's mother say when she addresses both of them? Rewrite the above paragraph using the **ihr**-form. Make any other necessary changes (**deine Freunde** becomes **eure Freunde**).

Julias Mutter sagt:—Julia und Karin, ihr _____

_____

_____

_____

_____

_____

Now Julia's mother is on the phone telling Julia's grandmother about the plans. What does she say? Rewrite the paragraph in the third person (**Julia, sie**). Make any other necessary changes. What happens to **deine Freunde**, for example?

Julias Mutter sagt:—Hallo, Mutter! Julia _____

_____

_____

_____

_____

_____

_____

6 Zwei Telefongespräche

Julia calls some of her friends to invite them to her party.

JULIA:	Hallo Claudia! Hier ist Julia.
CLAUDIA:	Hallo Julia!
JULIA:	Du Claudia, ich habe am Samstag eine Party. Ich möchte dich einladen. Kommst du?
CLAUDIA:	Ja, ich habe nichts vor. Ich komme gern! Wann beginnt die Party?
JULIA:	Um19 Uhr.
CLAUDIA:	Kann ich etwas mitbringen?
JULIA:	Ja, bring bitte ein paar Musikkassetten mit.
CLAUDIA:	Gut, das mache ich! Vielen Dank für die Einladung! Bis Samstag dann! Tschüs!
JULIA:	Auf Wiederhören!

****

JULIA:	Hallo Philipp! Hier ist Julia.
PHILIPP:	Tag, Julia! Was gibt's?
JULIA:	Am Samstag habe ich eine Party. Um 19 Uhr. Hast du etwas vor? Kannst du kommen?
PHILIPP:	Ach, schade! Ich kann leider nicht kommen. Wir fahren am Wochenende nach München und besuchen meinen Onkel.

JULIA: Ja, das ist schade! Nun aber viel Spass in München!
PHILIPP: Danke! Und viel Spass bei der Party!

hier ist Julia *this is Julia (on the phone)*
vor•haben *to have something on, have plans*
auf Wiederhören! *good-bye! (on the phone)*
was gibt's? *what's up?*
schade! *too bad!*
viel Spass! *have fun!*

ÜBUNG K

Hast du verstanden? Answer the questions based on the dialogues.

1. How does Julia say who's calling?

_____

2. How does she invite Claudia to the party?

_____

3. Does Claudia accept or decline the invitation?

_____

4. What does she say?

_____

5. What will Claudia bring along?

_____

6. How does she thank Julia for the invitation?

_____

7. How does each girl say goodbye?

_____

8. Can Philipp come to the party?

_____

9. What does he say? What excuse does he give?

_____

10. How does Julia respond?

_____

ÜBUNG L

Hör gut zu! You will hear Julia inviting some of her friends to her party. Listen to what each of her friends say in response to the invitation. Check off on Julia's list who can come and who can't.

	JA	NEIN
1. Astrid	_____	_____
2. Monika	_____	_____
3. Günther	_____	_____
4. Christof	_____	_____
5. Andreas	_____	_____

ÜBUNG M

Work with a partner. Use sentences from the four groups below to practice extending invitations. First you say what you are doing, then invite your partner. Your partner accepts or declines the invitation. Reverse roles.

I
Ich gehe ins Kino.
Ich habe eine Party.
Ich lade ein paar Freunde ein.

II
Ich möchte dich einladen.
Kannst du kommen?
Hast du schon etwas vor?

III
Ja, gern!
Ich komme gern!
Toll! Ich habe nichts vor.

IV
Es tut mir leid. Das geht nicht.
Schade!
Ich kann leider nicht kommen.

ÜBUNG N

After you have practiced, write out a dialogue. Use your imagination to expand on the above cues. For example, your partner could ask to bring something, or if he/she is not coming, explain why not. Practice your dialogue and present it to the class.

ÜBUNG O

Julia is also sending an invitation to her friends.

1. When is the party?

_____

2. What is Julia's address?

_____

3. What is her telephone number?

_____

PERSÖNLICHE FRAGEN

1. Hast du manchmal eine Party?

_____

2. Und deine Freunde? Haben sie auch Partys?

_____

3. Wen lädst du zu einer Party bei dir ein?

_____

4. Was gibt es alles zu essen und zu trinken?

_____

5. Was für Musik hört ihr?

_____

ÜBUNG **P**

Aufsatz. Write a paragraph about a party you are planning. Give the date of the party and when it begins. Name some of the people you are inviting and mention what you plan to have to eat and drink. You might also mention what kind of music you will have. (Remember, the present tense can be used to indicate future time in German.)

Ich habe am _____ um _____ eine Party. _____

_____

_____

_____

_____

_____

_____

_____

_____

KLASSENPROJEKT

Plan a class party. Design an invitation. Make a guest list. Decide what you'll have to eat and drink and write a shopping list.

WORTSCHATZ

die Erlaubnis *permission*
bitten um *to ask for*
an•rufen *to call up*
ein•laden *to invite*: er/sie lädt ein
ein•kaufen *to shop*
an•probieren *to try on*
vor•haben *to have something on, have plans*
mit•bringen *to bring along*

begrüssen *to greet*
die Einkaufsliste, -n *shopping list*
die Partysachen (pl.) *party things*
das Essen *food*
die Musikkassette, -n *music tape*
geht das? *is that okay?*
das geht schon, aber... *it's okay but . . .*
was gibt's? *what's up?*
viel Spass! *have fun!*

Diese Wörter kennst du schon

auf•räumen *to clean up*
vor•bereiten *to prepare*
planen *to plan*
feiern *to celebrate, party*
schreiben *to write*

der Gast, ⁀e *guest*
der Keller *basement*
der Kram *junk*
leider *unfortunately*
es tut mir leid *I'm sorry*

MODALS

sollen *to be supposed to; ought; should*: er/sie soll
wollen *to want to*: er/sie will
können *to be able to; can*: er/sie kann

dürfen *to be permitted, allowed to*: er/sie darf
müssen *to have to; must*: er/sie muss
mögen *to like*: er/sie mag

Und so sagst du das *Here's how to . . .*

invite someone

Ich möchte dich einladen. *I'd like to invite you.*
Ich lade dich ein. *I'm inviting you.*
Kannst du kommen? *Can you come?*

Hast du (schon) etwas vor? *Do you (already) have something on? Do you (already) have plans?*

accept an invitation

Ja, gern! *Yes, I'd love to!*
Ich komme gern! *I'd love to come!*

Toll! Ich habe nichts vor. *Great! I don't have anything planned.*

decline an invitation

Es tut mir leid. Das geht nicht. *I'm sorry. I can't.*
Ich kann (leider) nicht kommen. *(Unfortunately) I can't come.*
Schade! *Too bad!*
Ich habe schon etwas vor. *I already have plans.*

say who you are on the phone

Hallo! Hier ist... *Hello! This is . . .*

say good-bye on the phone

Auf Wiederhören! *Goodbye!*

Building your vocabulary

You can expand your vocabulary by recognizing prefixes. What do these words mean?

ab-		aus-		durch-	
durch-		durch-		mit-	**nehmen**
hin-		mit-		weg-	
mit-	**fahren**	weg-	**gehen**	zurück-	
weg-		weiter-			
weiter-		zurück-			
zurück-					

ÜBUNG Q

Satz-Schlangen-Spiel. Separable prefixes when separated from the rest of the verb come at the end of the sentence. Sentences in German can get very long! See how long you can make this sentence. Each student repeats what the student before has said and adds an element.

BEISPIEL: **Ich bringe Musikkassetten mit.**
Ich bringe Musikkassetten und... mit.

Suggestions: Add more names; add the time.

Ich lade dich ein.
Ich lade dich zu einer Party ein.
Ich lade dich und Robert zu einer Party ein.
Ich lade dich und Robert am Samstag zu einer Party ein.

KULTURECKE

If you go to a party in Germany you might be served **Chips,** (potato chips), **Salzstangen,** (pretzels), or **Nüsse,** (nuts). There will probably be a plate of **Wurst- und Käsebrote,** (sandwiches with cold cuts and cheese), **heisse Würstchen,** (frankfurters), or **Bratwürste,** (sausages). In southern Germany **Leberkäs** is often served—a mixture of beef, pork, onions, and spices all ground together until smooth, baked in a loaf form and served warm in thick slices. To go with the meat you'll have hearty dark bread, rolls, or perhaps big soft pretzels. And there will probably be a selection of salads: **Kartoffelsalat,** (potato salad), **Nudelsalat,** (noodle salad), **Gurkensalat,** (cucumber salad), **Tomatensalat,** (tomato salad), for example.

What will there be to drink? **Cola, Fanta, Mineralwasser, Apfelsaft**—soft drinks, mineral water, fruit juices. A popular party drink is a **Bowle,** a punch often made with fresh fruit such as strawberries for an **Erdbeerbowle** or peaches for a **Pfirsichbowle.** For adults a **Bowle** is often made with wine or champagne. For young people it is made with **Sprudel,** (seltzer), or **Limonade,** (carbonated soda usually citrus-flavored).

Erdbeerbowle

750 g Erdbeeren
Saft von 1 Zitrone
150 g Puderzucker
2 Flaschen Limonade
1 Flasche Sprudel

Erdbeeren waschen und die Stiele abdrehen. Die Beeren dann mit Zitronensaft beträufeln und mit Puderzucker überstreuen. Zugedeckt 1-2 Stunden kalt stellen. Kurz vor dem Servieren die Limonade und den Sprudel zugiessen.

Eis-Cocktail

Vanille-Es
4-8 Teel. Oragen-oder Zitronensaft
1 Flasche eisgekühilte Sinalco oder Cola

Das Eis in grosse Stücke scheiden auf vier Gläser verteilen. In jedes Glas 1-2 Teel. Orangen-oder Zitronensaft geben und mit Sinalco oder Cola auffüllen.

Party Punsch

1 Flasche Apfelsaft
1 Stück Stangenzimt
Saft von 2 Orangen
Saft von 2 Zitronen
50-75 g Zucker
Orangen-und Zitronenscheiben

Den Apfelsaft mit dem Zangenzimt erhitzen und 2-3 Minuten ziehen lassen. Orangen-und Zitronensaft und Zucker zugeben. Den Punsch nochmals erhitzen. Eine Orangen-oder Zitronenscheibe in jedes Glas legen und den heissen Punsch darüber giessen.

Wiederholung I

(Lektionen 1-5)

Lektion 1

a. When learning a language, it is helpful to know certain grammatical terms.

Gender refers to the class a noun belongs to, that is, if it is masculine, feminine, or neuter.

Number tells you if the noun is singular or plural.

Case tells you the function of a noun or a noun phrase in a sentence: the subject is in the nominative case: the direct object is in the accusative case.

Determiners precede a noun and distinguish whether you are talking about *the* book, for example, *this* book, *that* book, or perhaps just *any* book.

Here are some determiners:

- definite articles **der, die, das**   *the*
- indefinite articles **ein, eine**   *a, an*
- negative determiner **kein**   *no, none, not any*

MASCULINE		FEMININE		NEUTER		PLURAL	
NOM.	ACC.	NOM.	ACC.	NOM.	ACC.	NOM.	ACC.
der	den	die		das		die	
ein	einen	eine		ein		——	
kein	keinen	keine		kein		keine	

b. Noun plural must be learned with the noun. The plural article is **die**.

der Lehrer, *die* **Lehrer**
der Bleistift, *die* **Bleistifte**
das Buch, *die* **Bücher**
die Schule, *die* **Schulen**
der Kuli, *die* **Kulis**

Lektion 2

a. The basic form of the verb, the form listed in the dictionary, is the infinitive (**spielen,** **machen**). It consists of a stem (**spiel-, mach-**) and an infinitive ending (**-n** or **-en**). When the verb is used with a subject, the ending changes to match, or you could say agree, with that subject.

Ich spiele Klavier.
Mein Bruder spielt Geige.

	MACHEN STEM ENDING	SAMMELN STEM ENDING	ARBEITEN STEM ENDING	FINDEN STEM ENDING	HEISSEN STEM ENDING
ich	mach- e	samml- e	arbeit- e	find- e	heiss- e
du	mach- st	sammel- st	arbeit- est	find- est	heiss- t
er/sie/es	mach- t	sammel- t	arbeit- et	find- et	heiss- t
wir	mach- en	sammel- n	arbeit- en	find- en	heiss- en
ihr	mach- t	sammel- t	arbeit- et	find- et	heiss- t
sie, Sie	mach- en	sammel- n	arbeit- en	find- en	heiss- en

b. There are a number of verbs that have stem vowel changes in the **du-** and **er/sie-** forms.

	e → i	e → ie	a → ä	a → äu
	essen *to eat*	**sehen** *to see*	**fahren** *to ride*	**laufen** *to run*
ich	esse	sehe	fahre	laufe
du	**isst**	**siehst**	**fährst**	**läufst**
er/sie/es	**isst**	**sieht**	**fährt**	**läuft**
wir	essen	sehen	fahren	laufen
ihr	esst	seht	fahrt	lauft
sie, Sie	essen	sehen	fahren	laufen

Lektion 3

Possessive adjectives are another kind of determiner.

	NOMINATIVE				ACCUSATIVE			
	MASC.	FEM.	NEUT.	PL.	MASC.	FEM.	NEUT.	PL.
my	mein	meine	mein	meine	meinen	meine	mein	meine
your	dein	deine	dein	deine	deinen	deine	dein	deine
his, its	sein	seine	sein	seine	seinen	seine	sein	seine
her	ihr	ihre	ihr	ihre	ihren	ihre	ihr	ihre
our	unser	unsere	unser	unsere	unseren	unsere	unser	unsere
your	euer	eure	eure	eure	eueren	eure	euer	eure
their	ihr	ihre	ihr	ihre	ihren	ihre	ihr	ihre
your	Ihr	Ihre	Ihr	Ihre	Ihren	Ihre	Ihr	Ihre

In addition to the possessive adjectives, there are two other ways of showing relationship in German:

> **Erika ist *Gabis Mutter*.**
> **Erika ist die *Mutter von Gabi*.**

Lektion 4

A pronoun is a word that can take the place of a noun or a noun phrase.

	NOMINATIVE	ACCUSATIVE
I	ich	mich
you (*fam. sing.*)	du	dich
he	er	ihn
she	sie	sie
it	es	es
we	wir	uns
you (*fam. pl.*)	ihr	euch
they	sie	sie
you (*formal sing. & pl.*)	Sie	Sie

Lektion 5

a. Many verbs in German begin with a prefix. Some can be separated from the verb and others cannot. Those that can be separated from the verb are called separable prefixes. They have a meaning and can stand alone as words.

einladen   Wir *laden* euch *ein*.
mitkommen   Wir fahren in die Stadt. *Kommst* du *mit?*

aufräumen *to clean up*			
ich	räume auf	wir	räumen auf
du	räumst auf	ihr	räumt auf
er/sie/es	räumt auf	sie, Sie	räumen auf

b. The verb **einladen** has a separable prefix and also has a stem vowel change in the **du**- and **er/sie**-form.

Du *lädst* uns ein.
Er *lädt* dich ein.

c. Inseparable prefixes are never separated from the verb.

*be*grüssen   *ver*dienen   *ge*winnen

d. There are six modal verbs in German.

	sollen *should*	**wollen** *to want to*	**können** *can*	**müssen** *must*	**dürfen** *to be allowed to*	**mögen** *to like*
ich	soll	will	kann	muss	darf	mag
du	sollst	willst	kannst	musst	darfst	magst
er/sie/es	soll	will	kann	muss	darf	mag
wir	sollen	wollen	können	müssen	dürfen	mögen
ihr	sollt	wollt	könnt	müsst	dürft	mögt
sie, Sie	sollen	wollen	können	müssen	dürfen	mögen

Modals are usually used with the infinitive of another verb. If the meaning of the infinitive is clearly understood, it is sometimes omitted.

Willst du morgen ins Kino gehen?   —Ich *kann* nicht. (gehen)

ÜBUNG A

Fill in the correct sports and activities and the letters in the shaded area will also spell a word. Below the puzzle write a sentence telling if you do the sport or activity or not.

1. _____

2. _____

3. _____

4. _____

5. _____

6. _____

7. _____

8. _____

ÜBUNG **B**

Cross out the word in each box that doesn't fit.

Bleistift
Heftmaschine
Lineal
Apfelkuchen

Klavier
Skateboard
Geige
Trompete

Hähnchen
Pommes frites
Hamburger
Apfelsaft

Bruder
Mutter
Tochter
Tante

ÜBUNG **C**

Sort out the verbs with separable and inseparable prefixes and write them in the appropriate column. Put a slash between the prefix and the verb.

There are ten separable and ten inseparable prefix verbs in the box.

fernsehen	begrüssen	verkaufen	anprobieren	gebrauchen
verdienen	aufräumen	mitbringen	vergessen	anrufen
gewinnen	aussehen	einladen	beginnen	verdienen
vorhaben	einkaufen	bekommen	vorbereiten	beantworten

Separable   *Inseparable*

_____   _____

_____   _____

_____   _____

_____   _____

_____   _____

_____   _____

_____   _____

_____   _____

_____   _____

_____   _____

ÜBUNG D

Write the German equivalent for each English sentence. Use modals and an appropriate verb from the list given.

nach Hause gehen   **bleiben**   **fahren**
mitkommen   **üben**

1. I can't stay.

   _____

2. He's not allowed to drive.

   _____

3. We're supposed to go home.

   _____

4. She has to practice.

   _____

5. Do you want to come along?

   _____

ÜBUNG E

Work with a partner. You invite your partner to do the things listed on the left. Your partner says he or she can't and gives an excuse. Switch roles. Add to the invitations and excuses if you can.

Willst du...   **Ich kann nicht. Ich muss...**

Kannst du...   **Ich soll...**

ins Kino gehen   **meine Hausaufgaben machen**

Tennis spielen   **zu Hause bleiben**

Karten spielen   **Klavier üben**

ein Eis essen   **meine Grosseltern besuchen**

ÜBUNG F

Do Activity E again, this time addressing two classmates. What changes have to be made?

Proficiency Activities

Speaking

Practice the following situations with a partner. One takes the role of A, the other takes the role of B.

1. **A** You are in a department store buying school supplies. Politely ask the salesperson the price of three items you are interested in.
   B You are the salesperson. Answer A's questions.

2. **A** You and B are talking about sports, hobbies, and activities. Ask B what he or she does and respond to B's questions about what you do.
   B Respond to A's questions and ask about his or her sports, hobbies, and activities.

3. **A** You are getting to know a new classmate. Tell B about your family. Mention how many brothers and sisters you have. Give their names, ages, and tell what they like to do.
   B Tell A about your family.

4. **A** You and B are at a snack stand. Ask B what he or she wants to eat and drink.
   B Respond to A's questions and ask what A is going to have.

5. **A** You are having a party. Invite B to come. Tell when the party is, tell who else is coming, and mention something B can bring.
   B Accept or decline the invitation. If you decline, tell why you can't come.

Listening

Listen to the following bits of conversation and determine whether the response in each case makes sense or not. Check the appropriate column.

	MAKES SENSE	DOESN'T MAKE SENSE
1.	_____	_____
2.	_____	_____
3.	_____	_____
4.	_____	_____
5.	_____	_____

Reading

Read the following letter from a student in Germany looking for a pen pal. Then answer the questions.

Hallo! Ich heisse Alexander Reiter. Ich bin 14 Jahre alt. Ich wohne in Bremen. Das ist eine Stadt in Norddeutschland. Ich habe drei Geschwister: zwei Brüder und eine Schwester. Meine Brüder studieren schon auf der Universität. Markus ist in Hamburg, und Paul ist in Mainz. Meine Schwester ist 16. Sie geht aufs Gymnasium. Ich gehe auch aufs Gymnasium und bin in der 9. Klasse. Mathe, Biologie und Englisch sind meine Lieblingsfächer. In meiner Freizeit mache ich gern Sport, und ich habe auch viele Hobbys. Ich spiele Basketball, und ich schwimme viel. Ich fotografiere gern, ich sammle Comic-Hefte, ich spiele Computer, und ich höre Musik. Musik habe ich sehr gern! Ich spiele Gitarre und spiele immer mit ein paar Freunden zusammen. Unsere Band heisst "Mr. Pluto."

Read the questions and determine whether they are true or false based on what you have read. Check the appropriate column.

	JA	NEIN
1. Alexander studiert auf der Universität.	————	————
2. Er kommt aus Bremen.	————	————
3. Er hat drei Schwestern.	————	————
4. Er lernt Mathe, Biologie und Englisch gern.	————	————
5. Er macht keinen Sport.	————	————
6. Er spielt in einer Band.	————	————

Writing

1. At the beginning of the school year you go shopping for school supplies. Write five items you need to buy.

_____

_____

2. The teacher would like to know a little more about you. Write five things you like to do in your leisure time.

_____

_____

_____

3. Write a short paragraph about your family. Include your parents' names; whether you have brothers and sisters (if you do, tell their names and ages); whether you have pets (if you do, tell what you have and what you call them).

_____

_____

_____

_____

_____

4. List five things you like to eat or drink when you go to a fast food stand or restaurant.

_____

_____

_____

5. You are having a party. Write a note to a friend inviting him or her to come. Be sure to include the date and time of the party. Mention also what your friend can bring, who else will be there, some of the things you are planning to serve.

_____

_____

_____

_____

_____

2
Zweiter Teil

6
Die Ferien

Review: The Conversational Past; Time Expressions with Seasons, Months, and Parts of Days

1 Wortschatz

Was kannst du alles in den Ferien machen?

eine Reise machen—
nach Deutschland fliegen

einen Stadtbummel
machen

in den Bergen wandern

angeln

zelten

reiten

windsurfen gehen

segeln

**zu Hause bleiben
und faulenzen**

2 The students in Frau Heim's German class are discussing what they did during the last vacation. Read the dialogue and see what you remember about the conversational past.

FRAU HEIM: Was hast du in den Ferien gemacht, Monika?

MONIKA: Ich bin mit meinen Eltern nach Deutschland gereist. Wir sind nach Frankfurt geflogen, dann sind wir mit dem Zug nach München gefahren.

FRAU HEIM: Wie schön! Wie war* die Reise?

MONIKA: Die Reise war ganz toll! Wir haben viele alte Städte und Schlösser gesehen, und ich habe viel Deutsch gesprochen.

FRAU HEIM: Das ist grossartig! Hast du auch fotografiert?

MONIKA: Ja. Ich kann morgen meine Fotos mitbringen.

FRAU HEIM: Gut! Und du, Paul. Hast du auch eine Reise gemacht?

PAUL: Ich war in einem Ferienlager in den Bergen. Es hat viel Spass gemacht. Wir sind jeden Tag geschwommen. Ich bin auch windsurfen und segeln gegangen. Es war super!

FRAU HEIM: Windsurfen! Das habe ich noch nie gemacht. Habt ihr auch Wanderungen gemacht?

PAUL: Na klar! Wir sind viel gewandert. Wir haben auch gezeltet. —Und Sie, Frau Heim, was haben Sie in den Ferien gemacht?

FRAU HEIM: Ich bin zu Hause geblieben. Ich habe viel gelesen, habe im Garten gearbeitet, und ich habe auch einfach gefaulenzt! Es war herrlich!

alte Städte und Schlösser *old cities and castles*
das Ferienlager *vacation camp*

* This is a simple past tense form of the verb **sein**, *to be*. It means *was*. You will learn more about these forms later. For now, it is enough to recognize the forms **ich/er/sie/es war, du warst, wir/sie/Sie waren,** and **ihr wart** when you see them.

ÜBUNG A

Write a caption in German for each picture. Base your captions on the dialogue you just read.

BEISPIEL:

Frau Heim hat gefaulenzt.

1. _____

_____

2. _____

_____

3. _____

_____

4. _____

_____

5. _____

_____

6. _____

_____

7. _____

_____

8. _____

_____

3 In the dialogue on page 106, the students and their teacher are talking about their _____. The events happened in the _____. Most of the verbs in the dialogue are in the conversational past. Do you remember how to form the conversational past? It consists of two parts: the helping verb, either **haben** or **sein**, and the past participle.

hat gespielt
ist gegangen

Refresh your memory and conjugate the two helping verbs.

	haben	**sein**
ich	_____	_____
du	_____	_____
er/sie/es	_____	_____
wir	_____	_____
ihr	_____	_____
sie	_____	_____
Sie	_____	_____

It is best to learn the helping verb along with the past participle of each verb. It might be helpful to remember that verbs conjugated with **sein** often show a change of location or condition.

Now reread the dialogue and write down all the verbs in the conversational past.

Write the helping verb and the past participle.

BEISPIEL: **hast gemacht**

1. _____
2. _____
3. _____
4. _____
5. _____
6. _____
7. _____
8. _____
9. _____
10. _____
11. _____
12. _____
13. _____
14. _____
15. _____
16. _____
17. _____
18. _____
19. _____

Look at the past participles you wrote down. Some end in _____, and some end in _____. What do you think is the difference?

German verbs are referred to as weak (regular) or strong (irregular). The past participle of weak verbs ends in **-t**, the past participle of strong verbs ends in **-en**. The past participles of strong verbs may also have vowel and/or consonant changes. Look again at the verbs you wrote down. Which ones are weak and which ones are strong?

WEAK: _____

_____

STRONG: _____

_____

Can you give the infinitives of these verbs?

WEAK: _____

_____

STRONG: _____

_____

To form the past participle of weak verbs, add the prefix _____ to the **er/sie**-form of the verb.

INFINITIVE	VERB STEM	PRESENT TENSE	CONVERSATIONAL PAST
spielen	spiel-	er spielt	er hat gespielt
warten	wart-	er wartet	er hat gewartet

What do you notice about the verb **warten**? How are the **er**-ending and the past participle ending different from the endings on **spielen**? Why do you think this occurs? —Verbs with a stem ending in **-t** or **-d** add **-est** in the **du**-form and **-et** in the **er/sie**-form, the **ihr**-form, and in the past participle.

Let's see if you remember how to form the conversational past of the following weak verbs.

	machen	**angeln**	**arbeiten**
ich	_____	_____	_____
du	_____	_____	_____
er	_____	_____	_____
sie	_____	_____	_____
es	_____	_____	_____
wir	_____	_____	_____
ihr	_____	_____	_____
sie	_____	_____	_____
Sie	_____	_____	_____

The conversational past of the verb **fotografieren** is _____. The past participle does not have the prefix _____. Verbs ending in **-ieren** do not add **ge-** in the past participle:

> telefonieren   hat telefoniert
> probieren   hat probiert

4   Now let's review the conversational past of strong verbs.

INFINITIVE	VERB STEM	PRESENT TENSE	CONVERSATIONAL PAST
lesen	les-	er liest	er hat gelesen
nehmen	nehm-	er nimmt	er hat genommen
bleiben	bleib-	er bleibt	er ist geblieben
laufen	lauf-	er läuft	er ist gelaufen

Point out where the irregularities occur in these verbs. As you can see, the irregularities in strong verbs are generally not predictable. Therefore you must learn the irregularities as you learn each new verb.

On the vocabulary lists and in the vocabulary section at the back of this book, irregularities such as stem vowel changes, irregular past participles, and past participles with **sein** as a helping verb, will be indicated.

Here are some commonly used strong verbs you learned in Book I.

bleiben (bleibt, ist geblieben) *to stay*
essen (*isst*, hat gegessen) *to eat*
fahren (*fährt*, ist gefahren) *to ride*
geben (*gibt*, hat gegeben) *to give*
gehen (geht, ist gegangen) *to go*
helfen (*hilft*, hat geholfen) *to help*
kommen (kommt, ist gekommen)
   to come
laufen (*läuft*, ist gelaufen) *to walk*
lesen (*liest*, hat gelesen) *to read*
nehmen (*nimmt*, hat genommen)
   to take
reiten (reitet, ist geritten) *to ride*
   (a horse)

schlafen (*schläft*, hat geschlafen)
   to sleep
schreiben (schreibt, hat geschrieben)
   to write
**schwimmen (schwimmt, ist
   geschwommen)** *to swim*
sehen (*sieht*, hat gesehen) *to see*
sein (*ist*, ist gewesen) *to be*
singen (singt, hat gesungen) *to sing*
sprechen (*spricht*, hat gesprochen)
   to speak
stehen (steht, hat gestanden) *to stand*
trinken (trinkt, hat getrunken) *to drink*
tun (tut, hat getan) *to do*

Now write all the forms of the conversational past for the following verbs.

	essen	laufen	schreiben
ich			
du			
er			
sie			
es			
wir			
ihr			
sie			
Sie			

ÜBUNG B

Choose elements from each column below to write eight sentences in the conversational past.

ich	haben	Golf	gemacht
du	hat	eine Reise	gespielt
Claudia	habt	schwimmen	gegangen
wir	habe	segeln	
ihr	hast	einen Stadtbummel	
Hans und Uwe	seid	Tennis	
Herr Seiler	sind	Volleyball	
die Mädchen und Jungen	bin	eine Wanderung	
Otto	ist	windsurfen	
	bist		

BEISPIEL: **Wir haben eine Wanderung gemacht.**

1. _____

2. _____

3. _____

4. _____

5. _____

6. _____

7. _____

8. _____

ÜBUNG **C**

You and your friends went on a picnic. Match the words on the left with the verbs on the right and tell about what you did, using the conversational past.

ein Picknick	schwimmen
belegte Brote	trinken
Apfelsaft	spielen
Volleyball	laufen
im See	essen
um den See	kommen
bis 19 Uhr	machen
spät nach Hause	bleiben

BEISPIEL: **Wir haben ein Picknick gemacht.**

1. _____

2. _____

3. _____

4. _____

5. _____

6. _____

7. _____

ÜBUNG **D**

A classmate who didn't go along to the picnic asks one of your friends if he also did each of the things mentioned. Rewrite each of the sentences above, this time in the form of a question addressed to Hans.

BEISPIEL: **Hans, hast du auch ein Picknick gemacht?**

1. _____

2. _____

3. _____

4. _____

5. _____

6. _____

7. _____

ÜBUNG E

What did people do on their vacations? Write sentences with the words and phrases given.

BEISPIEL: **der Lehrer / nach England reisen**
 Der Lehrer ist nach England gereist.

1. ich / immer bis zehn Uhr schlafen

_____

2. Heike und Tim / jeden Tag Tennis spielen

_____

3. du / nur faulenzen

_____

4. wir / einen Stadtbummel machen

_____

5. ihr / segeln gehen

_____

6. Susanne / viel fotografieren

_____

5 Ein Brief

Read the following letter. What can you observe about the form? How is the date written? What is different from a letter written in English?

Stuttgart, den 10. September 1998

Liebe Karin!

Lange habe ich nichts von dir gehört. Hast du meine Postkarte bekommen? Ich war mit meinen Eltern in Österreich. Es war herrlich! Wir haben in einer kleinen Pension gewohnt. Die Wirtin, Frau Stiglmeier, war furchtbar nett und lustig. Jeden Tag haben wir etwas Schönes gemacht. Am Montag haben wir am Vormittag Tennis gespielt und sind am Nachmittag schwimmen gegangen. Am Abend haben wir Karten gespielt. Ich habe einmal sogar gewonnen! Am Dienstag haben wir eine grosse Wanderung in den Bergen gemacht. Das Wetter ist gut gewesen, sonnig, aber nicht zu warm. Abends waren wir dann sehr müde und sind gleich nach dem Abendessen ins Bett gegangen! Am Mittwoch bin ich mit meinem Bruder windsurfen gegangen. Das war vielleicht lustig! Wir haben das zum ersten Mal gemacht, und wir sind immer wieder ins Wasser gefallen!

Am Donnerstag hat es geregnet. Wir haben einen Stadtbummel gemacht, oder besser gesagt, einen Dorfbummel! Am Nachmittag haben wir in einem kleinen Café gemütlich Kaffee getrunken, und dann sind wir ins Kino gegangen. Und am Freitag, am 3. August, habe ich Geburtstag gehabt! Morgens beim Frühstück haben mir alle gratuliert, und Frau Stiglmeier hat Blumen auf den Frühstückstisch gestellt! Nach dem Frühstück sind wir mit Herrn Stiglmeier angeln gegangen, und am Nachmittag haben wir Minigolf gespielt. Abends haben wir in einem italienischen Restaurant ganz nett gefeiert. Und dann war es schon Samstag! Die Woche ist so schnell vorbeigegangen! Nach dem Mittagessen hat es ein grosses Volleyballspiel gegeben. Alle haben mitgespielt, und es hat viel Spass gemacht.

Und schon war es der letzte Abend. Im Dorf haben sie samstags immer einen Tanz. Wir haben viel getanzt und gesungen — ein schöner Abschied. Am nächsten Morgen sind wir dann leider nach Hause gefahren. Vielleicht können wir im Winter zum Schilaufen wieder hinfahren. Das wäre toll!

Und was hast du in den Ferien gemacht? Bist du wieder in England bei deinem Onkel gewesen? Da hast du sicher viel Englisch gelernt! Hoffentlich kommst du bald wieder nach Stuttgart. Bitte grüsse deine Eltern ganz herzlich von mir und schreib mal, wie es euch geht!

Herzliche Grüsse

deine Marianne

die Pension *guest house*
die Wirtin *landlady*
müde *tired*
zum ersten Mal *for the first time*
immer wieder *again and again*
das Dorf *village*
gemütlich *cozy, relaxed*
ein schöner Abschied *a nice farewell*
das wäre toll! *that would be great!*
grüssen *to greet, say hello to*

In an informal letter, the place you are writing from comes before the _____.
You have learned that when writing the date in German, the _____ comes
before the _____. How is the punctuation different from English? —The day
and the month are separated by a period rather than a comma, and there is no punctuation between the month and the year. The date is in the accusative case, which is
indicated by the form of the definite article, _____.

Write the following dates as they would appear on a German letter.

1. Stuttgart / May 3, 1994 _____

2. New York / July 31, 1990 _____

3. London / March 10, 1992 _____

4. Hamburg / December 24, 1993 _____

5. Berlin / January 1, 1995 _____

What else can you observe in this letter? —**Liebe** ends in -e because **Karin** is feminine.
If Marianne were writing to Robert, she would write _____ **Robert!**

How is the punctuation on the salutation different?

Now answer these questions about the letter to check your comprehension.

1. Who is writing the letter?

   _____

2. To whom is that person writing?

   _____

3. What is the person writing about?

   _____

6 In the letter, Marianne tells what she did on each day of her vacation. She often mentions whether it was in the morning, afternoon, or evening. Complete the following phrases.

am Morgen   *in the morning (early)*

_____ Vormittag   *in the morning (before noon)*

_____ Nachmittag   *in the afternoon*

_____ Abend   *in the evening*

You can also say **morgens, vormittags, nachmittags,** and **abends**.

Now complete the phrases with the days of the week.

am Montag   *on Monday*

_____ _____   *on Tuesday*

_____ _____   *on Wednesday*

_____ _____   *on Thursday*

_____ _____   *on Friday*

_____ _____   *on Saturday*

_____ _____   *on Sunday*

You can also say **montags, dienstags,** and so on. This usually suggests regularity, for example, that something happens every Monday.

ÜBUNG **F**

Reread Marianne's letter and fill in the chart showing what she did on each day of her vacation.

	am Vormittag	am Nachmittag	am Abend
am Montag	Tennis spielen		
am Dienstag			
am Mittwoch			
am Donnerstag			
am Freitag			
am Samstag			
am Sonntag			

ÜBUNG G

Now express what you have written in the chart in paragraph form, telling what Marianne did on each day of her vacation. If you start a sentence with a word or phrase other than the subject, for example, **am Montag**, don't forget to invert the word order.

Am Montag *hat Marianne* Tennis gespielt. _____

_____

_____

_____

_____

_____

7 The contraction **am (an dem)** is also used in dates. Find the sentence in Marianne's letter where she mentions her birthday. How does she express the date? _____ When is your birthday?

_____

Now write sentences telling your birthday and the birthdays of five of your friends or family members.

BEISPIEL: **Mein Bruder hat am 28. Oktober Geburtstag*.**
My brother's birthday is on October 28th.

1. Ich _____.

2. _____

3. _____

4. _____

5. _____

6. _____

*Read **"am achtundzwanzigsten Oktober."**

8 The contraction **im (in dem)** is used to express in what season or in what month something occurs.

> **im Sommer** *in the summer*
> **im Juli** *in July*
>
> BUT: **am 4. Juli** *on the 4th of July*

ÜBUNG **H**

Fill in the chart with sports and activities you do in each season of the year. Then write sentences telling what you do in each of the seasons.

Herbst	Winter

Frühling	Sommer

1. Im Herbst _____

   _____

2. _____

   _____

3. _____

   _____

4. _____

   _____

ÜBUNG I

Complete each sentence with the phrase expressing the correct month.

1. _____ beginnt die Schule.

2. _____ haben wir Sommerferien.

3. Halloween ist _____.

4. Thanksgiving ist _____.

5. Weihnachten ist _____.

6. Martin Luther King Day ist _____.

7. Washington und Lincoln haben _____ Geburtstag.

8. Muttertag ist _____.

9. Vatertag ist _____.

10. Mein Geburtstag ist _____.

ÜBUNG J

Hör gut zu! You will hear some students talking about their vacations. Some are talking about what they are doing now and some are telling what they did last year. Listen to each statement and determine if it is referring to what the person is doing now (the present) or if it is referring to what he or she did last year (the conversational past). Put a check mark in the appropriate column.

	NOW (PRESENT)	LAST YEAR (CONVERSATIONAL PAST)
1.	_____	_____
2.	_____	_____
3.	_____	_____
4.	_____	_____
5.	_____	_____
6.	_____	_____
7.	_____	_____
8.	_____	_____

ÜBUNG K

Here is part of a travel folder showing some of the things you can do at this particular vacation spot. Work with a partner. Pretend you just got back from the vacation spot described in this folder. You tell your partner all the things you can do. Your partner asks if you did each one and you respond. Follow the example on the next page.

Du: Du kannst schwimmen gehen.
Partner: Und bist du auch schwimmen gegangen?

Du: Ja,
    ich bin… schwimmen gegangen
        viel *a lot*
        jeden Tag *every day*
        manchmal *sometimes*

Nein,
    ich bin… schwimmen gegangen.
        nie *never*
        gar nicht *not at all*
        nicht einmal *not once*

ÜBUNG L

Aufsatz. Your family is spending a vacation at a summer resort. Write an entry in your travel diary for one of the vacation days, telling all the different things you did on that day. Use the conversational past.

_____, den 7. August

KLASSENPROJEKT

Make a travel folder or poster for an imaginary vacation resort or area. Draw or cut out pictures from magazines or travel folders. Use the formal **Sie**-form in the text. Make individual folders or posters or work in groups.

PERSÖNLICHE FRAGEN ?

1. Hast du schon eine Reise nach Deutschland gemacht? Wann? Mit wem? Wie lange bist du geblieben?

2. Was machst du gewöhnlich in den Sommerferien?

3. Was hast du in den letzten Ferien gemacht?

4. Welche Bücher hast du in den Sommerferien gelesen?

5. Welche Filme und Videos hast du gesehen?

6. Was hast du lieber: Sommerferien oder Winterferien? Warum?

ÜBUNG M

Interview a classmate, asking the above questions. Take notes and report what you learned to the class.

WORTSCHATZ A-Z

der Berg, -e *mountain*
in den Bergen *in the mountains*
das Ferienlager *vacation camp*
   in einem Ferienlager *in a vacation camp*
das photo, -s *photo*
der Stadtbummel *stroll through the city*
   einen Stadtbummel machen *to take
     a stroll through the city*
die Wanderung, -en *hike*
   eine, Wanderung, machen *to take
     a hike*

angeln (angelt, hat geangelt) *to fish*
faulenzen (faulenzt, hat gefaulenzt)
   to be lazy
fliegen (fliegt, ist geflogen) *to fly*
segeln (segelt, hat gesegelt) *to sail*
windsurfen gehen (geht w., ist w.
   gegangen) *to go windsurfing*

Diese Wörter kennst du schon*

die Ferien (pl.) *vacation*
die Reise, -n *trip*
   eine Reise machen *to take a trip*
der Zug, ̈-e *train*
   mit dem Zug *by train*
bleiben (bleibt, ist geblieben) *to stay,
   remain*
   zu Hause bleiben *to stay home*
fahren (fährt, ist gefahren) *to ride,
   go by vehicle*
fotografieren (fotografiert, hat fotografiert)
   to photograph
wandern (wandert, ist gewandert) *to hike*
zelten (zeltet, hat gezeltet) *to camp out
   (in a tent)*
am Morgen *in the morning (early)*

am Vormittag *in the morning
   (before noon)*
am Nachmittag *in the afternoon*
am Abend *in the evening*
morgens *in the morning (early);
   mornings*
nachmittags *in the afternoon; afternoons*
abends *in the evening; evenings*
am Montag (am Dienstag, etc.)
   on Monday
montags (dienstags, etc.) *on Monday;
   Mondays; etc.*
im Sommer *in the summer*
im Juli *in July*
am 4. Juli *on the 4th of July*

Und so sagst du das *Here's how to . . .*

express how much or how often

viel *a lot*
jeden Tag *every day*
manchmal *sometimes*
nie *never*

noch nie *never yet*
gar nicht *not at all*
nicht einmal *not once*

*Also study the list of verbs that were introduced in Book 1 on page 112.

express enthusiasm

wie schön! *how nice!*   super! *super!*
ganz toll! *really great!*   herrlich! *wonderful!, beautiful!*
grossartig! *terrific!*

say when it's your birthday

Ich habe am 28. Oktober Geburstag. *My birthday is on October 28th.*

write the date on a letter

Stuttgart, den 10. September 1998 *Stuttgart, September 10, 1998*

write the greeting on a friendly letter

Liebe (Marianne)! *Dear (Marianne),*   Lieber (Robert)! *Dear (Robert),*

write the closing on a friendly letter

Herzliche Grüsse *best regards*

Building your vocabulary

Nouns and verbs are sometimes related. If you know the verb, you can often figure out the meaning of the noun. If you know the noun, you can often tell the meaning of the verb. For example, in this chapter you learned the word **der Stadtbummel,** *a stroll through the city.* What do you think the verb **bummeln** means? It means *to stroll.* What do the following nouns and verbs mean?

die Reise _____   reisen _____

die Wanderung _____   wandern _____

das Foto _____   fotografieren _____

die Sammlung _____   sammeln _____

das Spiel _____   spielen _____

ÜBUNG N

Memory-Spiel: Was hast du in den Ferien gemacht? How long can you and your classmates keep the game going? Use as many phrases as possible.

angeln   **schwimmen**   **windsurfen**   **Wasserskilaufen**

In den Ferien bin ich segeln gegangen.
In den Ferien bin ich segeln und . . . gegangen.
In den Ferien bin ich . . .

Golf   **Volleyball**   **Basketball**   **Tischtennis**   **Karten**

In den Ferien habe ich Tennis gespielt.
In den Ferien habe ich Tennis und . . . gespielt.
In den Ferien habe ich . . .

KULTURECKE

Urlaub und Ferien

In German there are two words for vacation: **Urlaub** and **Ferien**. People who work and earn money have **Urlaub**; students have **Ferien** — for elementary and secondary school students (**Schüler**) it is called **Schulferien** and for university students (**Studenten**) it is called **Semesterferien**.

Most workers in Germany today get six weeks vacation a year as well as extra vacation pay. On their vacations, Germans love to travel. Many go to vacation areas in Germany — the North Sea coast, the Harz Mountains, the Black Forest, or the Bavarian Alps, for example. Many others go to Austria, Switzerland, France, Spain, and Italy. A wide variety of relatively inexpensive flights and vacation packages to the United States and other more far away places is available and very popular.

In Germany, school vacations are shorter but more frequent than in the U. S. There are six weeks of vacation in the summer, **die grossen Ferien**, one or two weeks in the fall, **die Herbstferien**, two weeks at Christmas, **die Weihnachtsferien**, two weeks at Easter, **die Osterferien**, and one week in June, **die Pfingstferien**. Because so many people travel during the summer, the states in Germany stagger their summer vacations in order to ease the congestion on the highways.

Here is the vacation schedule for the school year 1996-97 in the state of Baden-Württemberg. Compare the vacation dates with your own.

Ferientermine in Baden-Württemberg 1996-1997				
Herbstferien '96	**Weihnachten '96**	**Osterferien '97**	**Pfingstferien '97**	**Sommerferien '97**
26.10 – 30.10	23.12 – 10.1.97	1.4 – 4.4	20.5 – 31.5	31.7 – 13.9

7
Alles für den Sport
Conversational Past of Verbs with Separable and Inseparable Prefixes

1 Wortschatz

Im Sommer und Im Winter —- Sport macht Spass!

You probably know what most of the items pictured are in German. Write the number of the item in front of the label that goes with it. Some of the words are cognates, others are related to words you already know. Use the word-building skills you have been practicing.

_____ der Tennisschläger   _____ das Zelt   _____ das Snowboard

_____ die Tennisbälle   _____ der Schlafsack   _____ die Skier

_____ die Tennisschuhe   _____ der Rucksack   _____ die Skistiefel

_____ das Skateboard   _____ die Wanderstiefel   _____ die Schlittschuhe

_____ das Fahrrad   _____ der Badeanzug   _____ der Hockeyschläger

_____ die Rollschuhe   _____ die Badehose   _____ der Schlitten

_____ das Segelbrett   _____ die Wasserskier

ÜBUNG A

Here are some popular sports and activities. Organize them in the chart below.

Tennis spielen   **Skateboard fahren**   **schwimmen (gehen)**
zelten (gehen)   **Wasserski laufen**   **wandern (gehen)**
Schlittschuh laufen   **Ski laufen**   **windsurfen gehen**
Snowboard fahren   **Eishockey spielen**   **Schlitten fahren**
Rollschuh laufen   **Rad fahren**

SOMMER	SOMMER und WINTER	WINTER

ÜBUNG B

Draw lines matching the equipment with the appropriate sport or activity.

Skateboard fahren

Eishockey spielen

Schlitten fahren

Wasserski laufen

Rollschuh laufen

Rad fahren

Ski laufen

windsurfen gehen

Tennis spielen

wandern gehen

Snowboard fahren

Schlittschuh laufen

zelten gehen

schwimmen gehen

ÜBUNG C

From Übung B, choose six of the activities that you would like to do. Write what you need to do each one. Follow the example.

BEISPIEL: **Ich möchte Wasserski laufen.**
Ich brauche einen Badeanzug (oder eine Badehose) und Wasserskier.

1 _____

_____

2 _____

_____

3. _____

_____

4. _____

_____

5. _____

_____

ÜBUNG D

Work with a partner. Ask your partner if he or she does each of the activities listed. Take notes and report to the class.

2 Der Skiausflug

Der Skibus ist um 7 Uhr angekommen. Alle haben ihre Skier, Snowboards und Stiefel abgegeben und sind eingestiegen. Um 7 Uhr 30 ist der Bus pünktlich abgefahren. Aber Moment! Der Peter ist nicht mitgefahren! Er hat sein Snowboard vergessen, und er ist zurückgelaufen. Jetzt hat er leider den Bus verpasst!

Beantworte kurz die Fragen!

1. Wann ist der Skibus angekommen? _____

2. Wann ist er abgefahren? _____

3. Wer ist nicht mitgefahren? _____

4. Was hat er vergessen? _____

3 Read the text about the **Skiausflug** again. Underline the past participles. There are six verbs with _____ prefixes and two verbs with _____ prefixes. Write the past participle next to the corresponding infinitive below.

ankommen, ist _____   vergessen, hat _____

abgeben, hat _____   verpassen, hat _____

einsteigen, ist _____

abfahren, ist _____

mitfahren, ist _____

zurücklaufen, ist _____

What can you observe about the past participles? —In verbs with separable prefixes the _____ comes between the prefix and the rest of the past participle. In verbs with inseparable prefixes there is no _____ in the past participle.

ÜBUNG E

Complete each sentence, writing the correct form of the verb in parentheses in the present tense. Then rewrite the sentence in the conversational past.

BEISPIEL: (ankommen) **Der Skibus kommt um 7 Uhr an.**
            Der Skibus ist um 7 Uhr angekommen.

1. (abgeben)   Die Schüler _____ ihre Skier _____.

   _____

2. (einsteigen) Sie (*pl.*) _____ in den Skibus _____.

   _____

3. (abfahren)   Der Skibus _____ um 7 Uhr 30 _____.

   _____

4. (mitfahren)   Peter _____ nicht _____.

   _____

5. (vergessen)   Er _____ sein Snowboard.

   _____

6. (zurücklaufen) Er _____ schnell _____.

   _____

7. (verpassen)   Er _____ den Bus.

   _____

ÜBUNG F

Use the following phrases to write a short story. Use the conversational past.

aus dem Bus aussteigen	**im Bus singen**
ein Liftticket kaufen	**in den Bus einsteigen**
den ganzen Nachmittag Snowboard fahren	**mittags etwas essen**
den ganzen Vormittag Ski laufen	**um 9 Uhr 30 im Skigebiet ankommen**

Die 8. Klasse hat einen Skiausflug gemacht. Die Schüler...

4 Here are some verbs with separable prefixes you learned in **Lektion 5**. Complete the past participles.

anrufen, hat an___rufen   **einladen, hat ein___laden**

aufräumen, hat auf___räumt   **mitbringen, hat mit___bracht**

einkaufen, hat ein___kauft   **vorhaben, hat vor___habt**

Here are three more prefix verbs you learned. What do you notice about the past participles of these verbs?

begrüssen, hat begrüsst
anprobieren, hat anprobiert
vorbereiten, hat vorbereitet

The past participles of these verbs do not have a _____. Why not? —The prefix **be-** is inseparable (**begrüssen, vorbereiten**). The verb **anprobieren** ends in **-ieren**. Remember: verbs with inseparable prefixes and verbs ending in **-ieren** do not have **ge-** in the past participle.

ÜBUNG G

Practice some of the verbs you learned in **Lektion 5**. Julia's mother asks her if she has done everything for the party. Complete what she says. Follow the example.

BEISPIEL: **Du musst deine Freunde anrufen.**
          Hast du deine Freunde angerufen?

1. Du musst deine Freunde einladen.

   _____

2. Du musst den Keller aufräumen.

   _____

3. Du musst die Partysachen einkaufen.

   _____

4. Du musst das Essen vorbereiten.

   _____

5. Du musst deine Bluse anprobieren.

   _____

5 Infinitives are often used as nouns: **Wandern macht Spass. Schwimmen hält fit.** To form a noun from a verb, the infinitive form is simply capitalized. The gender of such nouns is always neuter. Verb phrases such as **Karten spielen** and **Ski laufen** are written as one word: **Karten spielen** becomes **das Kartenspielen**; **Ski laufen** becomes **das Skilaufen.**

Make nouns out of the following verbs. Also write the definite article.

1. schreiben _____

2. lesen _____

3. essen _____

4. Briefmarken sammeln _____

5. Skateboard fahren _____

6. Rad fahren _____

ÜBUNG H

Give your opinion about the following sports and activities and tell whether or not you like to do each one. Use the suggested phrases as needed.

Briefmarken sammeln	**turnen**	**wandern**
Tischtennis spielen	**radfahren**	**Ski laufen**
Karten spielen	**schwimmen**	

Was meinst du?   *What do you think?*
Wie findest du... ?   *What do you think of . . .?*

... **macht Spass**   . . . *is fun*   ... **ist gefährlich**   . . . *is dangerous*
... **hält fit**   . . . *keeps you fit*   ... **ist schwer**   . . . *is hard*
... **ist toll**   . . . *is great*   ... **ist teuer**   . . . *is expensive*
... **ist langweilig**   . . . *is boring*

BEISPIEL: **Kartenspielen ist toll. Ich spiele gern Karten.**
   OR **Kartenspielen ist langweilig. Ich spiele nicht gern Karten.**

1. _____

_____

2. _____

_____

3. _____

4. _____

_____

5. _____

_____

6. _____

_____

ÜBUNG I

Continue **Übung H** orally, asking your classmates how they like various sports and activities. You may add others to the list given.

ÜBUNG J

Write whether you have ever done the following sports.

BEISPIEL: **Wasserski laufen**
   Ja, ich bin schon Wasserski gelaufen.
OR **Nein, ich bin noch nie Wasserski gelaufen.**

1. Rollerblade fahren

_____

2. Golf spielen

_____

3. Skateboard fahren

_____

4. windsurfen gehen

_____

5. Ski laufen

_____

6. Hockey spielen

_____

ÜBUNG K

Work with a partner and ask if he or she has ever done the sports mentioned in the preceding activity.

Du: **Bist du schon Wasserski gelaufen?**
Partner: **Ja,...** OR **Nein,...**

ÜBUNG L

Hör gut zu! You will hear some bits of conversation. For each exchange you hear, determine whether the response to the comment or question makes sense or not. Check the appropriate column.

JA, PASST GUT.	NEIN, PASST NICHT.
1. _____	_____
2. _____	_____
3. _____	_____
4. _____	_____
5. _____	_____
6. _____	_____

PERSÖNLICHE FRAGEN ?

1. Gehst du gern zelten? Wo machst du das — an einem See? in den Bergen? auf einem Campingplatz? Mit wem gehst du zelten?

_____

_____

_____

2. Machst du gern Wintersport? Was machst du alles?

_____

_____

3. Was machst du im Sommer?

_____

_____

ÜBUNG M

Aufsatz. Write a short composition about the sports and activities mentioned in this chapter. What do you think of the various sports? Are they fun? Are they boring? Which ones do you do? Which ones have you never tried? Which ones would you like to try? Here are some phrases to start you off:

Ich finde...   **Ich habe/ bin... noch nie...**
Im Winter... ich...   **Ich möchte mal...**
Im Sommer... ich...

_____

_____

_____

_____

_____

_____

_____

_____

KLASSENPROJEKT

Design an ad or a display window for a sporting goods store. Draw items or cut out pictures from newspapers, catalogs, or magazines. Label the items.

WORTSCHATZ A-Z

der Ausflug, ⸚e *excursion, outing*
das Liftticket -s *lift ticket*
der Schlafsack, ⸚e *sleeping bag*
der Schläger *racquet*
   Tennisschläger *tennis racquet*
   Hockeyschläger *hockey stick*
der Schlitten *sled*
der Schuh, -e *shoe*
   Rollschuh *roller skate*
   Schlittschuh *ice skate*
   Tennisschuh *sneaker*
das Segelbrett, -er *windsurfing board*
das Skateboard, -s *skateboard*
das Snowboard, -s *snowboard*
der Ski, -er *ski*
das Skigebiet, -e *ski area*
der Stiefel *boot*
   Skistiefel *ski boot*
   Wanderstiefel *hiking boot*

ab•geben (gibt ab, hat abgegeben) *to check, hand in*
an•kommen (ist angekommen) *to arrive*

ein•steigen (steigt ein ist, eingestiegen) *to board, climb in*
finden (findet, hat gefunden) *to find*
meinen (meint, hat gemeint) *to think, have the opinion*
mit•fahren (fährt mit, er ist mitgefahren) *to drive, ride, go along*
verpassen (verpast, hat verpasst) *to miss*
zurück•laufen (läuft zurück, ist zurückgelaufen) *to run back*

Schlitten Skateboard Snowboard	fahren *to go*	*sledding* *skateboarding* *snowboarding*
Rollschuh Schlittschuh Ski Wasserski	laufen* *to go*	*roller skating* *ice skating* *skiing* *water skiing*

Moment! *just a minute!*
pünktlich *on time, punctual*
Sport hält fit *sports keep you in shape*

Diese Wörter kennst du schon

der Badeanzug, ⸚e *(woman's) bathing suit*
die Badehose, -n *swim trunks*
das Fahrrad, ⸚er *bicycle*
der Rucksack, ⸚e *backpack*
das Zelt, -e *tent*
ab•fahren (fährt ab, ist abgefahren) *to drive, ride away; depart*
Rad fahren (fährt Rad, ist Rad gefahren) *to ride on a bike, to bicycle*

vergessen (vergisst, hat vergessen) *to forget*
zelten (zeltet, hat gezeltet) *to go camping*
gefährlich *dangerous*
langweilig *boring*
macht Spass *is fun*
schwer *hard, difficult*
teuer *expensive*

*Ski fahren and Wasserski fahren are also used.

Und so sagst du das *Here's how to . . .*

ask for someone's opinion

Was meinst du?   *What do you think?*

Wie findest du (Skifahren)?   *How do like (skiing)? What do you think of . . . ?*

express your opinion

Ich finde (Skilaufen...   *I think (skiing) is . . .*

(Skilaufen) ist...   *(Skiing) is . . .*

Building your vocabulary

In **Lektion 6** you practiced recognizing the meaning of related words. For example, if you know the meaning of the noun, you can often figure out the meaning of the related verb and vice versa. Continue practicing this strategy by writing the verb each of the following nouns are based on.

der Schlafsack _____   das Zelt _____

das Fahrrad _____   das Segelboot _____

die Skier _____   die Wanderstiefel _____

Here are some more compound words. Say each compound word with the definite article and give the English meaning. Remember, compound words have the gender of the final part of the compound.

Tischtennis-   Tennis-   Schlitt-   Golf-   Tennis-   Hockey-

Fuss- ___ **-ball** ___ Golf-   **-schuh**   **-schläger**

Basket- ___   ___ Volley-   Roll- ___   ___ Tennis-   Golf- ___   ___ Tischtennis-

ÜBUNG N

Wortschatzspiele. Make flashcards with pictures of the equipment and clothing you learned in this chapter. **Spiel 1:** The class will be divided into two teams. The first person on Team A is shown a flashcard and must identify the item or give the related verb or use the related verb in a sentence (or do all three!) If the Team A student is wrong, the first person on Team B gets a chance. The team with the most correct answers wins. **Spiel 2:** Write the activity verbs (**Ski fahren**, and so on) on separate flashcards. Shuffle six pictured item-cards and six matching verb-cards. Line up the cards along the chalkboard so the pictures and verbs are not showing. Identify the cards by writing the numbers from one to twelve on the chalkboard. Then test your memory by matching the pictured item with the verb.

KULTURECKE

Young people in Germany like to participate in all kinds of sports and activities and there are many opportunities available through local clubs, church groups, and regional and national youth organizations.

Abenteuer-Radtour

für Mädchen und Jungen von 13-15 Jahren

Trekking durch Schwedisch Lappland Europas letzte Wildnis

Eissporthalle

für Eislauf täglich geöffnet 9.30-16.30
Abendlauf 20.00-21.30
jeden Mittwoch Eishockey

Gleitschirmfliegen auf der Schwäbischen Alb

Kanu-Freizeit

in Südfrankreich
Kanutouren
auch viel baden und Sport
Busfahrt, Unterkunft, Verpflegung,
Kanumiete, Versicherung, Programm
DM 560

SNOWBOARD-SCHULE

Anfänger und Fortgeschrittene
für Kids, Jugendliche und Erwachsene
Freestyle- und Freeride-Kurse und
Halfpipe Einführungskurse

8
Ein typischer Tag

Reflexive Verbs; Telling Time Using the 24-hour System

1 Wortschatz

Ein typischer Tag bei dem Schüler Thomas Schwarz

am Morgen

Er steht auf.

Er duscht *sich*.

Er zieht *sich* an.

Er frühstückt.

Er geht in die Schule.

Er beeilt *sich*.

tagsüber

8:00

In der Schule
konzentriert er *sich*.

9:30

In der Pause unterhält
er *sich* mit Freunden.

13:30

Er isst sein Mittagessen.

14:00

Er macht seine
Hausaufgaben.

16:00

Er zieht *sich* um.

16:15

Er spielt Fussball.

am Abend

18:30

Er isst sein Abendessen.

19:00

Er macht Hausaufgaben
und liest.

20:00

Er übt mit seiner Band.

21:30

Er sieht ein bisschen
fern.

22:00

Er zieht *sich* aus.

22:15

Er geht ins Bett und
schläft.

2 In Germany, as in many countries around the world, the 24-hour system of telling time is used. It is important to be familiar with this system in order to read such things as train, bus, and plane schedules, movie timetables, TV program listings, store hours, and school schedules. In everyday communication you can say, for example, **ein Uhr nachmittags** or **dreizehn Uhr; sieben Uhr abends** or **neunzehn Uhr.** The 24-hour clock starts with one o'clock in the morning, **ein Uhr,** and goes to twelve midnight, **vierundzwanzig Uhr** or **mitternacht.**

In the USA the 24-hour system is used primarily in the military. How do we in other situations distinguish between seven in the morning and seven in the evening? Look at the times given for Thomas Schwarz's day. How would you express the times in English?

ÜBUNG **A**

Here are some questions for Thomas. Read them and complete his responses by filling in the correct times.

1. Wann stehst du auf? — Ich stehe um _____ auf.

2. Wann duschst du **dich**? — Ich dusche **mich** um _____.

3. Wann ziehst du **dich** an? — Ich ziehe **mich** um _____ an.

4. Wann frühstückst du? — Ich frühstücke um _____.

5. Wann musst du **dich** beeilen? — Ich muss **mich** um _____ beeilen.

6. Wann konzentrierst du **dich**? — Um _____ bin ich in der Schule, und ich konzentriere **mich**.

7. Wann unterhältst du **dich**? — In der Pause um _____ unterhalte ich **mich**.

8. Wann isst du dein Mittagessen? — Ich esse um _____ mein Mittagessen.

9. Wann machst du am Nachmittag deine Hausaufgaben? — Ich mache um _____ meine Hausaufgaben.

10. Wann ziehst du **dich** um? — Ich ziehe **mich** um _____ um.

11. Wann spielst du Fussball? — Ich spiele um _____ Fussball.

12. Wann isst du dein Abendessen? — Ich esse um _____ mein Abendessen.

13. Wann übst du mit deiner Band? — Um _____ übe ich mit meiner Band.

14. Wann ziehst du **dich** aus? — Ich ziehe **mich** um _____ aus.

15 Und wann gehst du ins Bett? — Um _____ gehe ich ins Bett.

ÜBUNG B

Work with a partner. You take the role of Thomas. You partner asks you the questions in **Übung A** and you answer. Then switch roles.

3 Read how students enjoy themselves on the weekend.

Wie amüsieren *sich* Thomas und seine Freunde am Wochenende? Fragen wir sie mal!

Wie amüsiert ihr **euch**?	—Wie amüsieren wir **uns**? Wir…
Wir haben eine Party.	Wir tanzen.
Wir hören Musik.	Wir unterhalten **uns**.
Wir essen Pizza.	Wir sehen **uns** einen Videofilm an.

Look back at the preceding pages and the exchange above. Pay particular attention to the words in boldface. You will notice that certain verbs are used with an additional pronoun. One such verb is **sich amüsieren**, *to enjoy oneself, have a good time.* Can you fill in the correct pronouns?

ich amüsiere _____	*I enjoy myself*
du amüsierst _____	*you enjoy yourself*
er amüsiert _____	*he enjoys himself*
sie amüsiert _____	*she enjoys herself*
wir amüsieren _____	*we enjoy ourselves*
ihr amüsiert _____	*you enjoy yourselves*
sie amüsieren _____	*they enjoy themselves*

Verbs such as **sich amüsieren** are called reflexive verbs. The pronouns are called reflexive pronouns because they refer to the same person as the subject. Read the forms of **sich amüsieren** with their English equivalents. Underline the reflexive pronouns in English. Go back to pages 142-144 and circle the reflexive verbs. What do they mean in English? You will notice that reflexive verbs in German are not always reflexive in the corresponding English.

Look at the two boxes below. Draw lines matching the subject pronouns with the corresponding reflexive pronouns.

SUBJECT PRONOUNS (NOMINATIVE)

ihr	**er**
du	**ich**
wir	**sie** *(pl.)*
sie	

REFLEXIVE PRONOUNS (ACCUSATIVE)

sich	**uns**
dich	**euch**
sich	**sich**
mich	

What can you observe about the reflexive pronouns? —They are the same as the accusative (direct object) pronouns except for the third person, singular and plural.

DIRECT OBJECT PRONOUNS   REFLEXIVE PRONOUNS

	mich	
	dich	
ihn		
sie }		**sich**
es		
	uns	
	euch	
sie		**sich**

In the polite form, (the **Sie** form) the reflexive pronoun is **sich: Amüsieren Sie sich gut, Frau Meier?**

On vocabulary lists and in the end vocabulary, reflexive verbs will be listed in this way: **s. amüsieren.**

ÜBUNG **C**

Choose the correct pronouns for each form of the verb **sich unterhalten**, *to have a conversation*. What do you notice about this verb? Note that both verb forms and pronouns are listed randomly.

ich		_____ unterhält _____	uns	
	wir	_____ unterhalte _____		sich
ihr		_____ unterhalten _____	euch	
	er	_____ unterhaltet _____		mich
du		_____ unterhalten _____	sich	
	sie (*pl.*)	_____ unterhältst _____		dich

ÜBUNG **D**

Write seven sentences in the conversational past, using a word or phrase from each column for each sentence.

er	hast	sich	lange geduscht
meine Mutter	haben	mich	warm angezogen
wir	habt	dich	schnell umgezogen
du	haben	euch	gut konzentriert
ich	hat	sich	nett unterhalten
Ralf und Ilse	habe	uns	nicht beeilt
ihr	hat	sich	nach dem Sport ausgezogen

1. _____

2. _____

3. _____

4. _____

5. _____

6. _____

7. _____

ÜBUNG **E**

Fill in the present tense and conversational past.

	PRESENT	CONVERSATIONAL PAST

1. sich unterhalten

    ich _____   _____

    er _____   _____

2. sich beeilen

    wir _____   _____

    Frau Meier _____   _____

3. sich umziehen

    ihr _____   _____

    die Kinder _____   _____

ÜBUNG **F**

Here is a typical morning in the life of Thomas. Using the cues provided, write what Thomas's mother says and what he replies.

BEISPIEL: **(aufstehen) Du musst aufstehen!... Thomas, bist du aufgestanden?**
Ja, ich bin aufgestanden!

1. (sich duschen)

   MUTTER: _____

   THOMAS: _____

2. (sich warm anziehen)

   MUTTER: _____

   THOMAS: _____

3. (frühstücken)

   MUTTER: _____

   THOMAS: _____

4. (sich beeilen)

   MUTTER: _____

   THOMAS: _____

ÜBUNG **G**

After school Thomas's mother asks him some questions about his day. Thomas answers yes to everything. Write what he says in complete sentences.

1. Mutter: Hast du dich gut konzentriert?

   Thomas: Ja, ich _____.

2. Mutter: Hast du dich mit deinen Freunden unterhalten?

   Thomas: Ja, ich _____.

3. Mutter: Hast du dich nach der Schule umgezogen?

   Thomas: Ja, ich _____.

4. Mutter: Hast du deine Hausaufgaben schon gemacht?

   Thomas: Ja, ich _____.

ÜBUNG **H**

Work with a partner and prepare a scene between mother or father and daughter or son. Use the sentences in the preceding activities. Expand and improvise if you can. Present your scene to the class.

4 Here is a summary of word order in sentences with reflexive verbs. Note the position of the reflexive pronoun.

1ST POSITION	2ND POSITION	3RD POSITION		LAST POSITION
Ich	ziehe	mich	heute warm	an.
Ziehst	du	dich	heute auch warm	an?
Du	musst	dich	heute warm	anziehen!
Hast	du	dich	warm	angezogen?

5 What does Sarah do in the morning? Read what she says.

Ich putzte *mir* die Zähne.

Ich wasche *mir* die Haare.

Ich kämme *mir* die Haare.

Ich mache *mir* etwas zu essen.

Ich ziehe *mir* die Jacke an.

Ich setze *mir* die Mütze auf.

6 **Sarah will jetzt in die Schule gehen. Sie verabschiedet *sich* von ihrer Mutter.**

SARAH: Tschüs, Mutti! Ich geh' jetzt!

Mutter: Du gehst schon? Hast du **dir** die Zähne geputzt? Hast du **dir** die Haare gekämmt? Hast du **dir** etwas zu essen gemacht? Es ist heute kühl–hast du **dir** die Jacke angezogen und hast du **dir** auch die warme Mütze aufgesetzt?

SARAH: Ja, ja, Mutti, hab' ich alles gemacht! Ich muss **mich** jetzt beeilen! Wiedersehen! Bis später!

Read the above text again. What can you observe about the reflexive pronouns? —Not all are in the accusative; some are in the dative. Look at the following pairs. Why do you think the examples on the left are accusative and examples on the right are dative?

Ich wasche *mich*.	**Ich wasche *mir* die Haare.**
Ich kämme *mich*.	**Ich kämme *mir* die Haare.**
Ich ziehe *mich* an.	**Ich ziehe *mir* die Jacke an.**

The examples on the right have direct objects. Can you name them? In the sentences with a direct object, the reflexive pronoun is an indirect object and is in the dative case.

Reflexive Pronouns	
Accusative	**Dative**
mich	mir
dich	dir
sich	
uns	
euch	
sich	

As you can see, the accusative and dative reflexive pronouns are only different in the first and second person singular. Fill in the correct reflexive pronouns.

Ich wasche _____.   Ich wasche _____ die Haare.

Du wäschst _____.   Du wäschst _____ die Haare.

Er ⎫
Sie ⎬ wäscht_____.
Es ⎭

Er ⎫
Sie ⎬ wäscht _____ die Haare.
Es ⎭

Wir waschen _____.   Wir waschen _____ die Haare.

Ihr wascht _____. Ihr wascht _____ die Haare.

Sie waschen _____. Sie waschen _____ die Haare.

Sie (*formal*) waschen _____. Sie (*formal*) waschen _____ die Haare.

Note that in German the definite article is often used where English would use a possessive adjective.

Ich wasche mir *die* Haare. *I'm washing* my *hair.*
Zieh dir *die* Jacke an! *Put on* your *jacket!*

ÜBUNG I

Was macht Sarah? Look at the picture and write what Sarah is doing.

BEISPIEL:

Sie putzt sich die Zähne.

1.

_____

2.

_____

3. _____

4. _____

5. _____

ÜBUNG J

Tell Sarah what she has to do using the sentences in **Übung I** and changing them according to the example.

BEISPIEL: **Du musst dir die Zähne putzen!**

1. _____

2. _____

3. _____

4. _____

5. _____

ÜBUNG K

You're babysitting and have to be sure your little charge washes carefully before going to bed. Review the vocabulary for the parts of the body you learned in Book I; then, remind the child to wash well.

BEISPIEL: (*hand*)   **Wasch dir die Hände.**

1. (*neck*)   Wasch dir _____.

2. (*feet*)   Wasch dir _____.

3. (*face*)   Wasch dir _____.

4. (*legs*)   Wasch dir _____.

5. (*ears*)   Wasch dir _____.

der Arm, - e	*arm*
das Bein, e	*leg*
der Fuss, ¨e	*foot*
das Gesicht, -er	*face*
die Hand, ¨e	*hard*
der Hals, ¨e	*neck*
das Ohr, -en	*ear*

ÜBUNG L

What would you say if you were babysitting two children? Follow the example.

BEISPIEL: **Wascht euch die Hände!**

1. _____

2. _____

3. _____

4. _____

5. _____

ÜBUNG M

Fill in the correct pronouns.

Du fragst das Kind:

1. Hast du _____ gewaschen?

Das Kind sagt:

Ja, ich habe _____ gewaschen.

2. Hast du _____ die Zähne geputzt?   Ja, ich habe _____ die Zähne geputzt.

3. Hast du _____ die Haare gekämmt?   Ja, ich habe _____ die Haare gekämmt.

4. Hast du _____ ausgezogen?   Ja, ich habe _____ ausgezogen.

5. Hast du _____ den Schlafanzug angezogen?   Ja, ich habe _____ den Schlafanzug angezogen.

Du fragst zwei Kinder: **Die Kinder sagen:**

1. Habt ihr _____ gewaschen.   Ja, wir haben _____ gewaschen.

2. Habt ihr _____ die Zähne geputzt?   Ja, wir haben _____ die Zähne geputzt.

3. Habt ihr _____ die Haare gekämmt?   Ja, wir haben _____ die Haare gekämmt.

4. Habt ihr _____ ausgezogen.   Ja, wir haben _____ ausgezogen.

5. Habt ihr _____ den Schlafanzug angezogen?   Ja, wir haben _____ den Schlafanzug angezogen.

Die Mutter kommt nach Hause und fragt: **Du sagst:**

1. Haben _____ die Kinder gewaschen?   Ja, sie haben_____ gewaschen.

2. Haben _____ die Kinder die Zähne geputzt.   Ja, sie haben _____ die Zähne geputzt.

3. Haben _____ die Kinder die Haare gekämmt.   Ja, sie haben _____ die Haare gekämmt.

4. Haben _____ die Kinder ausgezogen?   Ja, sie haben _____ ausgezogen.

5. Haben _____ die Kinder den Schlafanzug angezogen.   Ja, sie haben _____ den Schlafanzug angezogen.

ÜBUNG N

Give the German equivalents. Remember, German often has a definite article where English has a possessive adjective.

1. *I have to wash my hair.*

   _____

2. *He is hurrying.*

   _____

3. *She is putting her jacket on.*

   _____

4. *We're fixing ourselves something to eat.*

   _____

7 In German, some verbs are always reflexive, for example, **sich beeilen** and **sich amüsieren**.

Some verbs can be used both reflexively and non-reflexively. Look at the following examples.

Ich wasche den Wagen.	*I'm washing the car.*
Ich wasche mich.	*I'm washing myself.*
Ich wasche mir die Hände.	*I'm washing my hands.*

Now you supply the English for the next sentences.

Ich ziehe das Kind an. _____

Ich ziehe mich an. _____

Ich ziehe mir die Schuhe an. _____

ÜBUNG O

Klassenumfrage In the evening after doing homework, many students watch TV. Practice the verb **sich etwas ansehen**, *to watch something,* by taking a poll in your class of favorite TV programs.

1. Select a moderator to come to the front of the class and write the days of the week in German across the board.

2. The moderator asks the class: **Was seht ihr euch am Montag an?** Students take turns responding with different programs they like to watch on that day. For example, **Wir sehen uns «Murphy Brown» an**. The moderator lists the programs under the column headed **Montag** and continues with the rest of the days of the week.

3. Select a new moderator to do a poll. He or she asks for a show of hands and writes the number of viewers next to each program: **Wer sieht sich «Murphy Brown» an? Heb bitte die Hand hoch!**

4. Tally the results and make a list of the most-frequently watched programs for your class: **Unsere Lieblingsfernsehsendungen.**

5. Select another new moderator to go around the room asking for individual favorites: **Was siehst du dir am liebsten an?** Individual students respond: **Ich sehe mir... am liebsten an.**

ÜBUNG P

Hör gut zu! You will hear some incomplete sentences. Write the number of the sentence beginning you hear in front of the appropriate completion below.

_____	die Haare.	_____	ihr Abendessen.
_____	die Jacke an.	_____	ihr Mittagessen.
_____	die Mütze auf.	_____	mit ihren Freunden.
_____	die Zähne.	_____	schläft.

PERSÖNLICHE FRAGEN ?

1. Wann stehst du auf?

_____

2. Wann gehst du in die Schule?

_____

3. Wann isst du dein Mittagessen?

_____

4. Wann kommst du nach Hause?

_____

5. Was machst du nach der Schule?

_____

6. Wann isst du dein Abendessen?

_____

7. Was machst du am Abend?

_____

8. Welche Fernsehsendungen siehst du dir an?

_____

9. Wann gehst du ins Bett?

_____

ÜBUNG Q

Aufsatz. Write a composition describing a typical day in your life.

Ein typischer Tag

_____

_____

_____

_____

_____

_____

_____

_____

_____

_____

KLASSENPROJEKT

Kinderbuch. Work in groups to create a children's book describing a typical day in a child's life. Write a simple text and illustrate it.

WORTSCHATZ A-Z

Ein typischer Tag *a typical day*

s. beeilen (beeilt sich, hat sich beeilt) *to hurry*

s. duschen (duscht sich, hat sich geduscht) *to shower*

  frühstücken (frühstückt, hat gefrühstückt) *to eat breakfast*

s. kämmen (kämmt sich, hat sich gekämmt) *to comb (one's hair)*

s. konzentrieren (konzentriert sich, hat sich konzentriert) *to concentrate*

s. verabschieden (verabschiedet sich, hat sich verabschiedet) *to say goodbye*

s. an•ziehen (zieht sich an, hat sich angezogen) *to get dressed*

  auf•stehen (steht auf, ist aufgestanden) *to get up*

s. aus•ziehen (zieht sich aus, hat sich ausgezogen) *to get undressed*

s. um•ziehen (zieht sich um, hat sich umgezogen) *to change (clothes)*

s. unterhalten (mit) (unterhält sich, hat sich unterhalten) *to have a conversation (with)*

s. waschen (wäscht sich, hat sich gewaschen) *to wash oneself*

s. die Haare kämmen *to comb one's hair*

s. die Zähne putzen (putzt sich d. Z., hat sich d. Z. geputzt) *to brush one's teeth*

s. die Mütze auf•setzen (setzt sich d. M. auf, hat sich d. M. aufgesetzt) *to put on one's cap*

s. etwas zu essen machen *to fix oneself something to eat*

s. die Haare waschen (wäscht sich die Haare, hat sich die Haare gewaschen) *to wash one's hair*

s. etwas an•sehen (sieht sich etwas an, hat sich etwas angesehen) *to watch something*

die Fernsehsendung, -en *TV program*

in die Schule gehen *to go to school*

in der Schule *in/at school*

in der Pause *during the break, recess*

nach der Schule *after school*

ins Bett gehen *to go to bed*

Diese Wörter kennst du schon

das Frühstück, -e *breakfast*	das Ohr, -en *ear*	die Hand, ¨e *hand*
das Mittagessen *lunch*	der Hals, ¨e *neck*	das Bein, -e *leg*
das Abendessen *supper*	der Arm, -e *arm*	der Fuss, ¨e *foot*
das Gesicht, -er *face*		

s. amüsieren, (amusiert sich, hat sich amusiert) *to enjoy oneself, have a good time*
üben (übt, hat geübt) *to practice*
fern•sehen (sieht fern, hat ferngesehen) *to watch TV*
schlafen (schläft, hat geschlafen) *to sleep*
ein bisschen *a little*
am liebsten *most of all*

Und so sagst du das *Here's how to . . .*

say goodbye

Tschüs *Bye, So long*   Wiedersehen *Bye*
Auf Wiedersehen *Goodbye*   Bis später *See you later*

tell time using the 24-hour clock

Es ist zwei Uhr. *It's 2 A.M.*   Es ist achtzehn Uhr dreissig. *It's 6:30 P.M.*
Es ist vierzehn Uhr. *It's 2 P.M.*

Taking a closer look

As you study the vocabulary list, answer the following questions.

1. Which verbs have a stem vowel change? What are the changes?

2. Which verbs have separable prefixes? Which ones have inseparable prefixes?

3. Which verbs have past participles that don't begin with **ge-**? Why?

4. Which verbs have a past participle with **sein**?

5. For each verb on the list, write the third person singular forms in the present and in the conversational past. Start with **sich beeilen: er beeilt sich, er hat sich beeilt.**

ÜBUNG R

Ratespiel: Was tue ich?   One student comes to the front of the class and acts out the various activities learned in this chapter. The rest of the class guesses what the activity is. For example, the student pantomimes brushing his teeth. The class calls out: **Du putzt dir die Zähne.**

KULTURECKE

A typical school day for a German high school student usually begins at 8:00 and goes until 1:00. Students go home for lunch, which in Germany is usually a warm meal, the main meal of the day. After lunch it's time for homework, sports, music lessons, and other activities.

Tanzschule

Rock 'n' Roll ist in!
Am Nachmittag fur Schüler.
Am Abend für Singles und Paare
Die heissen Rhythmen von

Elvis, Little Richard und Shakin Stevens

Jobs für Schüler:

Babysitting
Zeitungen austragen
Gartenarbeit

Klavierunterricht

auch Keyboard und Orgel

Tel: 07143/78720

Turn- und Sportverein Untermberg

Jugendvollversammlung
20. März 18 Uhr
Vereinsheim

NACHHILFE

für Schüler und Schülerinnen in Mathematik

Tel: 07143/37062

Musikverein "Stadtkapelle"

Jungend musiziert
10. April 14-16 Uhr
Musiksaal der Burgfeldschule

Computer-Klub

für alle Computer-Freaks
von 13-18

Tennisklub

mitttwochs
16 Uhr

Fahrschule Schutz

Schnell und sicher den Führerschein machen
Bietigheim. Bahnhofstr. 9
Anmeldung dienstags ab 18 Uhr

9
Wie geht es dir?

More Reflexive Verbs;
Verbs Used as Nouns;
Review: Dative Personal Pronouns;
Word Order in *wenn*-clauses

1 Wortschatz

Was ist passiert? Habt ihr euch verletzt?

Till

Ich habe mir das Bein gebrochen.

Ulrike

Ich habe mir den Knöchel verstaucht.

Und was ist hier los? Seid ihr krank?

ÜBUNG A

What's the matter with everyone? Answer the questions.

1. Was hat sich Till gebrochen? _____

2. Was hat sich Ulrike verstaucht? _____

3. Wer hat eine Erkältung? _____

4. Wer hat Fieber? Warum? _____

5. Was tut Martin weh? _____

6. Was ist mit Anna los? _____

7. Warum muss Jens zum Zahnarzt? _____

2 In **Lektion 8** you learned about reflexive verbs. Here are three more you can use to talk about an injury.

sich verletzen *to injure, hurt oneself*
sich (etwas) brechen *to break (something)*
sich (etwas) verstauchen *to sprain (something)*

Look again at what Till and Ulrike say. Underline the reflexive pronouns.

Are they in the dative or accusative case? Can you explain why? —When there is another object in the sentence, the reflexive pronoun is in the dative.

Fill in the correct reflexive pronouns.

1. Ich habe _____ die Hand verstaucht.

2. Hast du _____ den Fuss gebrochen?

3. Ulrike hat _____ den Knöchel verstaucht.

4. Wir haben _____ das Bein gebrochen.

5. Ihr habt _____ den Knöchel verstaucht.

6. Die zwei Schüler haben _____ den Arm gebrochen.

* Note that even if the subject is plural, the object is singular—unless, of course, you broke both legs!

Ich **habe mir** *das Bein* **gebrochen.** *I broke my leg.*
Wir **haben uns** *das Bein* **gebrochen.** *We each broke a leg.*

ÜBUNG B

Was ist passiert? Write sentences using the cues given. (Remember that German often uses a definite article where English uses a possessive adjective.)

BEISPIEL: *(foot)* **Der Sportlehrer** *hat sich den Fuss* **gebrochen.**

1. Ich _____ gebrochen. *(nose)*

2. Walter _____ gebrochen. *(tooth)*

3. Ihr _____ verstaucht. *(ankle)*

4. Du _____ verstaucht. *(hand)*

5. Wir _____ gebrochen. *(finger)*

6. Meine Schwester _____ verstaucht. *(arm)*

7. Die zwei Fussballspieler _____ gebrochen. *(leg)*

ÜBUNG C

Und was noch? And what else? The athlete pictured below is in bad shape! Describe his injuries.

die Schulter
der Rücken
der Ellbogen
das Handgelenk
das Knie

Der Sportler hat sich _____

_____

_____

_____

_____ .

ÜBUNG **D**

Now go around the room and take turns talking about an injury you have had (or someone you know has had). Tell if it was bad or not so bad. Use the following words:

sehr schlimm	**nicht so schlimm**
schlimm	**gar nicht schlimm**

BEISPIEL: **Ich habe mir mal den Knöchel verstaucht.**
Es war schlimm.

3 When talking about injuries you are often required to give more information. People will ask when and how the injury happened.

WERNER: Till, was ist passiert?
TILL: Ich habe mir beim Skilaufen das Bein gebrochen.

WERNER: Schade! Wann war das?
TILL: Letzte Woche, am Dienstag.

WERNER: Und wie ist das passiert?
TILL: Ich bin vom Lift gefallen!

WERNER: So ein Pech! Gute Besserung!

4 In **Lektion 7** you learned that infinitives can be used as nouns. The gender is always _____. The verb **spielen**, for example, becomes **(das) Spielen**.

Such nouns can be used with or without the definite article. Infinitives may also combine with other words to form nouns.

> **Tennisspielen** macht Spass.
> **Das Skilaufen** kostet viel Geld.

Note that even when the infinitive is written separately, the noun is written together.

Ski laufen *to go skiing*
das Skilaufen *skiing*

Look at the dialogue above. Underline the infinitive used as a noun. What word precedes it? What does the sentence mean in English? What does the phrase **beim Skilaufen** mean?

A phrase with **beim** and an infinitive used as a noun expresses the idea of "while."

beim Schwimmen *while swimming*
beim Essen *while eating*

Write phrases with **beim** and the following infinitives.

BEISPIEL: **Schlitten fahren   beim Schlittenfahren**

1. Rad fahren _____

2. Rollschuh fahren _____

3. Klavier spielen _____

4. Eis essen _____

5. Musik hören _____

6. reiten _____

ÜBUNG E

Write six sentences using the cues below.

du	beim Radfahren	die Hand	verstaucht
Thomas	beim Reiten	den Arm	gebrochen
sie (*pl.*)	beim Schwimmen	den Fuss	
ich	beim Skateboardfahren	den Knöchel	
Julia	beim Fussballspielen	das Handgelenk	
ihr	beim Basketballspielen	das Knie	
wir			

BEISPIEL: **Julia hat sich beim Reiten den Arm gebrochen.**

1. _____

2. _____

3. _____

4. _____

5. _____

6. _____

ÜBUNG F

Rewrite the sentences in **Übung E**, this time telling when the injury happened. Here are some time phrases you can use.

gestern *yesterday*
vorgestern *day before yesterday*
letzte Woche *last week*
letzten Monat *last month*
letztes Jahr *last year*

vor ein paar Tagen *a few days ago*
vor zwei Wochen *two weeks ago*
vor zwei Monaten *two months ago*
vor zwei Jahren *two years ago*

BEISPIEL: **Julia hat sich vor zwei Wochen den Arm gebrochen.**

1. _____

2. _____

3. _____

4. _____

5. _____

6. _____

ÜBUNG G

Lustige Sätze. Work in groups of three to come up with funny sentences. Then take turns reading them aloud to the class.

WER?		WIE/WANN?	WAS?
Jenny	hat sich	beim Hausaufgabenmachen	den Kopf verstaucht.
Frank	hat sich	beim Pizzaessen	die Zunge gebrochen.

ÜBUNG H

On the opening page of this lesson, you read about young people who didn't feel well. Practice asking your classmates how they feel.

Wie geht es dir?

Es geht mir...
{
prima
gut
so so
nicht so gut
schlecht
}

ÜBUNG I

Here are some students who are not feeling well. Each one tells what hurts. Write what they say. Use the phrase **weh tun** which you learned in Book 1. Don't forget: if the subject is plural, the verb **tun** is plural.

Der Fuss tut mir weh.   *My foot hurts (me).*
Die Füsse tun mir weh.   *My feet hurt.*

BEISPIEL: *(stomachache)*   **Der Bauch tut mir weh.**
Ich habe Bauchschmerzen.

1. *(headache)* _____

_____

2. *(earache)* _____

_____

3. *(eyes hurt)* _____

_____

4. *(sore throat)* _____

_____

5. *(toothache)* _____

_____

6. *(backache)* _____

_____

5 The phrases you used in the last two activities to talk about how you feel and what hurts have a pronoun in the _____ case.

Es geht **mir** nicht gut.
Der Kopf tut **mir** weh.

Certain phrases in German take the dative case. You learned the dative pronouns in Book 1. See if you can unscramble the pronouns and complete the sentences.

euch	ich	Sie	du	er	ihnen	uns
sie (*sing.*)	wir	ihr	mir	ihr		
dir	ihm	sie (*pl.*)		Ihnen		

Personal Pronouns (Nominative)	Personal Pronouns (Dative)
BEISPIEL: *Ich* **habe Kopfschmerzen.**	**Der Kopf tut** *mir* **weh.**
_____ hast Bauchschmerzen.	Der Bauch tut _____ weh.
_____ hat Rückenschmerzen.	Der Rücken tut _____ weh.
_____ hat Halsschmerzen.	Der Hals tut _____ weh.
_____ haben Ohrenschmerzen.	Die Ohren tun _____ weh.
_____ habt Zahnschmerzen.	Die Zähne tun _____ weh.
_____ haben Augenschmerzen.	Die Augen tun _____ weh.
_____ haben Fussschmerzen.	Die Füsse tun _____ weh.

The dative personal pronouns are only a little different from the dative reflexive pronouns. Complete these sentences and circle the pronouns that are different in the two columns.

Dative Reflexive Pronoun	Dative Personal Pronoun
Ich habe _____ den Fuss verstaucht.	Der Fuss tut _____ weh.
Du hast _____ die Hand verstaucht.	Die Hand tut _____ weh.
Er hat _____ das Knie verstaucht.	Das Knie tut _____ weh.
Anna hat _____ den Arm gebrochen.	Der Arm tut _____ weh.
Wir haben _____ die Schulter verstaucht.	Die Schulter tut _____ weh.
Ihr habt _____ das Bein gebrochen.	Das Bein tut _____ weh.
Sie (pl.) haben _____ den Finger verstaucht.	Der Finger tut _____ weh.

The dative reflexive pronouns are different from the dative personal pronouns in the
_____ person, singular and plural.

		DATIVE PRONOUNS	
		PERSONAL	REFLEXIVE
S I N G U L A R	1ST PERSON	mir	
	2ND PERSON	dir	
	3RD PERSON	ihm	sich
		ihr	sich
		ihm	sich
P L U R A L	1ST PERSON	uns	
	2ND PERSON	euch	
	3RD PERSON	ihnen	sich

ÜBUNG J

Was tut weh? Write sentences telling what hurts. Follow the example.

BEISPIEL: **Thomas hat Bauchschmerzen.**
Der Bauch tut ihm weh.

1. Cindy hat sich das Handgelenk verstaucht.

_____

2. Robert hat Zahnschmerzen.

_____

3. Rebecca und Susan haben Kopfschmerzen.

_____

4. Michael hat sich den Knöchel gebrochen.

_____

5. Mary, Richard und Max haben Halsschmerzen.

_____

6. Lydia hat Ohrenschmerzen.

_____

PARTNERARBEIT

When you don't feel well, people often give advice. Work with a partner. Write and practice exchanges. You complain about your health, your partner gives you advice. Choose one to present to the class.

Ich habe...	**Du musst...**
die Grippe	zum Arzt gehen
Fieber	Tee mit Honig trinken
eine Erkältung	viel schlafen
einen Husten	zum Augenarzt gehen
Zahnweh	viel trinken
Kopfschmerzen	Hustensaft nehmen
Augenschmerzen	im Bett bleiben
eine Halsentzündung	ins Krankenhaus gehen
mir das Bein gebrochen	Medizin nehmen
	eine Schmerztablette nehmen

ÜBUNG K

Now answer the following questions, telling what you do when you're sick. Refer to the advice in the preceding activity.

BEISPIEL: **Was machst du, wenn du krank bist? —Ich bleibe im Bett.**

Was machst du...

wenn du müde bist? _____

wenn du Fieber hast? _____

wenn du Kopfschmerzen hast? _____

wenn du Halsschmerzen hast? _____

wenn du Husten hast? _____

wenn du eine Erkältung hast? _____

wenn du Zahnweh hast? _____

 Look at the questions in the preceding activity. What can you observe about the word order in the clause beginning with **wenn**? What is the position of the verb? —The verb comes at the end of the clause. In Book 1 you learned that clauses introduced by conjunctions such as **wenn** (if, when, whenever), **weil** (because), **dass** (that), **ob** (if), take verb-last word order.

BEISPIEL: **Wenn ich krank bin, bleibe ich im Bett.**

What happens to the word order in the second part of the sentence above? The subject (**ich**), and the verb, (**bleibe**) are reversed. —Remember, if any element other than the subject begins a sentence, the subject and verb are inverted, that is, they are reversed.

1	2	3	
Ich	bleibe	im Bett.	
Heute	bleibe	ich	im Bett.
Wenn ich krank bin,	bleibe	ich	im Bett.

Now again practice saying what you do when you're sick. Use the answers you wrote to the questions in **Übung K**, beginning each sentence with the **wenn**-clause in the question.

1. Wenn ich krank bin, _____.

2. Wenn ich _____.

3. _____

4. _____

5. _____

6. _____

7. _____

8. _____

ÜBUNG L

Hör gut zu! You will hear parents calling school to report their child's absence. Write the number of the parent calling under the picture of his or her child.

7 Entschuldigungsbriefe

If you are absent from school you have to bring an excuse note. Read the notes below. Which one do you think is a valid excuse that a teacher would accept?

München, den 5. Februar

Liebe Frau Freundlich!

Bitte entschuldigen Sie meinen Sohn Peter, dass er gestern und vorgestern nicht in die Schule gekommen ist. Er hat eine schlimme Halsentzündung und auch Fieber gehabt. Er ist den ganzen Tag im Bett geblieben und hat viel geschlafen. Ich habe den Arzt angerufen, und er hat Medizin verschrieben. Heute geht es dem Peter viel besser.

Mit freundlichen Grüssen
Erika Sieboldt

Bietigheim, den 5. Februar

Lieber Herr Rittersmann!

Mein Sohn Oliver war gestern nicht in der Schule, weil er zu müde war. Er hat sich einen netten Film im Fernsehen angeschaut und ist sehr spät ins Bett gekommen. Am Morgen war er dann müde und konnte nicht aufstehen. Auch hat er keine Hausaufgaben gemacht, so ist er zu Hause geblieben.

Mit freundlichen Grüssen
Sophie Schwermut

Müllheim, den 5. Februar

Liebe Frau Ehrlich!

Meine Tochter Claudia ist gestern nicht in die Schule gekommen, weil das Wetter einfach zu herrlich war! Sie hat zu Weihnachten ein neues Snowboard bekommen und fährt so oft wie möglich ins Skigebiet. Sie kann schon sehr gut Snowboard fahren und hat den ersten Preis im Snowboard-Rennen gewonnen.

Mit freundlichen Grüssen
Roland Reichert

---

entschuldigen *to excuse*
verschreiben *to prescribe*
das Rennen *race*

1. Wie heissen die drei Lehrer?

   _____

2. Wie heissen die drei Schüler?

   _____

3. Wer hat Sport gemacht?

   _____

4. Wer hat ferngesehen und ist müde gewesen?

   _____

5. Wer ist krank gewesen?

   _____

6. Welchen Entschuldigungsbrief würdest du deinem Lehrer oder deiner Lehrerin bringen, den ersten Brief, den zweiten Brief oder den dritten Brief?

   _____

PERSÖNLICHE FRAGEN ?

1. Wann bist du das letzte Mal krank gewesen? Was hast du gehabt?

   _____

   _____

   _____

2. Hast du dir schon mal etwas gebrochen oder verstaucht? Wann und wo war das? Was ist passiert? Erzähl darüber!

   _____

   _____

   _____

   _____

ÜBUNG **M**

Aufsatz. You have been absent from school. Write an excuse note your mother or father can sign.

WORTSCHATZ A-Z

s. etwas brechen (bricht sich das Bein, hat sich das Bein gebrochen) *to break something*
   s. etwas verstauchen (verstaucht sich die Hand, hat sich die Hand verstaucht) *to sprain something*
s. verletzen (verletzt sich, hat sich verletzt) *to hurt, injure oneself*
entschuldigen (entschuldigt, hat entschuldigt) *to excuse*
husten (hustet, hat gehustet) *to cough*
schlucken (schluckt, hat geschluckt) *to swallow*
weh tun (tut weh, hat weh getan) D* *to hurt*

* Verbs and phrases used with the dative case will be indicated with a D.

der Bauch, ⸚e *stomach*
der Ellbogen *elbow*
das Handgelenk, -e *wrist*
das Knie *knee*
der Knöchel *ankle*
der Rücken *back*
die Schulter, -n *shoulder*
die Entzündung, -en *infection*
die Halsentzündung, -en *sore throat*
die Erkältung, -en *cold*
das Fieber *fever*
das Bauchweh *stomachache*
das Zahnweh *toothache*
der Husten *cough*
der Hustensaft, ⸚e *cough medicine*
die Medizin *medicine*

der Schmerz, -en *pain*
die Schmerztablette, -n *pain reliever*
der Tee mit Honig *tea with honey*
der Augenarzt, ⸚e *eye doctor*
der Zahnarzt, ⸚e *dentist*
krank *sick*
müde *tired*
schlimm *bad*
beim (Skilaufen) *while (skiing)*
den ganzen Tag *all day*
im Bett bleiben *to stay in bed*
so ein Pech! *what bad luck!*
vorgestern *day before yesterday*
letzte Woche *last week*
vor zwei Wochen *two weeks ago*

Und so sagst du das *Here's how to . . .*

ask what happened

Was ist passiert? *What happened?*   Was ist los? *What's the matter?*

complain that something hurts

Es tut mir weh. *It hurts (me).*   Mir tut der Kopf weh. *My head hurts.*
Ich habe Zahnschmerzen.   Er hat Bauchweh. *He has a stomachache.*
I have a toothache.

give advice when someone isn't feeling well

Wenn du eine Erkältung hast sollst du... *When you have a cold you should . . .*

wish someone a speedy recovery

Gute Besserung! *Get well soon!*

ask how someone feels and say how you feel

Wie geht es dir!	*How are you!*
Es geht mir...	*I'm feeling . . .*
prima!	*great!*
gut.	*good.*
soso.	*so-so.*
nicht so gut.	*not so good.*
schlecht.	*awful.*

Building your vocabulary

When talking about sickness and injury, two important words are **krank** and **Arzt**. What do the following words mean?

krank _____   der Arzt _____

die Krankheit _____   der Zahnarzt _____

der Krankenwagen _____   der Augenarzt _____

das Krankenhaus _____   der Hals-Nasen-Ohrenarzt _____

die Krankenschwester _____   _____

Practice your vocabulary-building skills. Write the compound words shown below and give their meanings.

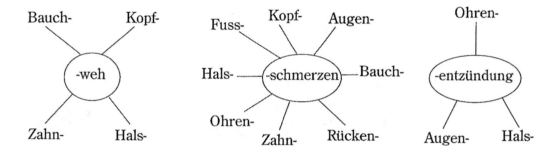

ÜBUNG N

Spiel: wer? was? wie? wann? Go around the room. Each student gives additional information. Then start a new sentence with a different subject and different information. The subject can be singular or plural, for example, **wir, mein Bruder, ihr.**

wer?   Ich

was?   Ich habe mir den Ellbogen verstaucht.

wie?   Ich habe mir beim Basketballspielen den Ellbogen verstaucht.

wann?   Ich habe mir vorgestern beim Basketballspielen den Ellbogen verstaucht.

KULTURECKE

Most homes in Germany have a **Hausapotheke**, *medicine chest*. Here are some things typically found in a **Hausapotheke**.

Heftpflaster	*Band Aids*
Verbandzeug	*bandages*
Jod	*iodine*
Antiseptikum	*antiseptic*
Brandsalbe	*ointment*
Schmerztabletten	*pain killer*
Halstabletten	*throat lozenges*
Magentabletten	*antacid*
Hustensaft	*cough medicine*
ein Thermometer	*thermometer*

And in most homes next to the telephone you will find a list of numbers **im Notfall**, *in case of an emergency*.

Gesundheitswesen
Gemeinde
74354 Besigheim

Ortsnetz
07143

Notruf
1 10
Unfall

Feuer   1 12

Polizei   30 88

Deutsches Rotes Kreuz Rettungsleitstelle—Notarzt	07142 / 192 22
Unfallchirurgie—Krankenhaus	07172 / 7 91
Stadtverwaltung Besigheim Zentrale	37 41
Giftzentrale (München)	(089) 41402211

Ärzte, Zahnärzte, Optiker

74354 Besigheim		Strasse	Tel.
Dr. Rieth, G.		Freudentalerstr. 1	351 54
Dr. Schuster, G		Bietigheimerstr. 2	228 04
Dr. Hennig, E	Augenarzt	Weinstr. 4	367 29
Dr. Lamorecht, W	Kinderarzt	Weinstr. 2a	780 31
Dr. Kienzle, E	Orthopädie	Hauptstr. 18	921 44
Dr. Rupf, W	Zahnarzt	Bahnhofstr. 2	635 78
APOTHEKER			
Stadtapotheke		Bahnhofstr. 11	358 49

10
Halt dich fit!

Review: The Imperative
The Interrogative *was für ein?*

1 Wortschatz

HALT DICH FIT!

Iss richtig!
Iss viel Obst und Gemüse!

Iss nicht zu viel Fleisch!

Bleib gesund!
Rauch nicht!

Beweg dich!
Geh zu Fuss!

Fahr nicht immer im Wagen!

Geh spazieren!

Mach Sport!

Sieh nicht so viel fern!

Sitz nicht so viel herum!

Fahr Rad!

Schlaf genug!

ÜBUNG A

What does the poster on the preceding page advise you to do? Here are the infinitives of the verbs used. You already know some of them. Can you figure out what the others mean?

sich bewegen	herumsitzen	schlafen
richtig essen	im Wagen fahren	spazierengehen
fernsehen	rauchen	Sport machen
sich fit halten	Rad fahren	zu Fuss gehen
gesund bleiben		

Now sort out the advice. What does the poster tell you to do and what does it tell you not to do? Use the verbs above in appropriate phrases.

Du sollst...

_____

_____

_____

_____

_____

_____

_____

Du sollst nicht...

_____

_____

_____

_____

2 The poster **"Halt dich fit!"** uses imperatives, also called command forms, to tell you what to do to stay healthy and fit. Imperatives can be used to:

give commands — *Geh* nach Hause!   *Go home!*
make requests — *Gib* mir *bitte* das Buch!   *Please give me the book!*
make suggestions — *Frag mal* deine Mutter!   *Why don't you ask your mother?*

There are three different command forms. The one you use depends on whom you're talking to.

—one person you address with **du:**   **Komm!**
—two or more people you address with **ihr:**   **Kommt!**
—one or more people you address with **Sie:**   **Kommen Sie!**

What is the ending on each command? What do you notice about the punctuation?

Here are some commands you hear and use in class every day. Write each one in the appropriate column.

Hör gut zu!
Wiederholt das!
Kommen Sie bitte!
Gib mir das Buch!

Setzen Sie sich bitte!
Steh auf!
Beantwortet die Fragen!
Gebt mir die Hausaufgaben!

Beeilt euch!
Schauen Sie mal!
Sei ruhig!
Vergessen Sie nicht!

DU   IHR   SIE

_____   _____   _____

_____   _____   _____

_____   _____   _____

_____   _____   _____

_____   _____   _____

_____   _____   _____

The following chart summarizes the command forms. You learned the command forms in Book I. This chart includes verbs with separable prefixes and reflexive verbs. Pay special attention to these verbs.

FAMILIAR SING.: **du**-form without ending	du kommst du rufst an du kämmst dich	komm! ruf an! kämm dich!
FAMILIAR PLURAL: **ihr**-form	ihr kommt ihr ruft an ihr kämmt euch	kommt! ruft an! kämmt euch!
FORMAL, POLITE: **Sie**-form	Sie kommen Sie rufen an Sie kämmen sich	kommen Sie! rufen Sie an! kämmen Sie sich!

Remember:

—If a verb has a stem vowel change (e ➤ i, e ➤ ie), it is also in the command.

If the vowel change is an umlaut (a ➤ ä, a ➤ äu) it is not in the command.

essen	du isst	*Iss!*	Esst!	Essen Sie!
fahren	du fährst	*Fahr!*	Fahrt!	Fahren Sie!

—The **du**- command of verbs ending in **-eln** or **-ern** is the same as the **ich**- form.

sammeln	ich sammle	*Sammle* mal Briefmarken!
füttern	ich füttre	*Füttre* den Hund!

—The command forms of **haben** and **sein** are:

haben	*Hab!*	*Habt!*	*Haben Sie!*
sein	*Sei!*	*Seid!*	*Seien Sie!*

—In German, commands always have an exclamation point.

ÜBUNG B

Complete the chart.

Infinitive	DU	IHR	SIE
essen	Iss!	Esst!	Essen Sie!
	Beeil dich!		
			Hören Sie zu!
sich fithalten			
		Habt keine Angst!	
			Schlafen Sie gut!
lesen			
	Steh auf!		
mitfahren			
		Steigt ein!	
ruhig sein			

Check over your completed chart.

1. Which verbs are reflexive? _____ Did you use the correct reflexive pronoun?

2. Which verbs have a separable prefix? _____

_____

Did you put the separable prefix in the correct place?

3. Did you put the proper punctuation at the end of each command?

ÜBUNG C

Look at the poster again at the beginning of the lesson. Which of the three command forms are used? —The poster is directed at one person, someone you would address with **du**. Redo the posters addressing one to your classmates using the **ihr**-command. Address the other to adults using the **Sie**-command.

Haltet euch fit!	**Halten Sie sich fit!**

3 Here are a few more things to note about imperatives.

—Sometimes the pronoun is included in the **du**- and **ihr**-commands to give the command special emphasis.

> **Frag den Lehrer!** *Ask the teacher.*
> **Frag du den Lehrer!** *You ask the teacher.*

—Words like **doch** and **mal** lend emphasis or can make a command more like a suggestion.

> **Frag doch den Lehrer!** *Go ahead and ask the teacher!*
> **Kauf dir mal ein neues T-shirt!** * *Why don't you buy yourself a new T-shirt?*
> **Frag du doch mal!** *Why don't you go and ask for a change!*

Rewrite the commands below, adding emphasis by inserting **doch, mal**, or **doch mal**. Then go around the room. One student reads the command on the left, the next student repeats the command, this time giving it more emphasis.

1. Iss einen Apfel! _____

2. Geh früher ins Bett! _____

3. Sei nicht so laut! _____

4. Mach die Tür zu! _____

5. Zieh dir eine Jacke an! _____

6. Kauf dir ein neues Heft! _____

* Note the position of the emphasis word in a sentence with a reflexive verb.

ÜBUNG D

Hör gut zu! To whom are these commands directed? Listen to each command and check the appropriate box.

1.			
2.			
3.			
4.			
5.			
6.			
7.			
8.			

4 Sometimes infinitives can be used to give commands. This way of giving commands is often found on signs in public places. What do the signs below mean? Give the English equivalent of each one.

Ruhig sein! _____

Nicht stören! _____

Tiere nicht füttern! _____

Nicht rauchen! _____

| Den Rasen nicht betreten! | _____ |

| Langsam fahren! | _____ |

| Nicht parken! | _____ |

| Nicht anhalten! | _____ |

betreten *to step on*
storen *to disturb*
anhalten *to stop*

Where might you see these signs? Write the German signs in the appropriate column. Some signs can be found in a number of places.

im Park	im Zoo	im Krankenhaus	in der Stadt

5 Read the following story about Charly and his friends.

Unser Freund Charly

Charly ist ein netter Kerl. Er ist aber immer müde. Er hat keine Energie. Er macht keinen Sport, er fährt nie Rad, er geht nicht spazieren. Er sitzt stundenlang vor dem Fernseher, trinkt Cola, isst Süssigkeiten und knabbert Kartoffelchips.

So sieht ein Tag bei Charly aus:
Der Wecker klingelt. Charly dreht sich um und schläft weiter. Er steht im letzten Moment auf, wäscht sich das Gesicht und zieht sich schnell an. Er frühstückt nicht. Er hat keine Zeit! Er rennt aus der Tür, setzt sich in den Wagen, und sein Vater fährt ihn in die Schule. In der Schule ist er schlapp und müde. Er kann sich nicht konzentrieren. Die Augen fallen ihm immer zu. Nach der Schule spielt er Computer und dann macht er ein paar Hausaufgaben. Abends sitzt er bis spät vor dem Fernseher.

Charlys Freunde machen sich Sorgen um ihn. Sie wollen ihm helfen. «Komm, Charly», sagen sie, «wir machen ein Fitness-Programm mit dir!» Charly ist nicht begeistert, aber er macht mit.

«So, Charly, pass mal auf! Du musst mehr Bewegung bekommen. Du darfst nicht immer herumsitzen!»

> —Geh spazieren! Komm! Wir machen einen Spaziergang!
> —Fahr Rad! Komm! Wir machen eine Radtour!
> —Spiel Fussball! Spiel Tennis! Mach Gymnastik!

Du musst auch richtig essen! Du darfst nicht so viel Süssigkeiten und Knabberzeug essen! Du darfst nicht immer nur Cola trinken!

> —Iss mehr Obst!
> —Kauf dir einen Joghurt!
> —Mach dir einen Salat!
> —Trink viel Wasser!

ein netter Kerl *a nice guy*
knabbern *to nibble, snack*
die Süssigkeiten (pl.) *sweets, candy*
sich Sorgen machen um *to be worried about*
begeistert *enthusiastic*
Bewegung bekommen *to get exercise*

ÜBUNG E

Beantworte die Fragen!

1. Warum ist Charly schlapp und müde?

    (a) Er macht keinen _____.

    (b) Er sitzt viel _____.

    (c) Er sieht viel _____.

    (d) Er isst zu viel _____.

    (e) Er trinkt zu viel _____.

2. Was soll Charly tun?

    (a) Er soll richtig _____.

    (b) Er soll mehr _____ bekommen.

    (c) Er soll Sport _____.

    (d) Er soll nicht so spät _____ gehen.

3. Hier ist Charlys Fitness-Programm. Seine Freunde machen jeden Tag etwas mit ihm. Sag, was sie jeden Tag machen.

Montag	Dienstag	Mittwoch	Donnerstag	Freitag	Samstag	Sonntag
Gymnastik	Schwimmen	Tennis	Schwimmen	Volleyball	Radtour	Spaziergang

(a) Am Montag machen sie _____.

(b) Am Dienstag _____.

(c) Am Mittwoch _____.

(d) Am Donnerstag _____.

(e) Am Freitag _____.

(f) Am Samstag _____.

(g) Am Sonntag _____.

6 The verb **sich fithalten** (to stay fit) is a reflexive verb with a separable prefix. It also has a stem vowel change. Do you know what it is? Read the paragraph and underline the forms of **sich fithalten**, including the subject and reflexive pronoun.

Charlys Freunde halten sich fit. Heidi sagt: «Ich halte mich fit. Ich esse richtig, und ich gehe jeden Tag zu Fuss in die Schule. Charly, wie hältst du dich fit?» Charly sagt nichts. Er hält sich nicht fit. «Ja», sagt er, «ihr seid gut. Ihr haltet euch fit. Ich bin zu faul!» «Oh, Charly», meinen seine Freunde, «das muss nicht sein! Wir halten uns fit, und wir fühlen uns auch gut. Komm! Halt dich mit uns fit!»

Now fill in the forms of the verb **sich fithalten**.

ich _____ _____ _____

du _____ _____ _____

er/sie/es _____ _____ _____

wir _____ _____ _____

ihr _____ _____ _____

sie/Sie _____ _____ _____

7 Charly and his friends go for something to eat. There are many different kinds of salads, soups, main courses, desserts, and beverages on the menu. What phrase do they use to ask "what kind of" salad each one will have?

Was für Salate gibt es?

Es gibt Tomatensalat, Kartoffelsalat, Fleischsalat, Kopfsalat und Obstsalat.

Was für ein Salat ist das?

Das da? Das ist ein Tomatensalat.

Hm, sieht gut aus! Ich esse einen Tomatensalat. Was für einen Salat nimmst du?

Ich nehme einen Obstsalat.

RESTAURANT AM MARKT
Speisekarte

Salate DM 4,00
Tomatensalat
Kartoffelsalat
Fleischsalat
Kopfsalat
Obstsalat

Suppen DM 3,00
Hühnersuppe
Zwiebelsuppe
Nudelsuppe
Gulaschsuppe
Gemüsesuppe

Hauptgerichte DM 8,00
Hamburger mit Pommes frites
Sauerbraten mit Kartoffelpüree
Gemüseplatte
Nudelauflauf mit Käse
Pizza mit Pepperoni
Pizza vegetarisch

Nachspeisen DM 3,00
Himbeereis
Gemischtes Eis
Apfelkuchen
Erdbeerkuchen
Vanillepudding
Schokoladenpudding

Getränke DM 2,00
Milch   Apfelsaft   Kaffee   Cola   Traubensaft   Mineralwasser

---

Kopfsalat *lettuce salad*
Nudelauflauf *noodle casserole*
Himbeereis *raspberry ice cream*
gemischtes Eis *two or three flavors of ice cream served in a dish*
Traubensaft *grape juice*

8 The interrogative **was für (ein)**, *what kind of (a)* can be used with a noun as the subject or direct object of a question.

	NOMINATIVE (SUBJECT)	ACCUSATIVE (DIRECT OBJECT)
MASC. DER/EIN	**Was für ein** Salat ist das? *What kind of a salad is that?*	**Was für einen** Salat nimmst du? *What kind of a salad are you having?*
FEM. DIE/EINE	**Was für eine** Suppe ist das? *What kind of a soup is that?*	**Was für eine** Suppe nimmst du? *What kind of a soup are you having?*
NEUT. DAS/EIN	**Was für ein** Eis ist das? *What kind of ice cream is that?*	**Was für ein** Eis nimmst du? *What kind of ice cream are you having?*
PLURAL	**Was für** Kartoffeln sind das? *What kind of potatoes are those?*	**Was für** Kartoffeln nimmst du? *What kind of potatoes are you having?*

ÜBUNG **F**

Look at the menu and answer the questions.

1. Was für einen Braten gibt es? _____

2. Was für eine Platte gibt es? _____

3. Was für einen Auflauf gibt es? _____

4. Was für eine Pizza magst du? _____

5. Was für ein Eis möchtest du haben? _____

6. Was für einen Kuchen isst du? _____

7. Was für einen Pudding nimmst du? _____

8. Was für einen Saft möchtest du? _____

ÜBUNG G

Complete the sentences with the correct form of **was für (ein)**. To do this, you must know the definite articles. They are listed below. Learn them!

der Salat	der Kuchen	die Suppe	die Milch	das Hauptgericht
der Hamburger	der Pudding	die Platte	die Cola	das Eis
der Braten	der Saft	die Pizza	die Nachspeise	das Getränk
der Auflauf	der Kaffee			das Mineralwasser

1. _____ Pudding ist das?

2. _____ Saft trinkst du?

3. _____ Nachspeise isst du am liebsten?

4. _____ Suppe isst du nicht gern?

5. _____ Braten gibt es?

6. _____ Pizza ist das?

7. _____ Eis möchtest du haben?

8. _____ Hauptgericht bestellst du?

ÜBUNG H

Heidi ist Vegetarierin. One of Charly's friends is a vegetarian. What does she select from the menu?

1. Was für einen Salat nimmt Heidi? _____

2. Was für einen Salat isst sie nicht? _____

3. Was für eine Suppe isst sie? _____

4. Was für eine Suppe isst sie nicht? _____

5. Was für ein Hauptgericht bestellt sie? _____

PARTNERARBEIT

Talk about the menu with a partner.

1. You ask what things are available. Your partner answers. Switch roles.

> DU: Was für Salate gibt es?
> PARTNER: Es gibt Tomatensalat…
> DU: Was für…

2. Now ask each other what you are going to order. Use the phrase **was für (ein)**.

> DU: Was für einen Salat nimmst du?
> PARTNER: Ich nehme einen…

ÜBUNG I

Ist das Charly? After two weeks Charly's friends notice a change! They make suggestions. Charly has a better idea! Write the suggestions and Charly's response. Use the inclusive command that you learned in Book 1:

Charlys Freunde:	Charly:
ein Stück Kuchen essen	einen Apfel essen
eine Cola trinken	einen Apfelsaft trinken
ein Eis essen	einen Joghurt essen
Computer spielen	Tennis spielen
fernsehen	eine Radtour machen
im Café sitzen	schwimmen gehen
ins Kino gehen	spazieren gehen
mit dem Bus fahren	zu Fuss gehen

BEISPIEL: CHARLYS FREUNDE: **Essen wir ein Stück Kuchen!**
  CHARLY: **Essen wir lieber einen Apfel!**

1. Freunde: _____

   Charly: _____

2. Freunde: _____

   Charly: _____

3. Freunde: _____

   Charly: _____

4. Freunde: _____

   Charly: _____

5. Freunde: _____

   Charly: _____

6. Freunde: _____

   Charly: _____

7. Freunde: _____

   Charly: _____

ÜBUNG J

Practice the exchanges you have written with a classmate.

PERSÖNLICHE FRAGEN ?

1. Was für Sport machst du?

   _____

2. Siehst du viel fern? Wieviel Stunden am Tag?

   _____

3. Wie kommst du in die Schule? Gehst du zu Fuss? Fährst du mit dem Rad? Fährst du mit dem Bus oder mit dem Wagen?

   _____

   _____

4. Isst du richtig? Was isst du alles am Tag? Isst du Obst? Gemüse? Brot? Joghurt? Süssigkeiten?

   _____

   _____

5. Bist du Vegetarier? Kennst du einen Vegetarier oder eine Vegetarierin? Was isst ein Vegetarier? Was isst er nicht?

_____

_____

ÜBUNG K

Aufsatz. Write a composition explaining how you stay fit. What do you do? What don't you do? What should you do?

Ich halte mich fit!

_____

_____

_____

_____

_____

_____

_____

_____

_____

_____

KLASSENPROJEKT

1. Design a "Fitness-Programm" for yourself, or work with a group to design one you could do together. List activities you will do each day and write a list of the foods you will eat.

2. Make a fitness poster. Draw, or cut out pictures of activities and food that belong in a healthy lifestyle. Label the poster.

WORTSCHATZ A-Z

die Bewegung, -en *movement, exercise:*
    Bewegung bekommen *to get exercise*
die Energie *energy*
die Gymnastik *gymnastics, exercises:*
    Gymnastik machen *to do gymnastics,*
      exercises
die Radtour, -en *bicycle tour, trip;*
    eine Radtour machen *to take a*
      bicycle trip
der Spaziergang, ⁻e *walk;* einen Spaziergang
    machen *to take a walk*
die Süssigkeit, -en *candy, sweets*

die Speisekarte, -n *menu*
das Hauptgericht, -e *main dish*
die Nachspeise, -n *dessert*
der Braten *roast*
die Gemüseplatte, -n *vegetable plate*
der Joghurt *yogurt*
das Kartoffelpüree *mashed potatoes*
der Nudelauflauf, ⁻e *noodle casserole*
der Pudding, -s *pudding*
der Traubensaft, ⁻e *grape juice*
der Vegetarier *vegetarian* (m.)
die Vegetarierin, -nen *vegetarian* (f.)

auf•passen (passt auf, hat aufgepasst) *to pay attention, watch out*
s. bewegen (bewegt sich, hat sich bewegt) *to get exercise*
s. fit•halten (hält sich fit, hat sich fitgehalten) *to keep fit*
mit•machen (macht mit, hat mitgemacht) *to participate, go along with*
rauchen (raucht, hat geraucht) *to smoke*
rennen (rennt, ist gerannt) *to run*
spazieren•gehen (geht spazieren, ist spazierengegangen) *to take a walk*
sitzen (sitzt, hat gesessen) *to sit, be sitting*
herum•sitzen (sitzt herum, hat herumgesessen) *to sit around*
s. setzen (setzt sich, hat sich gesetzt) *to sit (down)*
s. um•drehen (dreht sich um, hat sich umgedreht) *to turn around*

begeistert *enthusiastic*
gesund *healthy*
stundenlang *for hours*
vegetarisch *vegetarian*

s. Sorgen machen um A* *to worry about*
vor dem Fernseher sitzen *to sit in front of the TV*
was für (ein) *what kind of (a)*
zu Fuss gehen *to go on foot, walk*

Diese Wörter kennst du schon

das Fleisch *meat*
das Gemüse *vegetable*
das Obst *fruit*

der Salat, -e *lettuce; salad*
die Suppe, -n *soup*

genug *enough*
richtig *correct, right*

* The letter A indicates the word or phrase is followed by the accusative case. The letter D indicates the dative case.

Und so sagst du das *Here's how to . . .*

give a command

Haltet euch fit! *Stay fit!*

make a suggestion

Geh doch spazieren! *Why don't you go for a walk?*
Fahren wir Rad! *Let's ride bikes!*

make a request

Gib mir bitte das Buch! *Please give me the book.*

Taking a closer look

As you study the vocabulary list, answer the following questions.

1. Which verb has a stem-vowel change? What is it?
2. Which verbs are reflexive?
3. Which verbs have separable prefixes? Which one has an inseparable prefix?
4. What is the difference between **sitzen** and **sich setzen**? Give the conversational past of each one and use them in a sentence.
5. Write the conversational past of all the verbs on the list. Which verbs are weak and which ones are strong? How can you tell?
6. What do you notice about the verb **rennen**? It is called a mixed verb. Why?
7. How many cognates can you find on the list?

ÜBUNG L

Kommando-Spiel: Wer gibt das Kommando?

Practice commands.

1. One student comes to the front of the room and give commands to the class using the **ihr**-form. The class must do what **der Kommandant** says!
2. Now you come to the front of the class. Each student in the class then has the opportunity to give you a command that you must carry out. For this game the **du**-form is used since the command is directed at you.

Before you begin, brainstorm various commands that are appropriate for each game. For example:

1. Steht auf! Dreht euch um! Legt die Hand auf den Kopf! Legt die Finger auf die Nase! Hebt die rechte Hand! Setzt euch!
2. Steh auf! Geh an die Tür! Mach die Tür auf! Mach die Tür wieder zu! Geh an die Tafel! Nimm ein Stück Kreide in die Hand! Schreib deinen Namen an die Tafel!

KULTURECKE

Many Germans are health and fitness conscious. Although television, videos, and computers have indeed resulted in people being less active, a great deal of emphasis in recent years has been put on eating right and staying fit. Many magazines offer advice.

GUTE ERNÄHRUNG IST WICHTIG!

Jeden Tag sollen Sie etwas aus jeder Gruppe des Ernährungskreises essen — viel Getreide, Getreideproduckte, Obst und Gemüse, wenig Fett!

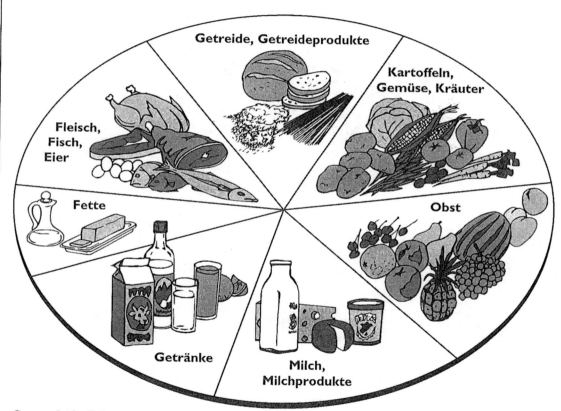

Sport hält fit!

Kalorien verbrennen ist besser als Kalorien sparen.

bei 30 Minuten	verbrennt der Korper
Radfahren	84 Kalorien
Wandern (5 km/h)	94 Kalorien
Rückenschwimmen (23 m/min)	150 Kalorien
Tischtennisspielen	165 Kalorien
Tennis, Einzel	225 Kalorien
Dauerlauf (8 km/h)	386 Kalorien

Wiederholung II
(Lektionen 6-10)

Lektion 6

a. The conversational past tense is commonly used in German to talk about things that happened in the past. This tense has two parts: the present tense of **haben** or **sein** and a past participle.

Past Participles	
WEAK VERBS (FOLLOW REGULAR PATTERN)	STRONG VERBS (HAVE SOME IRREGULARITIES)
ge + stem + **(e)t**	**ge** + stem + **en**
machen gemacht	laufen gelaufen
arbeiten gearbeitet	nehmen genommen

Ich *habe* meine Hausaufgaben schon *gemacht*.
I already did my homework.

Er *ist* schnell nach Hause *gelaufen*.
He quickly ran home.

Wir *haben* es nicht *genommen*.
We didn't take it.

b. Verbs ending in **-ieren** do not have a **ge-** in the past participle.

fotografieren   Du *hast* viel *fotografiert*.

Lektion 7

a. In verbs with separable prefixes, the **ge-** in the past participle is placed between the prefix and the rest of the verb.

WEAK VERBS		STRONG VERBS	
einkaufen	hat ein*ge*kauft	einladen	hat ein*ge*laden
aufräumen	hat auf*ge*räumt	einsteigen	ist ein*ge*stiegen

b. Verbs with inseparable prefixes do not have a **ge-** in the past participle.

begrüssen   **hat begrüsst**   **vergessen**   **hat vergessen**

c. Verbs with separable prefixes that end in **-ieren** do not have **ge-** in the past participle either.

anprobieren   **hat anprobiert**

Lektion 8

a. Reflexive verbs have a pronoun that refers back to the subject.

Infinitive: **sich waschen**

PRESENT TENSE	COMMAND	CONVERSATIONAL PAST
Ich wasche **mich.**		Ich habe **mich** gewaschen.
Du wäschst **dich.**	Wasch **dich!**	
Er / sie wäscht **sich.**		
Wir waschen **uns.**		
Ihr wascht **euch.**	Wascht **euch!**	
Sie waschen **sich.**	Waschen Sie **sich!**	

b. If there is more than one object in the sentence, the reflexive pronoun is dative.

Infinitive: **sich (etwas) kaufen**

PRESENT TENSE	COMMAND	CONVERSATIONAL PAST
Ich kaufe **mir** eine Tasche.		Ich habe **mir** ein Wörterbuch gekauft.
Du kaufst **dir** ein Heft.	Kauf **dir** ein Heft!	
Er / sie kauft **sich** ein Buch.		
Wir kaufen **uns** einen Kuli.		
Ihr kauft **euch** ein Wörterbuch.	Kauft **euch** ein Wörterbuch!	
Sie kaufen **sich** ein Computerspiel.	Kaufen Sie **sich** ein Computerspiel!	

Remember:

— Some verbs are always reflexive in German.
sich beeilen **Ich beeile mich.**

— Some verbs can be reflexive and non-reflexive.
Sie *zieht* das Kind *an*. *She dresses the child.*
Sie *zieht sich an*. *She dresses herself.*

— Some verbs are reflexive in German but not in English.
Sie *zieht sich um*. *She changes her clothes.*
Wir *unterhalten uns*. *We're having a conversation.*

Lektion 9

a. The following reflexive verbs are used to talk about an injury:

sich verletzen	**Ich habe mich verletzt.**
	I injured myself.
sich etwas brechen	**Er hat sich den Arm gebrochen.**
	He broke his arm.
sich etwas verstauchen	**Hast du dir den Knöchel verstaucht?**
	Did you sprain your ankle?

b. Infinitives can be used as nouns. They are capitalized and the gender is always neuter.

spielen *to play* **das Spielen** *playing*
Tennis spielen *to play tennis* **das Tennisspielen** *playing tennis*

A phrase with **beim** and the infinitive used as a noun expresses the idea of "while."

beim Skilaufen *while skiing*

c. There are a number of verbs and phrases in German that are followed by the dative case.

weh tun *to hurt* **es tut mir weh** *it hurts (me)*

DATIVE PERSONAL PRONOUNS			
Es tut *mir* weh.	*It hurts me.*	**Es tut *uns* weh.**	*It hurts us.*
Es tut *dir* weh.	*It hurts you.*	**Es tut *euch* weh.**	*It hurts you.*
Es tut *ihm* weh.	*It hurts him.*	**Es tut *ihnen* weh.**	*It hurts them.*
Es tut *ihr* weh.	*It hurts her.*	**Es tut *Ihnen* weh.**	*It hurts you. (formal)*

d. In clauses beginning with **wenn**, the verb comes at the end of the clause.

Ich gehe zum Arzt.   Ich bin krank.
Ich gehe zum Arzt, *wenn* **ich krank** *bin.*

If an element other than the subject begins the sentence, for example, a **wenn**-clause, the subject and verb are inverted in the main clause.

1	2	3	
Ich	gehe	zum Arzt,	wenn ich krank bin.
Wenn ich krank bin,	bleibe	ich	im Bett.

Lektion 10

a. Imperatives, also called command forms, can be used to give commands, make requests, and make suggestions.

Summary of Command Forms				
INFINITIVE	gehen	essen	sich fithalten	sein
FAM. SING.	Geh!	Iss!	Halt dich fit!	Sei ruhig!
FAM. PL.	Geht!	Esst!	Haltet euch fit!	Seid ruhig!
FORMAL	Gehen Sie!	Essen Sie!	Halten Sie sich fit!	Seien Sie ruhig!
INCLUSIVE	Gehen wir!	Essen wir!	Halten wir uns fit!	Seien wir ruhig!

d. The interrogative **was für (ein)** can be used with a noun as the subject or the direct object of a question.

	SUBJECT (Nominative)	DIRECT OBJECT (Accusative)
m. f. n.	Was für ein Saft ist das? Was für eine Suppe ist das? Was für ein Eis ist das?	Was für einen Saft trinkst du? Was für eine Suppe isst du? Was für ein Eis möchtest du?
pl.	Was für Äpfel sind das?	Was für Äpfel kaufst du?

ÜBUNG A

Match the following verbs to the proper group of expressions.

fahren   gehen   laufen   machen   spielen

1. eine Wanderung
   einen Spaziergang
   eine Radtour
   eine Reise
   einen Ausflug
   einen Stadtbummel

2. Tennis
   Golf
   Hockey
   Basketball
   Klavier
   Karten

3. schwimmen
   angeln
   windsurfen
   zelten
   spazieren
   wandern

4. Rad
   Schlitten
   Snowboard
   Skateboard

5. Rollschuh
   Schlittschuh
   Ski
   Wasserski

ÜBUNG B

Draw lines connecting the words that are opposite or nearly opposite in meaning, then complete the sentences below telling what **Schüler A** and **Schüler B** did.

faulenzen	s. bewegen
sich anziehen	verkaufen
aufstehen	abfahren
begrüssen	gehen
bleiben	sich fithalten
ankommen	ins Bett gehen
herumsitzen	sich verabschieden
kaufen	sich ausziehen

BEISPIEL: **Schüler A**
hat gefaulenzt.

Schüler B
hat sich fitgehalten.

1. _____   _____

2. _____   _____

3. _____   _____

4. _____   _____

5. _____   _____

6. _____   _____

7. _____   _____

ÜBUNG C

Fill out the following questionnaire and compare your answers with those of a classmate.

Umfrage

1. Was für eine Schule besuchst du? — eine Mittelschule? eine Oberschule?

_____

2. Was für Fächer hast du?

_____

3. Spielst du ein Instrument? Was für eins?

_____

4. Was für Musik hörst du gern?

_____

5. Was für Sport machst du?

_____

6. Was für einen Wagen kaufst du dir einmal?

_____

ÜBUNG **D**

Here are ads from two vacation spots. Compare what they offer by filling in the chart below.
Write the activities you can do at each place in the appropriate column. Write the activities
available at both places in the right column.

Ferienort A

Ferienort B

A	B	A + B

ÜBUNG E

Play the following game with one or more classmates. You will need one die and a marker each player can move along the game path. Each player in turn throws the die and moves his or her marker. If the marker lands on a picture, the player must describe in a sentence what the person in the picture is doing, for example, **Sie wäscht sich die Haare.** If the answer is correct, the player goes again; if not, the player returns to **Anfang**.

Variations: 1. Say the sentence in the conversational past: **Sie hat sich die Haare gewaschen.**
           2. Form a question
               a. in the present: **Wäscht sie sich die Haare?**
               b. in the conversational past: **Hat sie sich die Haare gewaschen?**
           3. Give a **du**-command: **Wasch dir die Haare!**

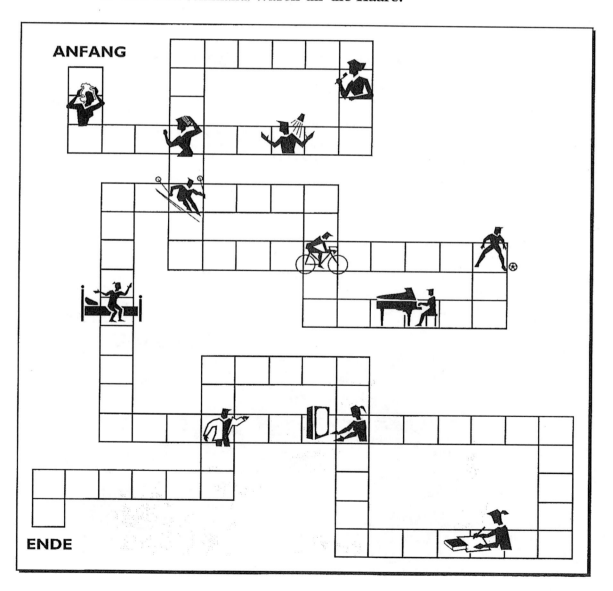

ANFANG

ENDE

Proficiency Activities

Speaking

Practive the following situations with a partner. You take the role of A, your partner takes the role of B.

1. A and B are talking about what they did during a recent vacation. A asks B where he or she went, who went along, and what he or she did. B respond to A's questions and asks about A's vacation.

2. A and B are talking about sports and activities. A asks B what he or she thinks about various sports and activities, what he or she does, and what he or she might like to do. B responds to A's questions and asks A about what he or she likes to do.

3. A and B want to get together this afternoon or this evening. A wants to know if B has time. A asks B what he or she is doing today. B responds to A's questions and asks about A's schedule. They then arrange a time when they can get together.

4. A was sick yesterday and didn't come to school. A explains his or her absence to the teacher. (B plays the role of the teacher.) B asks A why he or she wasn't in school yesterday and responds to A's explanation.

5. A is concerned that B is not taking good care of himself or herself. A asks B what he or she does to keep fit. B responds to A's questions. A then makes suggestions to B about things B should and shouldn't do to keep fit.

Listening

A friend is showing you pictures of his vacation. Write the number of what you hear under the picture your friend is describing.

Reading

Look over the following newspaper ads and answer the questions in English.

Ihr Fachhändler:

All Terrain Bike
Life Bike
Moutain
Tour Bike
City Cruiser
Jugend- u. Kinderräder

Fahrrad-Shop-Bauer
Bahnhofstr. 24
Tel: 6 72 89

Immer 200 Räder auf Lager.
Viele Ersatzteile, Zubehör
und Bekleidung.
— Viele aktuelle Angebote —

Wir nehmen Ihr altes Rad in Zahlung.

Dance-Center

Aerobic – Stretching – Fitnessgymnastik

Uhr	Montag	Dienstag	Donnerstag
17-18	**Stretching** (gesielte Dehnung)		**Stretching** (gezielte Dehnung)
18-19	**Aerobic-Power** (für Sportler)	**Aerobic II** (Mittelstufe)	**Aerobic-Power** (für Sportler)
19-20	**Aerobic-Weights** (m. Gewichtsmannschetten)	**Fitness-Gymnastik**	**Fitness-Gymnastik**
20-21	**Aerobic-I** (für Einsteiger)		**Aerobic II** (für Sportler)

Kein Vertragszwang – keine Anmeldung
Jede Stunde DM 4,50 (10er Abo DM 40,-)
modernes Sonnenstudio

Fitness-Center Bremen
Hauptmann Strasse 52 • Telefon 0 65 22

Squash

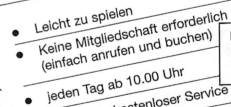

- Leicht zu spielen
- Keine Mitgliedschaft erforderlich (einfach anrufen und buchen)
- jeden Tag ab 10.00 Uhr
- Sauna als kostenloser Service

SPORT-HALLE
Lauterbachstr. 38
REGENSBURG
Tel. 3 56 66

Nach unserer Renovierung ist ab Sonntag unsere
Minigolfbahn weider geöffnet!
Fam. Tauber Schulstr. 4 Ulm Tel: 6 79 03

1. What are the four activities advertised here?

   _____

2. At what time and on what days can you do **Fitness-Gymnastik** at the **Fitness-Center** in Bremen?

   _____

3. If you wanted to play miniature golf, what number would you call to find out the hours and prices?

   _____

4. Where can you play squash?

   _____

5. If you went to the bicycle shop advertised on this page, what kind of a bike would you be interested in?

   _____

Writing

1. You are going on a camping trip with some friends. Make a list of at least five things you need to take along.

   _____

   _____

   _____

2. Staying fit and healthy is very important. Write five things you do to stay fit.

   _____

   _____

   _____

3. Write a paragraph describing what you do in the morning before going to school. Include at least five different activities.

_____

_____

_____

_____

_____

_____

4. Your sister fell while bike riding. She broke her arm, so you and your mother are taking her to the doctor. Write a note to leave for your father explaining what happened.

_____

_____

_____

_____

_____

_____

5. Write a short letter to a friend telling about what you did on your summer vacation. Mention at least four activities. Comment on the weather. Did you have a good time or was it boring? You can write about what you actually did or make something up.

_____

_____

_____

_____

_____

3
Dritter Teil

11

Wann hast du Geburtstag?

More on Ordinal Numbers;
The Dative Case; The Verb *werden*

1 Wortschatz

Mein Kalender

JUNI						
Montag	Dienstag	Mittwoch	Donnerstag	Freitag	Samstag	Sonntag
1 *Feiertag keine Schule*	2	3	4	5 *Schulausflug*	6	7
8 *Mutter Geburtstag*	9	10	11	12 *Konzert*	13	14 *Vatertag*
15	16	17	18 *Tim Geburtstag*	19	20 *Party für Tim*	21
22	23 *Lehrerkonferenz keine Schule*	24	25 *Sportfest*	26 *Ferienbeginn*	27	28
29	30					

Note that German calendars begin with Monday, not Sunday, as American calendars do.

2 To express dates you have to know ordinal numbers:

Montag ist der *erste* Juni.
Am *ersten* Juni machen wir einen Schulausflug.

In Book 1 you learned the cardinal numbers (one, two, three, and so on) and the ordinal numbers (first, second, third, and so on). Most ordinal numbers follow a regular pattern. There are a few exceptions. Fill in the missing numbers below.

1 eins	der 1. der erste	am 1. am ersten
2 _____	der 2. der zweite	am 2. am zweiten
3 drei	der 3. der dritte	am 3. am dritten
4 _____	der 4. _____	am 4. _____
5 _____	der 5. _____	am 5. _____
6 _____	der 6. _____	am 6. _____
7 sieben	der 7. der siebte	am 7. am siebten
8 _____	der 8. _____	am 8. _____
9 _____	der 9. _____	am 9. _____
10 _____	der 10. _____	am 10. _____
11 _____	der 11. _____	am 11. _____
12 _____	der 12. _____	am 12. _____
13 _____	der 13. dreizehnte	am 13. _____
18 _____	der 18. _____	am 18. _____
20 _____	der 20. der zwanzigste	am 20. am zwanzigsten
21 einundzwanzig	der 21. _____	am 21. _____
25 _____	der 25. _____	am 25. _____
30 _____	der 30. der dreissigste	am 30. am dreissigsten
31 _____	der 31. _____	am 31. _____

Look at the numbers on the facing page. What patterns can you observe?—Most of the numbers from 1 to 19 add _____ to form the ordinal number in the nominative and _____ in the phrase with **am**. The exceptions are: _____, _____, and _____. Cardinal numbers ending in **-ig** add _____ in the nominative and _____ in the phrase with **am**.

ÜBUNG **A**

Now look at the calendar on page 217 and answer the questions.

1. Wann hat Paul's Mutter Geburtstag?   am _____

2. Wann beginnen die Ferien?   _____

3. Wann ist Vatertag?   _____

4. Wann ist das Sportfest?   _____

5. Warum hat Paul am 1. Juni keine Schule?   _____

6. Warum hat er am 16. keine Schule?   _____

7. Wann hat Tim Geburtstag?   _____

8. Wann ist die Party für Tim?   _____

9. Wann ist der Schulausflug?   _____

10. Wann ist ein Konzert?   _____

ÜBUNG **B**

Do you remember the months in German? Write the months under the corresponding season.

Juni	November	Oktober	Februar	Juli	Mai	September	April
Dezember		August		Januar		März	

WINTER	FRÜHLING	SOMMER	HERBST
_____	_____	_____	_____
_____	_____	_____	_____
_____	_____	_____	_____
_____	_____	_____	_____

ÜBUNG C

Wann hast du Geburtstag? One student comes to the front of the room and asks each classmate: **Wann hast du Geburtstag?** Write the information for each of your classmates in a chart like the one below.

wer?	zu welcher Jahreszeit?	in welchem Monat?	an welchem Tag?
Jenny	im Herbst	im Oktober	am 15.

ÜBUNG D

Hör gut zu! You will hear a student talking about various things she has coming up in the month of May. Fill in her calendar by writing each activity or occasion in the appropriate space.

MAI						
Montag	Dienstag	Mittwoch	Donnerstag	Freitag	Samstag	Sonntag
			1	2	3	4
5	6	7	8	9	10	11
12	13	14	15	16	17	18
19	20	21	22	23	24	25
26	27	28	29	30	31	

ÜBUNG E

Work with a partner and compare what you have written on your calendars. The name of the student you heard in the listening activity is Barbara. You and your partner ask each other questions about Barbara's calendar. If your information doesn't match, ask another student what he or she has. If necessary, listen to the activity again.

BEISPIEL: **Was macht Barbara am 14.?**
Wann geht Barbara ins Kino?

ÜBUNG F

Bilderrätsel— Solve the following puzzle and write the solution in the space provided.

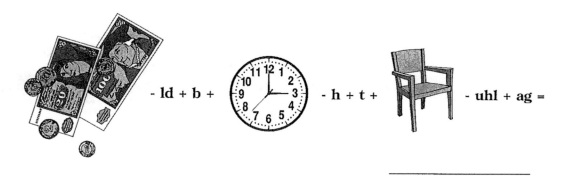

- ld + b +   - h + t +   - uhl + ag =

_____

3 Julian and Marta are talking about how old they are.

JULIAN: Ich habe nächste Woche Geburtstag.
MARTA: Ja, wirklich! Wie alt wirst du?
JULIAN: Ich werde vierzehn. Bist du schon vierzehn?
MARTA: Nein, ich werde erst im März vierzehn.

1. Wie alt ist Julian? _____

2. Wann wird Julian vierzehn? _____

3. Wie alt ist Marta? _____

4. Wann wird Marta vierzehn? _____

4 In the dialogue on the preceding page and in the questions that follow it, which words express "will be" or "will become?" Underline them.

You have underlined the forms of the verb **werden** (will be, will become).

Here are all the forms.

ich	werde	wir	werden
du	*wirst*	ihr	werdet
er/sie/es	*wird*	sie/Sie	werden

The verb **werden** has a stem vowel change in the _____-form and in the_____ -form. The _____ changes to _____. What else do you notice about the spelling of these two forms?

ÜBUNG **G**

All of the following students have birthdays in the summer. Write how old they are and how old they will be on their next birthday.

BEISPIEL: **(Maria / 13 / 4. Juni)**
Maria is dreizehn Jahre alt. Sie wird am 4. Juni vierzehn.

1. (Dieter / 13 / 23. Juni) _____

2. (Felix / 15 / 15. Juli) _____

3. (Susi / 17 / 29. Juli) _____

4. (Günter / 11 / 3. August) _____

5. (Erika / 16 / 22. August) _____

ÜBUNG **H**

Write how old these students were on their last birthdays. (Note that the conversational past of **werden** is **ist geworden.**)

BEISPIEL: **(Sabine / 10 / 16. September)**
Sabine ist am 16. September zehn geworden.

1. (Benji / 12 / 20. Oktober) _____

2. (Frank / 13 / 1. September) _____

3. (Tanja / 11 / 3. November) _____

4. (Ilse / 14 / 10. Oktober) _____

5. (Brigitte 18 / 30. September) _____

ÜBUNG I

Kettenübung   Go around the room asking your classmates about their age. The first student asks the second student. He or she responds and then asks the third student.

Schüler A   Bist du schon vierzehn?

Schüler B   Ja, ich bin (im Januar) vierzehn geworden.
            or
            Nein, ich werde erst (im April) vierzehn.
                        (nächstes Jahr)
                        (in zwei Jahren)

5 Tim hat Geburtstag

Tim's birthday is coming up. Two of his friends, Manuela and Kristen, are wondering what to give him.

Du, Kristin, was schenkst du dem Tim zum Geburtstag?

Ich habe ihm eine Kassette gekauft.

Was soll ich ihm schenken? Hast du eine Idee?

Gib ihm ein Buch, ein T-shirt, eine CD, einen Taschenrechner.

Hm. vielleicht. . .

Oder schenk ihm Pralinen oder Blumen.

Du spinnst! Ich kann doch dem Tim keine Blumen geben!

ÜBUNG J

Hast du verstanden? Answer the questions.

1. Was hat Kristin für Tim gekauft?

   _____

2. Was für Geschenkideen hat Kristin?

   _____

   _____

3. Findet Manuela Blumen gut?

   _____

ÜBUNG K

Practice the illustrated dialogue with a partner. Pretend you are both friends of Tim's. Suggest different items—those pictured and any others you can think of—and respond to each suggestion.

6 You have learned about the nominative, accusative, and dative cases:

—the **nominative** signals the **subject** of a sentence.
—the **accusative** signals the **direct object** of a sentence.
—the **dative** signals the **indirect object** of a sentence.

Let's take another look at the dative case. The dative expresses the idea of "to someone" or "for someone."

Ich gebe **dem Tim** ein Buch. { *I'm giving a book to Tim.*
                                 I'm giving Tim a book.

Ich kaufe **der Alice** eine CD. { *I'm buying a CD for Alice.*
                                   I'm buying Alice a CD.

Here are the dative case forms of the definite articles and the third person pronouns.

	DEFINITE ARTICLE	THIRD PERSON PRONOUN
MASC.	Ich gebe *dem* Tim ein Buch.	Ich gebe *ihm* ein Buch.
FEM.	Ich gebe *der* Alice eine CD.	Ich gebe *ihr* eine CD.
NEUT	Ich gebe *dem* Kind ein Spiel.	Ich gebe *ihm* ein Spiel.
PLURAL	Ich gebe *den* Kinder*n** ein Spiel.	Ich gebe *ihnen* ein Spiel.

* In the dative plural, an **-n** is added to the noun if it doesn't already end in **-n**.

Which interrogative would you use to ask the questions *to whom?* or *for whom?* Would you use **wer? wen?** or **wem?**

Wem schenkst du die Blumen?   *To whom are you giving the flowers?*
Wem kaufst du ein Buch?   *For whom are you buying a book?*

Fill in the correct interrogative pronoun.

_____ hat heute Geburtstag?   _____ kannst du fragen?

_____ gibst du die Kassette?

What letter alerts you to the dative case?

Reread the dialogue on pages 223-224 and underline the dative case forms.

ÜBUNG L

A classmate would like to know whom the presents are for. Write what your classmate asks and what you respond. Follow the example.

BEISPIEL: — **Wem gibst du das Buch?**
— **Dem Martin.**

1. _____

_____

2. _____

_____

3. _____

_____

4. _____

_____

5. _____

_____

ÜBUNG **M**

Now practice the following conversation with a partner. Use the pictures in the preceding activity as cues.

DU: **Ich schenke dem Martin ein Buch.**
PARTNER: **Wie bitte?* Was schenkst du ihm?**
DU: **Ich schenke ihm ein Buch.**

* If·you would like something repeated because you didn't hear or you didn't understand, use the phrase **wie bitte?** *how's that again?* or *what did you say?*

PERSÖNLICHE FRAGEN ❓

1. Wann hast du Geburtstag? _____

2. Schau auf einen Kalender! Wann ist dieses Jahr Muttertag? _____

3. Was schenkst du der Mutter zum Muttertag? _____

4. Wann ist dieses Jahr Vatertag? _____

5. Was schenkst du dem Vater zum Vatertag? _____

KLASSENPROJEKT

In Germany families often have a special calendar to remind them of birthdays. Make a class birthday calendar with the birthdays of your classmates or make your own individual family birthday calendar with the birthdays of your own friends and family members.

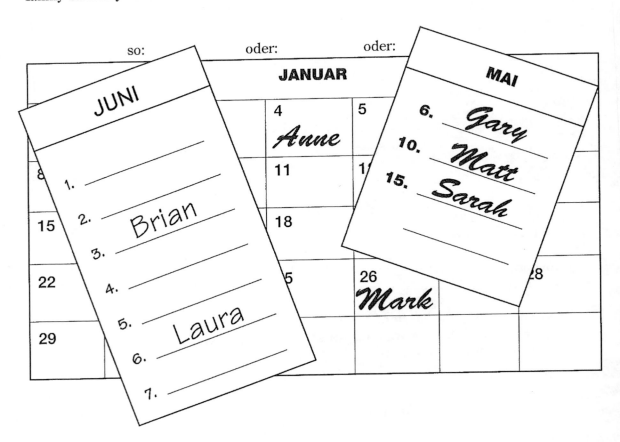

WORTSCHATZ A-Z

die Idee, -n *idea*
der Feiertag, -e *holiday*
der Kalender *calendar*
der Muttertag, -e *Mother's Day*
die Praline, -n *fancy chocolate candy*
der Vatertag, -e *Father's Day*

schenken *to give as a gift*
werden (wird, ist geworden) *will be, will become*
erst *only**
wem *to whom, for whom*
zum Geburtstag *for (your) birthday*

Diese Wörter kennst du schon

schon *already*
die Blume, -n *flower*
der Monat, -e *month*
der Tag, -e *day*
die Jahreszeit, -en *season*
Geburtstag haben: er hat Geburtstag *it's his birthday*
der erste Juni *June 1st, the first of June*

am ersten Juni *on June 1st; on the first of June*
der dritte *the third*
der siebte *the seventh*
der vierzehnte *the 14th*
am vierzehnten *on the 14th*
der zwanzigste *the 20th*
am zwanzigsten *on the 20th*

Und so sagst du... *Here's how to . . .*

respond to a suggestion

gute Idee *good idea*
nicht schlecht *not bad*
vielleicht *maybe*

meinst du? *do you think so?*
du spinnst! *you're crazy!*

ask for something to be repeated

wie bitte? *how's that again?, what did you say?*

to express future time

im (April) *in (April)*
nächste Woche *next week*
nächstes Jahr *next year*

in (zwei) Wochen *in (two) weeks*
 Tagen *days*
 Monaten *months*
 Jahren *years*

---

* The word **erst** means "only" in certain contexts. It implies there is an expectation of more to come. For example: **Sie ist erst vierzehn.** (She is only fourteen but expects eventually to be older.) **Es ist erst sieben Uhr.** (It is only seven o'clock but it will eventually be later.) Note the difference between:

Ich habe *nur* fünf Dollar. *I only have five dollars (so I can't buy the CD I want).*
Ich habe *erst* fünf Dollar. *I only have five dollars (at this point, but I am saving my money to buy the CD and will eventually have enough).*

ÜBUNG N

Spiel: Wem schenkst du was?   Prepare two stacks of cards: one set will contain your classmates' names, the other will have drawn-or-pasted pictures of items you would give as presents. (Pretend that money is no object and include some items accordingly: **ein Fahrrad, ein Moped, eine Gitarre, eine Reise nach Deutschland,** and so on.) Divide the class into two teams. Each teammate will take turns drawing a card from each stack to form sentences telling what he/she gives to whom. The winning team will be the one with the most correct sentences.

KULTURECKE

Certain birthdays are significant milestones in a young person's life. These birthdays bring with them certain rights and responsibilities. Read the following summary. What rights and responsibilities do you have now? Which birthdays will be milestones in your life?

Alter *Age*	Rechte *Rights*	Pflichten *Responsibilities*
6 6-11 7-18	• Children have the right to an education. • Children may attend movies designated "**ab 6 Jahren**" if the movie is over by 8 P.M. • Until the age of 18, children and young people can only sign a contract with the permission of a parent or guardian. • They have the right to spend their allowance as they want to.	• **Schulpflicht:** Children must go to school; until the age of 15.
12	• Children may attend movies designated "**ab 12 Jahren**" if the movie is over by 8 P.M. • From the age of 12, children cannot be forced to change their religion.	
14	• From 14-17, young people are legally responsible for their actions and can be prosecuted in juvenile court. • Young people have the right to choose their own religion. • They may attend movies that are over by 10 P.M.	
16	• Young people may attend movies designated "**ab 16 Jahren**" if the movie is over by midnight. • They are allowed to smoke in public. • They may go to a bar or dance until midnight without being accompanied by an adult. • Marriage is permitted without parental consent.	• **Ausweis oder Pass:** From the age of 16, everyone must have a valid I.D. or passport.
18	• **Volljährigkeit:** Young people are legally of age and have all the rights and responsibilities of adults. • **Wahlrecht:** They have the right to vote. • **Führerschein:** They may get a driver's license.	• **Wehrpflicht:** Young men must serve in the military or do alternative service.

12

Geschenke, Geschenke, Geschenke

Reviewing: Possessives and Personal Pronouns; Dative Case; Dative Prepositions *von* and *zu*; Verbs with Objects in the Dative Case

1 Wortschatz

Der Geburtstagstisch

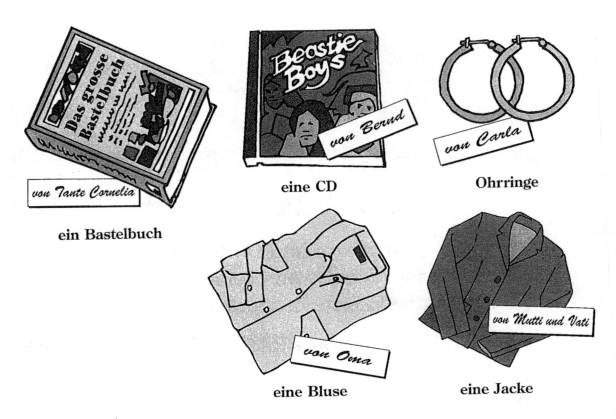

ein Bastelbuch

eine CD

Ohrringe

eine Bluse

eine Jacke

ÜBUNG A

Let's ask Gabi what she got for her birthday. Fill in the blanks in her response.

Gabi, was hast du zum Geburtstag bekommen und von wem?

1. Was hast du von **deinen** Eltern bekommen?

   Von _____ Eltern habe ich _____ bekommen.

2. Was hast du von **deiner** Oma bekommen?

   Von _____ Oma habe ich _____ bekommen.

3. Was hast du von **deinem** Bruder Bernd bekommen?

   Von _____ Bruder habe ich _____ bekommen.

4. Was hast du von **deiner** Schwester Carla bekommen?

   Von _____ Schwester habe ich _____ bekommen.

5. Was hast du von **deiner** Tante Cornelia bekommen?

   Von _____ Tante Cornelia habe ich _____ bekommen.

ÜBUNG **B**

Now you tell a classmate what Gabi got and from whom. Complete the sentences.

Was hat Gabi zum Geburtstag bekommen?

1. Von ihren Eltern hat sie . . .
2. Von ihrem Bruder Bernd hat sie . . .

2 In the preceding chapter you reviewed the definite articles and the third-person personal pronouns in the dative case. Here are the forms of the possessive adjectives in the dative. Did you use the correct ones in the activities you just did? Why did you have to use the dative case after the preposition **von** (*from*)?

DATIVE CASE			
	DEFINITE ARTICLE	INDEFINITE ARTICLE	POSSESSIVE ADJECTIVE
MASCULINE	dem	einem	meinem*
FEMININE	der	einer	meiner
NEUTER	dem	einem	meinem
PLURAL	den	———	meinen

* Also: **deinem, seinem, ihrem, unserem, eurem, ihrem,** and **Ihrem.**

The preposition **von** is always followed by the dative case. Do you remember the other dative prepositions you learned in Book 1?

ÜBUNG **C**

Draw lines matching the personal pronoun on the left and the corresponding possessive adjective on the right.

ÜBUNG D

Write the German equivalents for the following pronouns.

1. *my* _____

2. *our* _____

3. *your* (sing.) _____

4. *your* (pl.) _____

5. *his* _____

6. *her* _____

7. *their* _____

ÜBUNG E

Complete the sentences describing who's giving what to whom. In each case use possessive adjectives that correspond to the subject.

1. Ich kaufe **meinem** Vater eine CD.

   _____ Mutter Ohrringe.

   _____ Grosseltern Pralinen.

2. Du schenkst _____ Onkel ein Buch.

   _____ Tante Blumen.

   _____ Geschwistern ein Spiel.

3. Er (Michael) gibt _____ Freund eine lustige Geburtstagskarte.

   _____ Freundin eine Musikkassette.

   _____ Eltern einen Kalender.

4. Sie (Julia) kauft _____ Schwester eine Bluse.

   _____ Bruder eine Mütze.

   _____ Verwandten Pralinen.

5. Wir geben _____ Lehrer das Buch.

   _____ Lehrerin den Taschenrechner.

   _____ Klassenkameraden die Antworten.

6. Ihr kauft _____ Kusine ein Eis.

_____ Vetter eine Cola.

_____ Freunden Kartoffelchips.

7. Sie (die Eltern) kaufen _____ Tochter ein Fahrrad.

_____ Sohn einen Tennisschläger.

_____ Kindern einen Hund.

3 Gabis Geburtstag

Read the story about Gabi's birthday. Did she get what she wished for?

Heute ist ein besonderer Tag. Gabi hat Geburtstag! Von ihren Eltern hat sie sich ein Fahrrad gewünscht. Morgens kommt sie ganz gespannt ins Wohnzimmer. Ihre Eltern, ihr Bruder Bernd und ihre Schwester Carla stehen alle um den Geburtstagstisch und gratulieren ihr.

«Guten Morgen, Gabi! Wir wünschen dir alles Gute zum Geburtstag! Schau, die schönen Blumen und die viele Post! » sagt ihre Mutter und gibt ihrer Tochter einen Kuss. Gabi freut sich über alles: über die Blumen, die Post, die Glückwünsche und natürlich über die Geschenke. Sie macht die Geschenke auf und bedankt sich.

«Bernd, ich danke dir für die CD! Die Beastie Boys! Das ist meine Lieblings-gruppe!»

«Und Carla – Ohrringe! Wie schön! Vielen Dank!»

Von der Oma bekommt Gabi eine schöne Bluse und von Tante Cornelia ein Bastelbuch. Sie muss ihnen einen Brief schreiben und sich bedanken.

«Hier, Gabi», sagt Vati, «ein Geschenk von Mutti und von mir. Hoffentlich gefällt es dir!» Gabi ist enttäuscht. Sie hat sich ein Fahrrad gewünscht, und das Paket ist viel zu klein! Aber Gabi lächelt und sagt: «Was kann das sein?» Sie macht das Paket auf: eine Jacke! Gabi probiert die Jacke sofort an. «Schau! Die Jacke passt prima, und sie gefällt mir gut! Vielen, vielen Dank!»

«Kommt jetzt», sagt Mutti, «wir wollen frühstücken. Ihr müsst in die Schule gehen.» Alle gehen in die Küche. «Gabi, hol bitte die Zeitung vom Briefkasten», bittet Vati. Gabi läuft schnell aus dem Haus. Moment mal! Was ist das? Dort vor der Tür steht ein nagelneues Fahrrad. «Wem gehört das tolle Fahrrad?» fragt sie? «Das Fahrrad gehört dir natürlich!» ruft ihr Vater von der Küche. «Alles Gute zum Geburtstag!»

ÜBUNG F

Hast du verstanden?   Read the statements and determine if each one is true or false. Write **richtig** after the statement if it is true, write **falsch** if it isn't.

1. Heute hat Gabi Geburtstag. _____

2. Sie hat sich ein Skateboard gewünscht. _____

3. Von ihrem Bruder hat sie eine CD bekommen. _____

4. Von ihrer Schwester hat sie Ohrringe bekommen. _____

5. Gabis Grossmutter hat ihr Blumen geschenkt. _____

6. Heute ist ein Schultag. _____

7. Gabi ist sehr enttäuscht. Sie hat kein Fahrrad zum Geburtstag bekommen.

_____

ÜBUNG G

Take a little closer look at the story and answer the following questions.

1. What phrase tells you that Gabi is excited and eager to see her presents when she comes into the living room?

_____

2. What does Gabi's mother say to wish her a happy birthday?

_____

3. There are presents from Gabi's grandmother and aunt. How is Gabi going to thank them?

_____

4. What word tells you how Gabi feels when her parents give her a present that is obviously not the bicycle she had wished for? What does it mean in English?

_____

5. Gabi wants to know who the bike belongs to. How does she ask and what does her father say? What verb do they use?

_____

_____

ÜBUNG **H**

Complete each sentence with an appropriate verb from the list given.

dankt   **gefällt**   **gehört**   **gratuliert**   **wünscht**

1. Gabis Schwester _____ ihr zum Geburtstag.

2. Sie _____ ihr alles Gute.

3. Gabi _____ ihrer Schwester für die Ohrringe.

4. Die Jacke von ihren Eltern _____ ihr gut.

5. Das neue Fahrrad _____ ihr!

4 Look again at the verbs in the preceding activity. Look at the object of each verb. What case is the object in? _____.

There are a number of verbs in German that always have an object in the dative case. Here are several common ones. You are already familar with some of them.

danken *to thank someone*   **gratulieren** *to congratulate someone*
gefallen* *to please someone*   **wünschen** *to wish someone*
gehören *to belong to someone*

ÜBUNG **I**

Gabi got lots of presents for her birthday and she thanks everyone. Write what she does and what she says. Follow the examples. If necessary, review the dative pronouns on page 202.

BEISPIEL: **Carla hat ihr Ohrringe gegeben.**
             Gabi tut: Sie dankt ihr.
             Gabi sagt: Carla, ich danke dir für die Ohrringe.

1. Bernd hat ihr eine CD geschenkt.

  Gabi tut: _____

  Gabi sagt: _____

*Remember, the verb **gefallen** has a stem vowel change. In the **du**- and **er/sie**- form the **a** changes to **ä**.

2. Die Oma hat ihr eine Bluse geschickt.

Gabi tut: _____

Gabi sagt: _____

3. Gabi hat von Tante Cornelia ein Bastelbuch bekommen.

Gabi tut: _____

Gabi sagt: _____

4. Die Eltern haben ihr ein Fahrrad gekauft.

Gabi tut: _____

Gabi sagt: _____

5. Der Lehrer hat ihr eine Geburtstagskarte gegeben.

Gabi tut: _____

Gabi sagt: _____

ÜBUNG J

Express the answer to each question in a different way. Use the verb **gehören**.

BEISPIEL: **Wem gehört das Buch?   —Das ist mein Buch.**
Das Buch gehört mir.

1. Wem gehört das Fahrrad?   —Das ist sein Fahhrad.

_____

2. Wem gehört der Hund?   —Das ist unser Hund.

_____

3. Wem gehört die Mütze?   —Das ist deine Mütze!

_____

4. Wem gehören die CDs?   —Das sind eure CDs!

_____

5. Wem gehört das Haus?   —Das ist ihr (*their*) Haus.

_____

6. Wem gehört der Tennisschläger?   —Das ist ihr (*her*) Tennisschläger.

_____

ÜBUNG K

Write sentences using one word or noun phrase from each column.

WAS?		WEM?	
das Geschenk die Musik der Film die Schuhe das Essen die neue Schule die Computerspiele	gefällt gefallen	mir meinem Bruder der Lehrerin den Kindern uns ihren Eltern dir	gut nicht

BEISPIEL: **Die Musik gefällt ihren Eltern nicht.**

1. _____

2. _____

3. _____

4. _____

5. _____

6. _____

ÜBUNG L

Komplimente. Express the compliments below in a different way using the verb **gefallen**.

BEISPIEL: **Ich mag deine Bluse!**
          Deine Bluse gefällt mir!

1. Ich mag dein T-Shirt.

_____

2. Ich finde dein Haus schön.

_____

3. Ich mag deine Freunde.

_____

4. Dein Haar sieht sehr gut aus!

_____

ÜBUNG M

Read the thank you note that Gabi has written to her grandmother. Fill in the missing words.

bekommen	den	gelacht	Kuchen
besuchst	Fahrrad	Geschenke	Liebe
Bluse	gefällt	getragen	mir
Dank	gefeiert	Grüsse	Party
danke	gefreut	gut	Spass

Marburg, _____ 5. April

_____ Oma!

Vielen herzlichen _____ für die schöne _____! Ich habe mich darüber sehr _____! Die Bluse passt prima und _____ mir wirklich gut.

Mein Geburtstag war wunderbar! Ich habe viele _____ bekommen. Von Mutti und Vati habe ich ein _____ bekommen — toll! Bernd hat _____ eine CD von meiner Lieblingsgruppe gegeben und von Carla habe ich schöne Ohrringe _____.

Am Samstag habe ich mit meinen Freunden _____. Ich habe eine kleine _____ gehabt. Es hat viel _____ gemacht. Mutti hat einen tollen _____ gebacken. Wir haben viel getanzt, viel gegessen und viel _____. Ich habe die neue Bluse von dir _____. Die Bluse hat meinen Freunde auch _____ gefallen.

Ich hoffe, es geht Dir gut! Wann _____ du uns wieder? Wir haben dich lange nicht mehr gesehen!

Ich _____ dir nochmals ganz ganz herzlich für dein Geburtstagsgeschenk und für deine lieben Glückwünsche!

Herzliche _____
Deine Gabi

5 Feste und Feiertage

Was feierst du?

1

2

3

4

5

6

7

8

9

Wir gratulieren...

10

11

12

13

14

15

Alles gute...

16

17

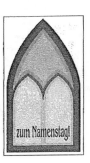

18

Wir wünschen euch...

19

20

21

The preposition **zu**, like **von**, is always followed by the dative case. The contractions **zum** and **zur** are often used.

$$zu + dem = zum$$
$$zu + der = zur$$

ÜBUNG **N**

Write the number of the card on the preceding pages next to the corresponding occasion listed below.

1. Easter _____

2. Christmas _____

3. Name Day _____

4. Birthday _____

5. New Baby _____

6. Father's Day _____

7. Hanukkah _____

8. Wedding _____

9. Engagement _____

10. Wedding Anniversary _____

11. New Year's _____

12. Kwanza _____

13. 50th Wedding Anniversary _____

14. New Job _____

ÜBUNG **O**

Hör gut zu! Write the number of the good wishes you hear under the corresponding picture.

_____   _____   _____   _____   _____   _____

PERSÖNLICHE FRAGEN

1. Was feiert ihr in eurer Familie? Geburtstage? Hochzeitstage? Chanukah? Weihnachten? Kwanza? Ramadan?

_____

2. Schau auf Seiten 241-242 Was für Glückwunschkarten schickst du in den nächsten Wochen und Monaten? Hat jemand Geburtstag? Erwartet jemand ein Baby? Heiratet jemand in deiner Familie oder in deinem Freundeskreis? An wen schickst du diese Karten?

_____

_____

_____

3. Was wünscht du dir zum Geburtstag?

_____

ÜBUNG P

Aufsatz. Write a thank you note for a present you recently received from a family member—grandparent, aunt, uncle, godmother (**Patentante**), godfather (**Patenonkel**), and so on. You may write about a real present or an imaginary one.

_____

_____

_____

_____

_____

_____

_____

_____

_____

_____

_____

_____

_____

_____

KLASSENPROJEKT

Design and draw birthday cards in German for family and friends. The items pictured are associated with good luck in German.

ALLES GUTE ZUM GEBURTSTAG!

WIR GRATULIEREN ZUM 16. GEBURTSTAG!

HERZLICHEN GLÜCKWUNSCH ZUM GEBURTSTAG!

WORTSCHATZ A-Z

das Bastelbuch, ¨er *crafts book*
die Geburtstagskarte, -n *birthday card*
der Geburtstagskuchen *birthday cake*
der Geburtstagstisch, -e *table with birthday presents, mail, etc.*
das Glück *happiness; good luck*

der Glückwunsch, ¨e *good wishes*
der Kuss, ¨e *kiss*
der Ohrring, -e *earring*
das Paket, -e *package*
die Post *mail*

auf•machen (macht auf, hat aufgemacht) *to open*
s. bedanken (bedankt sich, hat sich bedankt) *to say thank you*
bitten (bittet, hat gebeten) *to ask, request*
gehören D (gehört, hat gehört) *to belong to*
gratulieren (gratuliert, hat gratuliert) D *to congratulate*
hoffen (hofft, hat gehofft) *to hope*
lächeln (lächelt, hat gelächelt) *to smile*
lachen (lacht, hat gelacht) *to laugh*
passen D (passt, hat gepasst) *to fit*
(s.) wünschen D (wünscht [sich], hat [sich] gewünscht) *to wish (for)*

enttäuscht *disappointed*
ganz gespannt *eagerly anticipating*
glücklich *happy*
herzlich *heartfelt*

hoffentlich *hopefully*
nagelneu *brand new*
vor der Tür *in front of the door*

Diese Wörter kennst du schon

der Brief, -e *letter*
der Feiertag, -e *holiday*
das Geschenk, -e *present*
danken D (dankt, hat gedankt) *to thank*
feiern (feiert, hat gefeiert) *to celebrate*
s. freuen (freut sich, hat sich gefreut) (über A) *to be happy (about)*
gefallen (gefällt, hat gefallen) D *to be pleasing to someone*
schauen (schaut, hat geschaut) *to look*
von D *from*
zu D *to, for, on the occasion of*

Und so sagst du das... *Here's how to . . .*

express thanks

vielen Dank! *thank you! many thanks!*   ich bedanke mich *thank you*
ich danke dir *I thank you*

express good wishes

alles Gute zum Geburtstag *best wishes for your birthday*
        zum Muttertag   *for Mother's Day*
        zum Vatertag   *for Father's Day*
herzlichen Glückwunsch *best wishes*
viel Glück *good luck; (I wish you) much happiness*
wir gratulieren zur Verlobung *congratulations on your engagement*
        zur Hochzeit   *on your wedding*
        zum 50. Hochzeitstag   *on your 50th wedding anniversary*
        zum neuen Baby   *on the birth of your baby*
wir wünschen euch ein glückliches Neues Jahr *we wish you a happy New Year*
        ein frohes Weihnachtsfest   *a merry Christmas*
        ein frohes Chanukahfest   *a happy Hanukkah*

express hopes

ich hoffe *I hope*   hoffentlich *hopefully*

Taking a closer look

1. There are three reflexive verbs on the list. Name them. Which ones take the dative? Which one takes the accusative?

   _____

2. Which verb has a stem vowel change? What is the change?

   _____

3. Which verb has a separable prefix? Write a sentence in the present and in the conversational past using that verb.

   _____

   _____

Building your vocabulary

Write the compound words you can form. What do they mean in English?

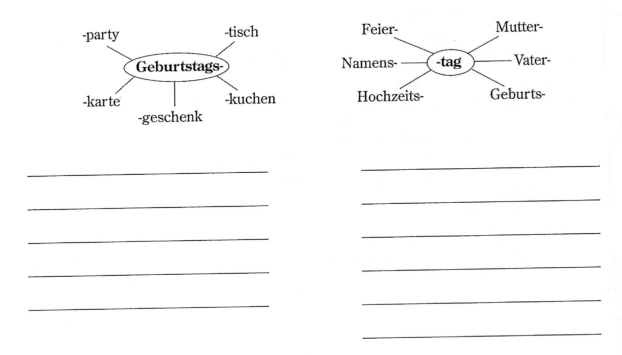

_____   _____

_____   _____

_____   _____

_____   _____

_____   _____

                                          _____

Recognizing related words helps you figure out what they mean. Fill in the related words and give the meanings.

1. hoffen _____   _____

2. Glück _____   _____

3. Feiertag _____   _____

4. Wunsch _____   _____

5. Dank _____   _____

ÜBUNG Q

Spiel: Alles Gute!   Write the different holidays and special occasions mentioned in this chapter on large cards — or draw pictures to symbolize them. Divide the class into two teams. Students on each team take turns picking a card and expressing good wishes for that occasion.

KULTURECKE

Here are some announcements of important family events. Can you tell what each one is for?

Wir sind umgezogen!

Unsere neue Adresse

Jürgen und Julia Baumann
Silberburgstr. 6
70199 Stuttgart

Tel: (0711) 2679607

Wir heiraten

**Markus Sieber
Sybille Sieber**
geb. Schmidt
den 15. September 1998

Kirchliche Trauung um 13 Uhr
in der Michaelis-Kirche,
Hamburg

Wir freuen uns über die Geburt unseres Sohnes

**Alexander Friedrich Beyer
8. Juli 1997**

Ursula und Roland Beyer
mit Kristin und Jan-Niklas

am Burgweg 2
76185 Karlsruhe

Wir haben uns verlobt!
**Bettina Hoffmann
Martin Wirth**
Tübingen, den 21. Mai 1997

13
Mode für sie, Mode für ihn

dieser-words;
More Verbs followed by the Dative Case

1 Wortschatz

Karsdorf Mode für junge Leute von heute!

Modehits zum Superpreis!

schick!

hübsch!

modisch!

preiswert!

bequem!

Alle Jeans jetzt im Angebot!

Jedes T-Shirt nur 12DM!

Tops in allen Farben!
Welche Farbe für Sie?

Pullis
aus Baumwolle
aus Wolle
aus Acyrl

Alle Grössen: S, M, L, XL und auch XXL

Schmuck ist in!
Wir haben

Halsketten Armbänder

Ohrringe Anhänger

Kapuzen-Sweatshirts

36DM ohne Kapuze 30DM

Baseball-Jacken

Mix-und-Match:

Kombinieren Sie mal dieses Polohemd

mit diesen Shorts oder mit diesem Jeans-Rock

= zwei tolle Outfits!

Anoraks **Westen**

Besuchen Sie auch unsere Schuh–Boutique!
neu: Schicke Sandalen für die heissen Sommertage!

ÜBUNG **A**

Look at the ad and answer the questions.

1. What is the name of the store?

   _____

2. What can you buy at this store?

   _____

3. You can see from this ad that fashion in Germany is very much influenced by the USA. List all the English words mentioned.

   _____

   _____

4. Clothes for young people often come in American sizes. What is the German word for size? How did you know?

   _____

5. List the adjectives used to describe the clothing in this ad. What do you think these adjectives mean in English?

   _____

   _____

ÜBUNG **B**

Do you remember the colors in German? Write the corresponding English equivalent for each of the following colors.

1. gelb _____   5. grün _____   9. weiss _____

2. orange _____   6. blau _____   10. grau _____

3. rot _____   7. lila _____   11. braun _____

4. rosa _____   8. schwarz _____   12. beige _____

Can you figure out what these three colors are?

13. hellblau _____   15. knallrot _____

14. dunkelblau _____

ÜBUNG C

You have already learned some items of clothing. Look at the list below and label the pictures.

der Anzug, ⸚e	das Hemd, -en	der Mantel, ⸚	der Schuh, -e
die Badehose, -n	die Hose, -n	die Mütze, -n	die Socke, -n
der Badeanzug, ⸚e	der Hut, ⸚e	der Pullover	der Stiefel
die Bluse, -n	die Jacke, -n	der Regenmantel, ⸚	das Sweatshirt, -s
der Gürtel	das Kleid, -er	der Rock, ⸚e	das T-Shirt, -s
der Handschuh, -e	die Krawatte, -n	der Schal, -s	der Turnschuh, -e

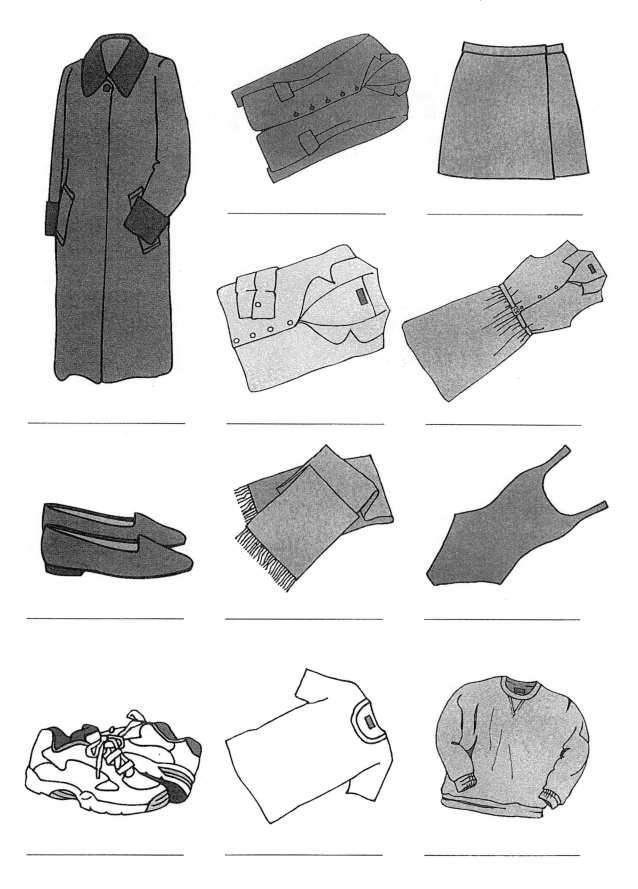

Die Grössen (Sizes). German sizes are different than American sizes:

	GIRLS — SKIRTS, DRESSES, COATES, PANTS							
USA	3/4	5/6	7/8	9/10	11/12	13/14	15/16	
Germany	32	34	36	38	40	42	44	
	GIRLS — BLOUSES							
USA	30	32	34	36	38	40		
Germany	38	40	42	44	46	48		
	GIRLS — SHOES							
USA	4–4½	5–5½	6–6½	7–7½	8–8½	9–9½	10–10½	
Germany	35	36	37	38	39	40	41	
	BOYS — SUITS, PANTS, COATS							
USA	26	28	30	32	34	36	38	40
Germany	36	38	40	42	44	46	48	50
	BOYS — SHIRTS							
USA	14	14½	15	15½	16	16½	17	
Germany	36	37	38	39	40	41	42	
	BOYS — SHOES							
USA	7	7½	8	8½	9–9½	10–10½	11–11½	
Germany	39	40	41	42	43	44	45	

2 Im Kaufhaus Karsdorf

Silvia is shopping. Does she find what she's looking for?

SILVIA: Was kostet dieses T-Shirt, bitte?
VERKÄUFERIN: Jedes T-Shirt kostet heute nur 12 Mark.
SILVIA: Und dieser Rock? Was kostet er?
VERKÄUFERIN: Welchen Rock meinen Sie?
SILVIA: Diesen.
VERKÄUFERIN: Ach, ja. Dieser kostet 55 Mark.
SILVIA: Hm, das is mir ein bisschen zu teuer.
VERKÄUFERIN: Dort drüben kosten alle Röcke nur 30 Mark.
SILVIA: Gut. Ich schau mal. Noch eine Frage. Haben Sie diese Bluse in Weiss?
VERKÄUFERIN: Ich glaube ja. Welche Grösse haben Sie?
SILVIA: Ich brauche Grösse 38.
VERKÄUFERIN: Schauen Sie! Grösse 38 in Weiss!
SILVIA: Prima! Diese Bluse nehme ich!
VERKÄUFERIN: Schön. Sie können hier an der Kasse zahlen.

3 In the dialogue above you will notice the words **dieser, jeder, welcher,** and **alle.** Reread the dialogue and underline these words. What do you think they mean? Why do you think the endings are sometimes different?

The words **dieser, jeder, welcher,** and **alle** are called demonstrative adjectives, or just demonstratives. They are used like definite articles but are a little more specific in meaning. Instead of just saying *the* t-shirt, demonstratives tell you if it's *this* t-shirt, *each* t-shirt, *which* t-shirt, or *all* t-shirts. The demonstratives are also called **dieser**-words because their endings are the same as **dieser.** The endings are also similar to those of definite articles.

> **dieser, diese, dieses** *this, that*
> **jeder, jede, jedes** *each*
> **welcher, welche, welches** *which*
> **alle** *all*

	MASCULINE	FEMININE	NEUTER	PLURAL
NOMINATIVE	der dieser	die diese	das dieses	die diese
ACCUSATIVE	den diesen	die diese	das dieses	die diese
DATIVE	dem diesem	der dieser	dem diesem	den diesen

Note also that **dieser**-words and definite articles can be used alone as pronouns to refer to something already mentioned.

> **Welchen Anorak kaufst du?**   **Diesen.**
> *Which anorak are you buying?*   *This one.*
>
> **Diese Bluse ist Grösse 38.**   **Prima! Die nehme ich!**
> *This blouse is size 38.*   *Great! I'll take it. (or I'll take that one.)*

The signs below are like ones you might see in a department store. Look at the endings on the **dieser**-words and determine the gender of each noun. Write the nouns in the appropriate column on the next page.

Diese Shorts stark reduziert!
Heute nur DM18.

Jedes Top
DM12.

Dieser Anorak
DM125.

Alle Jeans jetzt im Angebot!

Welche Weste für Sie?

Diese Baseball-Jacke
für nur DM90.

Alle Sandalen
DM50.

Grosses Schmuck-Angebot:
Jeder Anhänger DM10.
Jede Halskette DM12.
Jedes Armband DM8.
Alle Ohrringe DM7.

Welchen Pulli kaufen Sie?

MASCULINE	FEMININE
_____	_____
_____	_____
_____	_____
_____	_____

NEUTER	PLURAL
_____	_____
_____	_____
_____	_____
_____	_____

ÜBUNG D

Im Kaufhaus. Complete the exchanges using the pictures as cues. Use **dieser-** words. Follow the examples.

BEISPIEL: **Was kostet *dieser Rock*?** **Welcher Rock gefällt dir?** *Jeder Rock* kostet DM30. *Alle Röcke* gefallen mir!

1. Was kostet _____? _____ kostet DM15.

   _____ gefällt dir? _____ gefallen mir!

2. Was kostet _____? _____ kostet DM9.

   _____ gefällt dir? _____ gefallen mir!

3. Was kostet _____? _____ kostet DM10.

_____ gefällt dir? _____ gefallen mir!

4. Was kostet _____? _____ kosten DM20.

_____ gefällt dir? _____ gefallen mir!

5. Was kostet _____? _____ kostet DM125.

_____ gefällt dir? _____ gefallen mir!

6. Was kostet _____? _____ kostet DM15.

_____ gefällt dir? _____ gefallen mir!

7. Was kostet _____? _____ kostet DM12.

_____ gefällt dir? _____ gefallen mir!

8. Was kostet _____? _____ kostet DM95.

_____ gefällt dir? _____ gefallen mir!

ÜBUNG E

Fill in the correct form of **welch-** and **dies-**. What case are the **dieser**-words in? Why?

BEISPIEL: ***Welchen* Mantel kaufst du?**   *Diesen.*

1. _____ Hut kaufst du? _____

2. _____ Jeans magst du? _____

3. _____ Pulli probierst du an? _____

4. _____ Schuhe nimmst du? _____

5. _____ Kleid findest du schöner? _____

6. _____ Hose möchtest du haben? _____

ÜBUNG **F**

Look at the drawings and write what the salesperson in the store suggests you can combine to make outfits. Remember, the preposition **mit** (with) is always followed by the dative case.

BIESPIEL: **Sie können *diese* Bluse mit *diesem* Rock kombinieren.**

1. _____

2. _____

3. _____

4. _____

5. _____

6. _____

7. _____

ÜBUNG G

Make a "clothing wheel" to practice new vocabulary. Cut a large circle out of poster board. On the outer section of the circle paste small pictures of clothing items you have learned in this chapter and in Book I. You may cut pictures from magazines or draw them. Then cut out a smaller circle of poster board. Divide it into pie-shaped wedges and color in each wedge with a different color. With a paper fastener fasten the smaller circle to the larger circle. Work with a partner to practice vocabulary. Take turns playing the roles of salesperson and costumer in a clothing store. Here are some examples. Practice them and other exchanges using your clothing wheel to cue the item of clothing and the color.

BEISPIEL: —**Haben Sie diese Weste in Schwarz?**
—**Wir haben diese Weste nicht in Schwarz.**

—**Diese Hose gefällt mir nicht in Dunkelblau.**

—**Dieser Pulli in Grün steht Ihnen gut.**

—**Diesen Mantel haben wir nur in Braun.**

4 Wie gefällt dir diese Bluse?

Before buying the blouse, Silvia would like to try it on. Her friend Petra is along and gives her opinion.

SILVIA: **Darf ich diese Bluse anprobieren?**
VERKAUFERIN: **Ja, dort drüben.**

Ihre Freundin Petra sagt:

—Die Bluse gefällt mir gut!   ODER   —Die Bluse gefällt mir nicht.
—Ich finde die Bluse schön!   —Ich finde die Bluse nicht schön!
—Sie steht dir gut!   —Sie steht dir nicht!
—Sie sieht gut aus!   —Sie sieht nicht gut aus!
—Sie passt dir gut!   —Sie passt dir nicht! Sie ist dir...

zu eng!

zu weit!

zu kurz!

zu lang!

zu gross!

zu klein!

In the shopping scene, Petra is giving her opinion about the blouse her friend is trying on.

1. How can Petra say she likes the blouse?

_____

_____

2. How can she say the blouse doesn't suit Silvia, it doesn't look good on her?

_____

_____

3. How can Petra say to Silvia that the blouse fits her very well?

_____

4. How can she tell Silvia that the blouse is too big for her?

_____

The verbs **gefallen, stehen,** and **passen** are used with the _____ case. Underline these verbs in the shopping scene and the dative case form that follows each one.

ÜBUNG H

Write ten sentences using words from each box.

das T-Shirt
          das Outfit
    die Jeans
        der Pulli
die Weste
          die Schuhe
      der Mantel
das Top
      die Halskette
	passt
	passen
	steht
	stehen
	gefällt
	gefallen
		meiner Mutter
		          ihm
		      mir
		dir
		          seinem Freund
		Ihnen
		          deiner Schwester
		ihr
		          ihrem Vater
		      uns
			gut
			nicht

1. _____

2. _____

3. _____

4. _____

5. _____

6. _____

7. _____

8. _____

9. _____

10. _____

ÜBUNG I

You are shopping with friends. Give your opinion as they try on different things.

1. _____

_____

2. _____

_____

4. _____

_____

4. _____

_____

ÜBUNG J

Hör gut zu! You will hear people commenting on items in a store. Do you think they will buy the item or not? Mark the appropriate box.

	KAUFT	KAUFT NICHT
1.		
2.		
3.		
4.		
5.		
6.		

ÜBUNG K

Komplimente. Everyone likes to receive a compliment. In Germany, however, it is not customary to say thank you if someone pays you a compliment. You would say something like :

Wirklich? **Meinst du?** **Ja? nicht zu... ?**

—and the person complimenting you would reassure you with something like:

Ja, wirklich! **Überhaupt nicht zu (klein, gross, usw.)!**

Now go around the room. You compliment a classmate. That person asks for assurance —**ja wirklich?, meinst du?**—and you give it. Then your classmate compliments you and you respond! Here are some examples:

BEISPIEL: **Dein Hemd gefällt mir!** **Diese Farbe steht dir gut!**
Deine Bluse sieht schick aus! **Ich finde dein T-Shirt toll!**

GESPRÄCH

Write a dialog in a clothing store. Request an item in a specific color and inquire about the price. The salesclerk does not have the color, so ask for another color and decide whether you'll take it or not. Here are some phrases you might want to use.

VERKÄUFER/IN	KUNDE
Kann ich Ihnen helfen?	**Was kostet... ?**
Wie gefällt Ihnen diese... ?	**Haben Sie diese... in... ?**
Welche Grösse haben Sie?	**Was kostet... ?**
Es steht Ihnen...	**Ich nehme...**
Es passt Ihnen...	**Ich nehme... nicht ... ist mir zu...**

_____

_____

_____

_____

_____

_____

_____

_____

_____

_____

PERSÖNLICHE FRAGEN

1. Wo kaufst du deine Kleidung? Wie heissen die Geschäfte?

_____

2. Gehst du gern einkaufen?

_____

3. Wer geht mit, wenn du einkaufen gehst?

_____

4. Was ist deine Lieblingsfarbe?

_____

5. Was hast du dir in letzter Zeit zum Anziehen gekauft?

_____

6. Was brauchst du? Was möchtest du dir in nächster Zeit kaufen?

_____

KLASSENPROJEKT

Design clothing ads and make a bulletin board display.

WORTSCHATZ A-Z

der Anhänger *pendant*
der Anorak, -s *anorak, parka*
das Armband, ‐er *bracelet*
die Halskette, -n *necklace*
die Jeans (pl.) *jeans*
die Kapuze, -n *hood*
das Outfit, -s *outfit*
das Polohemd, -en *polo shirt*
der Pulli, -s *(pullover) sweater*
die Sandale, -n *sandal*
die Shorts (pl.) *shorts*
das Top, -s *top* (clothing)
die Weste, -n *vest*
die Grösse, -n *size*
die Leute (pl.) *people*
kombinieren (kombiniert, hat kombiniert)
  to combine
zahlen (zahlt, hat gezahlt) *to pay*
dieser (diese, dieses) *this*
jeder (jede, jedes) *that*

welcher (welche, welches) *which*
alle *all*
bequem *comfortable*
eng *tight*
modisch *fashionable*
preiswert *reasonable (in price)*
prima *great, terrific*
schick *chic, smart*
weit *wide, big*
dunkelblau *dark blue*
hellblau *light blue*
knallrot *bright red*
an der Kasse *at the register*
aus Baumwolle *made of cotton*
  Wolle *wool*
  Acryl *acrylic*
ich glaube ja *I think so*
ich schau mal *I'll take a look*
junge Leute *young people*
noch ein *another*

Diese Wörter kennst du schon

das Angebot *special*; im Angebot *on sale*
die Farbe, -n *color*
die Mode, -n *fashion*
der Ohrring, -e *earring*
der Schmuck *jewelry*
(See also items of clothing, p. 252.)

an•probieren (probiert an, hat anprobiert)
  to try on
besuchen (besucht, hat besucht) *to visit*
meinen (meint, hat gemeint)
  to think, be of the opinion
schauen (schaut, hat geschaut)
  to look

heiss *hot*
hübsch *pretty*
teuer *expensive*
billig *cheap*
mit D *with*
ohne A *without*
kurz *short*
lang *long*
gross *big*
klein *small*

Und so sagst du das... *Here's how to . . .*

pay a compliment

Dein Hemd ist schön. *Your shirt is nice.*   Du siehst hübsch aus. *You look pretty.*
Deine Bluse gefällt mir *I like your blouse.*

to respond to a compliment

Wirklich? *Really?*   Nicht zu... ? *Not too . . . ?*
Meinst du? *Do you think so?*

use phrases with the dative to give your opinion on clothes

es gefällt mir *I like it*   es steht dir *it suits you, it looks good on you*
es passt dir *it fits you*   es ist dir zu (gross) *it's too (big) for you*

Taking a closer look

Fashion for young people is very much influenced by the United States. Write all the cognates you can find on this vocabulary list.

Building your vocabulary

When you think of colors, there are certain combinations that always seem to go together. Can you figure out what these words mean? Write the English.

1. grasgrün _____   5. himmelblau _____

2. blutrot _____   6. kanarienvogelgelb _____

3. kohlrabenschwarz _____   7. silbergrau _____

4. kaffeebraun _____   8. schneeweiss _____

ÜBUNG L

Einkaufsspiel. Who needs what? What are you going to buy? How long can you and your classmates keep this game going?

Ich brauche ein T-Shirt.
Ich brauche ein T-Shirt und eine...

Ich kaufe diesen Anorak.
Ich kaufe diesen Anorak und diese...

KULTURECKE

What do these colors represent in English? Can you guess what they represent in German?

Rot ist die Liebe.
Blau ist die Treue.
Gelb ist der Neid.
Grün ist die Hoffnung.
Schwarz ist die Trauer.
Weiss ist die Unschuld.

Here is a popular German folk song. You can substitute the color and professions of the original lyrics with the ones below:

Alle meine Kleider

1. Grün, grün, grün sind al=le mei=ne Klei=der, grün, grün, grün ist al=les, was ich hab. Dar=um lieb ich al=les, was so grün ist, weil mein Schatz ein Jäger, Jä=ger ist.

Bäcker, weiss
Schornsteinfeger, schwarz
Feuerwehrmann, rot
Matrose, blau

14
Unsere Freunde: die Tiere

Two-way Prepositions

1 Wortschatz

Use your knowledge of cognates and your vocabulary-building skills to describe the picture. Write the number on the picture in front of the corresponding sentence that follows.

_____ Herr Vogelmann sitzt im Sessel.

_____ Ein Vogel sitzt auf seinem Kopf.

_____ Ein Hamster sitzt auf seiner Schulter.

_____ Eine Maus ist zwischen seinen Füssen.

_____ Hinter dem Sessel steht eine Lampe.

_____ Neben dem Sessel ist ein Tisch.

_____ Ein Aquarium steht auf dem Tisch und im Aquarium schwimmt ein Fisch.

_____ Eine Katze liegt auf dem Tisch und beobachtet den Fisch.

_____ Eine Schlange hängt vom Leuchter über dem Tisch.

_____ Ein Frosch und eine Schildkröte unterhalten sich unter dem Tisch.

_____ Ein Fernseher steht in der Ecke.

_____ Ein Hund sitzt vor dem Fernseher und sieht fern.

_____ Am Fenster ist ein Fensterbrett.

_____ Ein Meerschweinchen sitzt zwischen den Blumentöpfen auf dem Fensterbrett.

_____ Am Fenster hängen auch Gardinen, und ein Kaninchen versteckt sich hinter den Gardinen.

_____ Eine Spinne an der Wand spinnt ihr Netz.

ÜBUNG A

Answer each question with the correct phrase.

BEISPIEL: **Wo liegt die Katze?**   **auf dem Tisch**

1. Wo ist die Maus? _____

2. Wo steht das Aquarium? _____

3. Wo schwimmt der Fisch? _____

4. Wo sitzt Herr Vogelmann? _____

5. Wo sitzt das Meerschweinchen? _____

6. Wo steht die Lampe? _____

7. Wo steht der Fernseher? _____

8. Wo steht der Tisch? _____

9. Wo ist das Fensterbrett? _____

10. Wo hängen die Gardinen? _____

11. Wo versteckt sich das Kaninchen? _____

12. Wo sitzt der Vogel? _____

13. Wo unterhalten sich der Frosch und die Schildkröte? _____

14. Wo hängt die Schlange? _____

15. Wo sitzt der Hamster? _____

16. Wo ist das Meerschweinchen? _____

2 The phrases you used in the preceding activity to describe the picture on page 272 all begin with a preposition. When these prepositions answer the question **wo?** they are followed by the dative case.

When the prepositions **an** and **in** are followed by the dative definite article **dem**, they form contractions.

$$an + dem = am$$
$$in + dem = im$$

Do you remember the dative case forms? Fill in the missing ones in the chart.

	DEFINITE ARTICLE	INDEFINITE ARTICLE	POSSESSIVE PRONOUN
MASCULINE	dem	_____	_____
FEMININE	_____	_____	meiner
NEUTER	_____	einem	_____
PLURAL	denen	_____	_____

ÜBUNG B

Answer the questions with prepositional phrases describing each picture.

1. Wo ist der Vogel?

_____

_____

_____

_____

2. Wo ist die Katze?

_____

_____

_____

_____

_____

3 Herr Vogelmann is trying to find Hansi. Where is he?

Wohin fliegt Hansi?

Wo ist er jetzt?

Er fliegt in *die* Küche und
setzt sich auf *den* Tisch.

Er ist in *der* Küche und
sitzt auf dem Tisch.

Er fliegt *ins* Wohnzimmer
und fliegt unter *die* Lampe.

Er ist *im* Wohnzimmer und
sitzt unter *der* Lampe.

Er fliegt in *den* Garten und
fliegt *ins* Vogelhaus.

Er ist *im* Garten und sitzt
im Vogelhaus.

Er fliegt wieder *ins* Haus, *ins* Esszimmer, und setzt sich zwischen *die* Blumen.

Er ist *im* Esszimmer und sitzt zwischen *den* Blumen in der Blumenvase.

Read the captions under each picture again and underline the prepositional phrases. The phrases on the left answer the question _____, (where to) and describe where Hansi is flying to. The pictures on the right answer the question _____, (where) and describe where Hansi is.

What do you notice about the articles following the prepositions? The ones on the left indicating motion are in the _____ case. The ones on the right indicating location are in the _____ case.

The prepositions you have been using in this chapter are called two-way prepositions because they can be followed by the accusative or the dative case, depending on the situation.

ACCUSATIVE (motion toward a place)   DATIVE (location)

an	**Er hängt das Bild an die Wand.**	**Das Bild hängt an der Wand.**
	He hangs the picture on the wall.	*The picture is hanging on the wall.*
auf	**Er legt das Buch auf den Tisch.**	**Das Buch liegt auf dem Tisch.**
	He lays the book on the table.	*The book is lying on the table.*
hinter	**Der Hund rennt hinter das Sofa.**	**Der Hund sitzt hinter dem Sofa.**
	The dog runs behind the sofa.	*The dog is sitting behind the sofa.*

in	Die Katze rennt in die Küche. *The cat runs into the kitchen.*	Die Katze ist in der Küche. *The cat is in the kitchen.*
neben	Er stellt das Fahrrad neben den Baum. *He places the bike next to the tree.*	Das Fahrrad steht neben dem Baum. *The bike is standing next to the tree.*
über	Der Vogel fliegt über das Haus. *The bird flies over the house.*	Die Lampe hängt über dem Tisch. *The lamp is hanging over the table.*
unter	Der Hamster rennt unter den Tisch. *The hamster runs under the table.*	Der Hamster sitzt unter dem Tisch. *The hamster is sitting under the table.*
vor	Ich stelle den Stuhl vor die Tür. *I'm placing the chair in front of the door.*	Der Stuhl steht vor der Tür. *The chair is standing in front of the door.*
zwischen	Ich setze mich zwischen meinen Bruder und meine Schwester. *I sit down between my brother and my sister.*	Ich sitze zwischen meinem Bruder und meiner Schwester. *I'm sitting between my brother and my sister.*

Note the similar but different verbs that are used to indicate motion and location.

MOTION ⟶

LOCATION X

legen *to lay* (er/sie legt, hat gelegt)

liegen *to lie* [das Buch] (liegt, hat gelegen)

stellen *to place, put* (er/sie stellt, hat gestellt)

stehen *to stand, be standing* [die Vase] (steht, hat gestanden)

setzen *to set (down)* (er/sie setzt, hat gesetzt)

sitzen *to sit, be sitting* (sitzt, hat gesessen) [die Katze]

sich setzen *to sit (down)* (er/sie setzt sich, hat sich gesetzt)

hängen *to hang* (er/sie hängt, hat gehängt)

hängen *to hang, be hanging* [das Bild] (hängt, hat gehangen)

ÜBUNG C

Practice using the verbs that indicate motion and location. Look at the picture and word cues below. For each group of cues, write a sentence in the present tense and in the conversational past.

Was machst du?
Was hast du gemacht?

Wie ist das?
Wie ist das gewesen?

1.

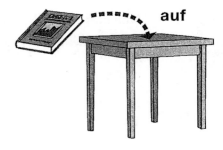

legen

Ich _____

_____

Ich _____

_____

liegen

Das Buch _____

_____

Das Buch _____

_____

2.

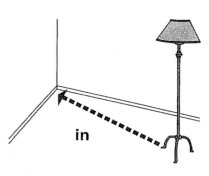

stellen

Ich _____

_____

Ich _____

_____

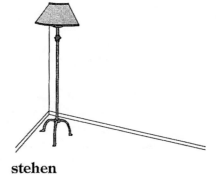

stehen

Die Lampe _____

_____

Die Lampe _____

_____

3.

setzen

Ich _____

_____

Ich _____

_____

sitzen

Die Katze _____

_____

Die Katze _____

_____

4.

sich setzen

Ich _____

_____

Ich _____

_____

sitzen

Ich _____

_____

Ich _____

_____

5.

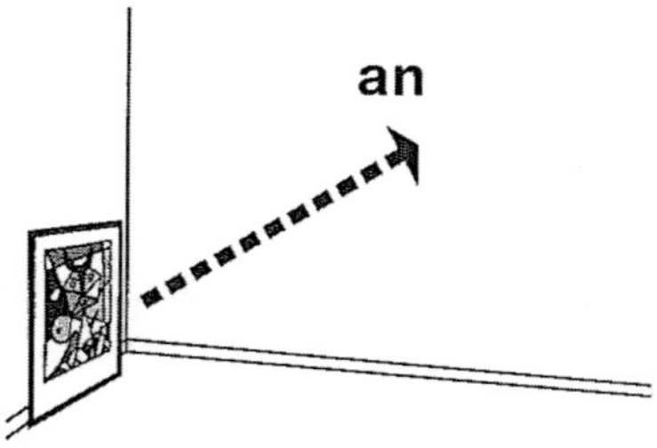

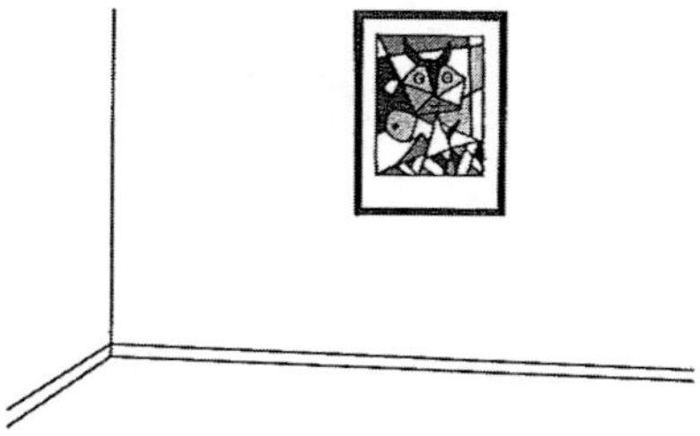

hängen

Ich _____

_____

Ich _____

_____

hängen

Das Bild _____

_____

Das Bild _____

_____

ÜBUNG D

Read the following story and fill in the missing definite articles, asking yourself whether the prepositional phrase answers the question **wo?** or **wohin?** and then choosing the dative or accusative case. After completing the paragraph, write each prepositional phrase in the correct column below.

Wir haben hinter _____ Haus einen schönen Garten. In _____ Garten sind viele Blumen. Jeden Tag geht meine Mutter in _____ Garten, holt ein paar Blumen und bringt die Blumen in _____ Haus. Sie stellt die Blumen in _____ Vase und setzt die Vase auf _____ Tisch oder auf _____ Klavier. Unsere Katze liebt auch Blumen. Sie sitzt neben _____ Mutter und schaut zu, wie sie die Blumen richtet. Wenn eine Blume auf _____ Boden fällt, nimmt sie die Blume, rennt in _____ Wohnzimmer und rennt hinter _____ Sofa. Sie liegt ganz glücklich unter _____ Sofa und frisst die Blume. Meine kleine Schwester sitzt neben _____ Sofa und schaut zu. Sie findet das ganz lustig. Manchmal geht sie in _____ Garten, holt noch eine Blume und gibt sie der Katze.

Wo? (Dative)	**Wohin?** (Accusative)
_____	_____
_____	_____
_____	_____
_____	_____
_____	_____
	_____
	_____
	_____

4 Mein Zimmer

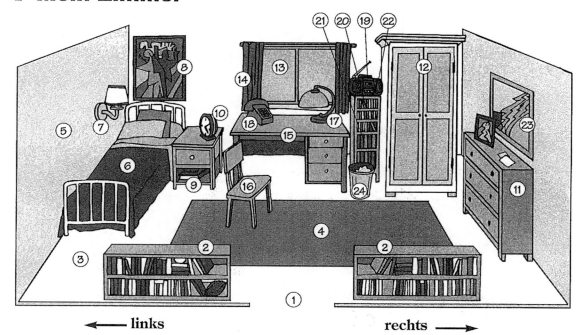

links ← → rechts

1-die Tür	7-die Lampe	13-das Fenster	19-der CD-Spieler
2-das Bücherregal	8-das Poster	14-die Gardinen	20-die CDs
3-der Boden	9-der Nachttisch	15-der Schreibtisch	21-die Musikkassetten
4-der Teppich	10-der Wecker	16-der Stuhl	22-der Lautsprecher
5-die Wand	11-die Kommode	17-die Lampe	23-der Spiegel
6-das Bett	12-der Schrank	18-das Telefon	24-der Papierkorb

ÜBUNG E

This room belongs to Marion Müller, who is fourteen years old. Read the description she has written of her room. Refer to the picture to fill in the words that are missing. Notice that Marion is describing the location of various things in her room so the dative case is used after the prepositions.

Das ist mein Zimmer. Schön und gemütlich, nicht wahr? Neben der Tür stehen rechts und links ein _____. An der Wand links ist _____. Über dem Bett hängen eine Lampe und ein _____. Neben dem Bett steht der _____, und auf dem _____ steht _____. An der Wand rechts steht die _____. Ein _____ hängt über der Kommode. In der Ecke rechts steht der _____. Links neben dem Schrank steht ein Regal. Der _____ und zwei _____ stehen auf dem Regal. Zwischen dem Regal und dem Nachttisch ist ein grosses _____. Am Fenster links und rechts hängen die _____. Ein _____ steht unter dem Fenster, und ein _____ steht vor dem Schreibtisch. Auf dem Schreibtisch stehen eine Lampe und das _____. Der _____ steht rechts neben dem Schreibtisch. Auf dem Boden liegt ein _____.

ÜBUNG F

Marion's hamster got out of his cage and has run into Marion's room. Follow the arrows and describe where he goes. Use the accusative case after the prepositions because the phrases describe motion toward a place.

Der Hamster rennt ins Zimmer. Er rennt _____

_____

_____

_____

_____

_____

_____

_____

_____

_____

_____

_____

_____

_____ .

ÜBUNG G

Hör gut zu! Listen to the following statements and determine whether they answer the question **wo?** or **wohin?** Mark the corresponding box.

	1	2	3	4	5	6	7	8
WO? (DATIVE)								
WOHIN? (ACCUSATIVE)								

PERSÖNLICHE FRAGEN ?

1. Was für ein Haustier hast du — oder hast du keins?

_____

_____

2. Wie heisst dein Tier?

_____

3. Wer sorgt für dein Tier?

_____

4. Wo schläft dein Tier?

_____

5. Was für ein Tier möchtest du haben?

_____

6. Hast du ein eigenes Zimmer oder teilst du ein Zimmer mit einer Schwester oder mit einem Bruder?

_____

7. Was für Möbelstücke hast du in deinem Zimmer?

_____

_____

ÜBUNG H

Aufsatz. Draw a diagram of your room (or of your "dream" room) and write a description to accompany your diagram: **Mein Zimmer**   or   **Mein Traumzimmer**

_____

_____

_____

_____

_____

_____

_____

_____

_____

KLASSENPROJEKT

1. Make cards and label all the items in your classroom. Look up words you don't know in a German-English dictionary. You may divide the room into sections and work in groups, each group taking a different section.

2. After everything is labeled, write a description of the room as a whole-class activity.

3. One student takes the role of director, another takes the role of mover. The director tells the mover where to put various items. (Take turns so everyone gets a chance to be a director and a mover.)

BEISPIEL: DIREKTOR/IN: **Stell das Wörterbuch ins Bücherregal!**
ARBEITER/IN: _(after placing the dictionary in the bookcase)_
Das Wörterbuch ist im Bücherregal.

DIREKTOR/IN: **Leg den Bleistift auf den Schreibtisch!**
ARBEITER/IN: _(after laying the pencil on the desk)_
Der Bleistift liegt auf dem Schreibtisch.

WORTSCHATZ

der Hamster *hamster*
das Kaninchen *rabbit*
das Meerschweinchen *guinea pig*
die Schildkröte, -n *turtle*
die Schlange, -n *snake*
die Spinne, -n *spider*
die Möbel (*pl.*) *furniture*
das Möbelstück, -e *piece of furniture*
das Aquarium, die Aquarien *aquarium*
der Blumentopf, ¨e *flowerpot*
die Blumenvase, -n *flower vase*
der Boden, ¨ *floor*
das Bücherregal, -e *bookcase*
der CD-Spieler *CD player*
das Fenster *window*

das Fensterbrett, -er *windowsill*
die Gardinen (*pl.*) *curtains*
die Kommode, -n *dresser*
der Lautsprecher *loudspeaker*
der Leuchter *chandelier*
der Nachttisch, -e *night table*
der Papierkorb, ¨e *wastepaper basket*
das Poster *poster*
der Schreibtisch, -e *desk*
der Spiegel *mirror*
der Teppich, -e *carpet, rug*
das Vogelhaus, ¨er *birdhouse*
die Wand, ¨e *wall*
der Wecker *alarm clock*

Diese Wörter kennst du schon

das Tier, -e *animal*
das Haustier, -e *pet*
der Fisch, -e *fish*
der Frosch, ¨e *frog*
der Hund, -e *dog*
die Katze, -n *cat*
die Maus, ¨e *mouse*
der Vogel, ¨ *bird*
das Bett, -en *bed*
die Ecke, -n *corner*
das Esszimmer *dining room*

die Küche, -n *kitchen*
die Lampe, -n *lamp*
der Schrank, ¨e *closet*
der Sessel, -n *easy chair*
das Sofa, -s *sofa*
der Stuhl, ¨e *chair*
das Telefon, -e *telephone*
der Tisch, -e *table*
die Tür, -en *door*
das Wohnzimmer *living room*
das Zimmer *room*

beobachten (beobachtet, hat beobachtet) *to observe*
rennen (rennt, ist gerannt) *to run*
Spinnen: die Spinne spinnt ihr Netz *the spider spins its web*
s. verstecken (versteckt sich, hat sich versteckt) *to hide oneself*

legen (legt, hat gelegt) *to lay*
liegen (liegt, hat gelegen) *to lie, recline*
stellen (stellt, hat gestellt) *to place, put*
stehen (steht, hat gestanden) *to stand*

setzen (setzt, er hat gesetzt) *to set, put*
s. setzen (setzt sich, er hat sich gesetzt) *to sit down*
sitzen (sitzt, er hat gesessen) *to sit, be sitting*
hängen (hängt, er hat gehängt) *to hang*
hängen (hängt, er hat gehangen) *to hang, be hanging*

Two-way Prepositions

an *on*	in *in, into*	unter *under*
auf *on (top of)*	neben *next to*	vor *in front of*
hinter *behind*	über *over*	zwischen *between*

wo? *where?*	gemütlich *cozy, comfortable*	rechts *right, on the right*
wohin? *where to?*	links *left, on the left*	nicht wahr? *isn't that so?*

Building your vocabulary

1. Write the compound words you can form. What do they mean in English?

Nacht-   Schreib-
Bastel- —— (-tisch) —— Arbeits-
Ess- Zeichen- Garten-

Wohn-   Ess-
Bade- —— (-zimmer) —— Schlaf-
Bastel- Spiel- Arbeits-

_____   _____

_____   _____

_____   _____

_____   _____

_____   _____

_____   _____

2. List all the cognates you can find on this list.

_____

_____

ÜBUNG I

Bingo-Spiel. Make a set of bingo cards with either animal items or furniture items you have learned in this chapter. Each student makes a bingo card with nine spaces, filling each space with either the German words or with pictures. The teacher or a student reads randomly from the vocabulary list either animals or items of furniture. The first one to fill his or her bingo card is the winner. The winner could also be the first one to get three items in a row horizontally, vertically, or diagonally.

BINGO		
Maus	Katze	Frosch
Vogel	Schlange	Fisch
Hund	Meerschweinchen	Hamster

BINGO		
Lampe	Sofa	Bett
Stuhl	CD-Spieler	Kommode
Telefon	Schreibtisch	Wecker

KULTURECKE

Germans are very fond of animals and many people have pets. In Germany, dogs are allowed in many hotels and restaurants. Many German proverbs have to do with cats and dogs. Read the ones below. Can you think of equivalent ones in English?

- Bei Nacht sind alle Katzen grau.

- Hunde, die viel bellen, beissen nicht.

- Der Hund ist oft schlauer als sein Herr.
- Wer mich liebt, liebt auch meinen Hund.
- Wenn die Katze nicht zu Hause ist, tanzen die Mäuse.

- Wer mit dem Hund zu Bett geht, darf sich nicht wundern, wenn, er mit Flöhen aufsteht.

- Tote Hunde beissen nicht.

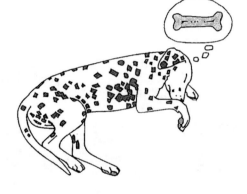

- Schlafende Hunde soll man nicht wecken.

15
In der Stadt

Summary of Prepositions

1 Wortschatz

Stadtplan von Grünstadt

1-das Hotel	19-die Bäckerei	37-das Schwimmbad
2-das Café	20-die Marktstr.	38-das Museum
3-die Bank	21-das Restaurant	39-die Gartenstr.
4-die Post	22-die Apotheke	40-der Schlossgarten
5-der Bahnhof	23-der Imbiss-Stand	41-der Kinderspielplatz
6-der Blumenladen	24-das Musikgeschäft	42-der Zoo
7-das Schloss	25-das Rathaus	43-die Tankstelle
8-der Schlossplatz	26-der Brunnen	44-die Schule
9-die Bahnhofstr.	27-der Marktplatz	45-die Brunnerstr.
10-der Park	28-die Hauptstr.	46-der Gemüseladen
11-das Theater	29-die Wilhelmsstr.	47-das Krankenhaus
12-die Schillerstr.	30-die Fleischerei	48-das Fotogeschäft
13-die Peterskirche	31-die Buchhandlung	49-der Parkplatz
14-der Petersplatz	32-der Jeans-Shop	50-das Verkehrsamt
15-das Kaufhaus	33-die Steinerstr.	51-die Kirchstr.
16-der Supermarkt	34-das Kino	52-der See
17-das Sportgeschäft	35-die Bibliothek	
18-die Lindenstr.	36-der Sportplatz	

ÜBUNG A

Was gibt es alles in Grünstadt? What can you find in the town of Grünstadt? Look at the map and list all the things you see. You are already familiar with most of the words. Do you remember what they mean? What do you think the new words mean?

Es gibt ein Hotel, ein Café, einen Park, _____

_____

_____

_____

_____

_____

_____

_____

_____.

ÜBUNG B

Why would you go to various places in Grünstadt? Write the number of the place on the left in front of the most appropriate statement on the right.

Ich gehe...

1. zur Post.
2. ins Krankenhaus.
3. ins Kaufhaus.
4. ins Restaurant.
5. zum Supermarkt.
6. auf den Sportplatz.
7. zur Apotheke.
8. ins Fotogeschäft.
9. in die Bäckerei.
10. ins Kino.

_____ Ich möchte ein Brot und ein paar Brötchen kaufen.
_____ Ich brauche Briefmarken.
_____ Ich möchte Fussball spielen.
_____ Ich möchte einen Film für meine Kamera kaufen.
_____ Ich habe mir den Arm gebrochen.
_____ Ich habe Hunger.
_____ Ich möchte den neuen Action-Film sehen.
_____ Ich brauche Lebensmittel.
_____ Ich brauche Hustensaft.
_____ Ich brauche eine neue Jacke für den Winter.

ÜBUNG C

Make a list of all the places on the map of Grünstadt. You will recognize most of them from Book I. List the places under the following headings to help you review them more easily. Be sure you know the gender and meaning of each word. After you have completed your list, compare it with a classmate's — or you may want to work in pairs to write the list in the first place. Ask each other what the words mean.

Geschäfte (Businesses)	Öffentliche Stellen (Public Places)	Unterhaltung (Entertainment/ Recreation)	Sehenswürdigkeiten (Places of Interest)

ÜBUNG D

Again looking at the map of Grünstadt, write where the following things are located. Use these phrases:

in der ...strasse
am ...platz
an der Ecke ...strasse und ...strasse

BEISPIEL: **Wo ist das Rathaus?**   **Am Marktplatz.**

1. Wo ist die Apotheke? _____

2. Wo ist der Zoo? _____

3. Wo ist eine Tankstelle? _____

4. Wo ist die Bank? _____

5. Wo ist die Peterskirche? _____

6. Wo ist der Jeans-Shop? _____

ÜBUNG E

Now let's get a little more specific. How much information can you give about where the various places in Grünstadt are located? Here are some phrases to help you. Remember to use the dative case after these prepositions describing location!

gegenüber *across from*   **vor** *in front of*
neben *next to*   **hinter** *behind*
zwischen *between*

BEISPIEL: **Wo ist der Gemüseladen?**
          In der Hauptstrasse *gegenüber* der Fleischerei.

1. Wo ist ist der Kinderspielplatz?

_____

2. Wo ist die Post?

_____

3. Wo ist ein Sportgeschäft?

_____

4. Wo ist das Schwimmbad?

_____

5. Wo ist das Kaufhaus?

_____

6. Wo ist ein Parkplatz?

_____

ÜBUNG F

Hör gut zu! You will hear statements describing where various things in Grünstadt are located. Look at the map as you listen and determine whether the statement is correct or not. Mark the appropriate box.

	1	2	3	4	5	6	7	8	9	10	11	12
STIMMT												
STIMMT NICHT												

ÜBUNG G

Partnerarbeit   Work with a partner. Looking at the map, take turns asking each other where different places in Grünstadt are located. Give as much information as possible. As a variation, describe where a place is located and have your partner tell you what the place is.

2 Wie komme ich zum... ?

Paul is new in Grünstadt and doesn't know his way around. He is looking for a music store. Read how he asks for and gets directions.

PAUL: Entschuldigung! Wo ist hier ein Musikgeschäft?

POLIZIST: Ein Musikgeschäft. Moment mal! Ich glaube, am Marktplatz gibt es eins.

PAUL: Und wie komme ich zum Marktplatz, bitte? Ist es weit?

POLIZIST: Nein, es ist nicht weit. Du gehst rechts in die Hauptstrasse bis zum Marktplatz. Gleich um die Ecke links ist das Musikgeschäft.

PAUL: Danke schön.

POLIZIST: Bitte schön.

Here are some expressions you need to know to ask for directions:

Wie komme ich zum Marktplatz?
zur Hauptstrasse?
zum Rathaus?

and how to give directions:

Du gehst **geradeaus** – – ➔ – – ➔

diese Strasse entlang bis zur Ampel – – ➔

bis zur Hauptstrasse – – ➔ Hauptstrasse

bis zum Schloss – – ➔ – – ➔

an der Schule vorbei
– – ➔ – – ➔

am Krankenhaus vorbei
– – ➔ – – ➔ – – ➔

am Park vorbei
– – ➔ – – ➔ – – ➔

Du gehst die nächste Strasse

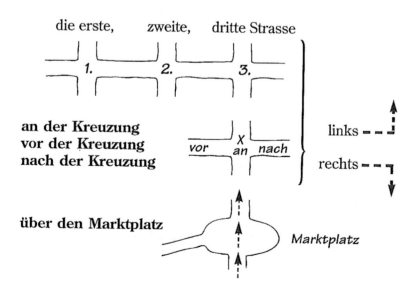

die erste, zweite, dritte Strasse

1.   2.   3.

an der Kreuzung
vor der Kreuzung   vor   X   nach
nach der Kreuzung   an

links – – ┘

rechts – – ┐

über den Marktplatz   Marktplatz

Remember that certain prepositions form contractions with the definite article.

an + dem = _____   in + dem = _____   zu + dem = _____

an + das = _____   in + das = _____   zu + der = _____

bei + dem = _____   von + dem = _____

ÜBUNG H

Hör gut zu!   Visitors to the city of Grünstadt come to the **Verkehrsamt** (tourist office) to get information about the city and to ask directions to various places. Look at the **Stadtplan** as you listen to the directions each one is giving and write down where that person is going.

1. _____

2. _____

3. _____

ÜBUNG I

Complete the directions below by filling in the missing words. Refer to the map of Grünstadt.

1. Wir stehen hier vor dem Verkehrsamt. Du gehst hier _____ bis zur

   Schillerstrasse, dann _____ die Schillerstrasse entlang. Gleich vor

   dem Fotogeschäft siehst du die _____. Da gehst du wieder

   _____ bis zum _____. Dort ist die Peterskirche.

2. Du willst zur Post? Da gehst du hier die _____ geradeaus, über

   den_____, immer geradeaus die Hauptstrasse entlang bis zur

   _____. Du gehst _____ in die Bahnhofsstrasse, und

   dort rechts direkt neben dem _____ ist die Post.

ÜBUNG J

Partnerarbeit Work with a partner and take turns asking for and giving directions to the places in Grünstadt listed.

WO? **Ihr seid auf dem Marktplatz.**

WOHIN? **zum Schloss** **zum Zoo** **zur Buchhandlung**
zum Supermarkt **zum Theater** **zur Tankstelle**

BEISPIEL: **Du: Wie komme ich zum Schloss?**
Partner: Das Schloss ist am Schlossplatz. Du gehst hier die Hauptstrasse entlang bis zur Bahnhofsstrasse, dann rechts in die Bahnhofsstrasse und immer geradeaus bis zum Schlossplatz.

3 In Book I you learned about prepositions that are always followed by the accusative case and prepositions that are always followed by the dative case.

PREPOSITIONS FOLLOWED BY THE ACCUSATIVE CASE	PREPOSITIONS FOLLOWED BY THE DATIVE CASE
durch *through*	**aus** *out of, from (a place)*
für *for*	**ausser** *besides, except for*
gegen *against*	**bei** *at; near; at the home or place of*
ohne *without*	**gegenüber** *across from*
um *around, about; at (in expressions of time)*	**mit** *with; by means of*
	nach *after, toward; according to*
	seit *since*
	von *of, from, by*
	zu *to*

In the preceding lesson of this book, Lesson 14, you learned about the two-way prepositions, the ones followed by the dative case when talking about location and the accusative case when talking about motion toward a place.

PREPOSITIONS FOLLOWED BY THE DATIVE OR THE ACCUSATIVE CASE		
an *at, on*	**in** *in, into*	**unter** *under*
auf *on, on top of*	**neben** *beside, next to*	**vor** *before, in front of*
hinter *behind*	**über** *over, above*	**zwischen** *between*

The prepositions are listed here for reference and it is a good idea to memorize them. The important thing, however, is to be able to use them. By practicing the situations in this lesson and Lesson 14, as well as throughout the book, you will learn the prepositions easily!

4 Die Umgebung von Grünstadt

Herr and Frau Bahr live outside of Grünstadt. They are driving to the city today. Read about their trip on the next page and then with a pencil trace their route on the map below.

1-der Wald	6-der Parkplatz	11-das Stadion
2-der See	7-die Bahnhofsstrasse	12-der Fluss
3-die Berge	8-die Gartenstrasse	13-der Tunnel
4-die Brücke	9-das Einkaufszentrum	14-der Flughafen
5-der Park	10-das Haus von Freunden	15-die Fabrik

Herr und Frau Bahr wohnen in der Nähe von Grünstadt. Heute wollen sie mit dem Wagen nach Grünstadt fahren. Sie setzen sich in den Wagen und fahren aus der Garage. An der Kreuzung fahren sie links durch den Wald und um den See bis zum Fluss. Da fahren sie über die Brücke und durch den Park bis zur Stadtmitte. Sie fahren auf den Parkplatz hinter dem Kaufhaus. Sie steigen aus dem Wagen und gehen einkaufen. Nach einer Stunde kommen sie zurück und fahren weiter. Sie fahren rechts in die Gartenstrasse und immer geradeaus bis sie aus der Stadt heraus sind.

Jetzt wollen sie noch im Einkaufszentrum ein paar Sachen kaufen. Sie fahren schnell zum Einkaufszentrum. Nach dem Einkaufen besuchen sie Freunde. Diese Freunde wohnen ganz in der Nähe vom Einkaufszentrum. Bei den Freunden trinken sie Kaffee. Jetzt wird es aber spät! Herr und Frau Bahr müssen nach Hause! Sie verabschieden sich von den Freunden und steigen wieder in den Wagen. Sie fahren um das Stadion und durch einen Tunnel. Der Tunnel führt unter den Fluss. Nach dem Tunnel müssen sie rechts fahren. Sie fahren an dem Flughafen vorbei. Rechts sehen sie den Wald. Links ist eine Fabrik. Bald sind sie wieder zu Hause.

ÜBUNG **K**

Reread the selection about Herr and Frau Bahr's trip to Grünstadt. Underline all the prepositional phrases. Indicate with a capital D or a capital A above the phrase whether it is in the dative or accusative case.

ÜBUNG **L**

Write the prepositional phrases. Don't forget to use appropriate contractions.

1. Wir gehen durch...

    (das Haus) __**durch das Haus**__

    (die Stadt) _____

    (der Wald) _____

    (die Schule) _____

    (das Kaufhaus) _____

2. Ich bin ohne... gekommen.

    (der Stadtplan) _____

    (der Mantel) _____

    (die Kamera) _____

    (das Buch) _____

    (das Geld) _____

3. Der Bus fährt um…

(der See) _____

(die Stadt) _____

(der Flughafen) _____

(der Wald) _____

(das Stadion) _____

4. Die Bushaltestelle ist gegenüber… .

(die Schule) _____

(das Hotel) _____

(der Supermarkt) _____

(das Rathaus) _____

(die Buchhandlung) _____

5. Du gehst gleich nach… links.

(die Ampel) _____

(der Sportplatz) _____

(die Kreuzung) _____

(das Schwimmbad) _____

(die Kirche) _____

6. Gehen Sie immer geradeaus bis zu… .

(die Post) _____

(der Bahnhof) _____

(der Marktplatz) _____

(das Krankenhaus) _____

(die Bäckerei) _____

7. An… müsst ihr nach links.

(der Schlossplatz) _____

(die Ampel) _____

(das Theater) _____

(die Tankstelle) _____

(das Museum) _____

8. Gehst du heute in... ?

     (die Stadt) _____

     (das Kino) _____

     (die Schule) _____

     (der Zoo) _____

     (das Museum) _____

9. Hinter... ist ein Parkplatz.

     (das Kaufhaus) _____

     (die Schule) _____

     (das Restaurant) _____

     (der Blumenladen) _____

     (der Supermarkt) _____

5 Wie komme ich hin? Ist es weit?

When you ask for directions, people can't always help you out. What do they say?

Wie komme ich zum Einkaufszentrum?

Ich weiss es nicht.   **Ich kenne mich hier nicht aus.**
Tut mir leid.   **Ich bin nicht von hier.**

Sometimes what you are looking for is farther away than you thought.

Wie komme ich hin? Ist es weit?

Kann ich zu Fuss gehen  **oder muss ich mit dem Bus**

fahren **?**

Du kannst nicht zu Fuss gehen. Es ist zu weit!

Du musst... fahren.

    mit dem Bus

    mit dem Zug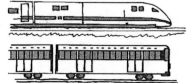

    mit der U-Bahn

    mit dem Wagen

ÜBUNG M

Using the cues given, describe how different people get where they are going.

WER?	WIE?	WOHIN?
ich		ins Theater fahren
1. ihr		in die Schule gehen
2. wir		zum Flughafen fahren
3. meine Tante		nach Berlin fahren
4. der Lehrer		in die Schweiz fahren
5. die Kinder		in den Wald fahren
6. du		nach Spanien fliegen

BEISPIEL: **Ich fahre mit der U-Bahn ins Theater.**

1. _____
2. _____
3. _____
4. _____
5. _____
6. _____

ÜBUNG N

Go around the class. Each student tells how he or she got to school that day.

Wie bist du heute in die Schule gekommen?
Bist du zu Fuss gekommen oder bist du mit dem Bus gefahren?

Ich bin ...

ÜBUNG O

The people pictured below are asking for directions. In some cases the person asked can help them out, in other instances the person asked doesn't know. Write the conversations using the cues as a guide. Be sure to use the appropriate form of address — **du, ihr,** or **Sie** — depending on the situation.

A: _____

B: _____

_____

A: _____

B: _____

_____

A: _____

B: _____

_____

A: _____

B: _____

_____

PERSÖNLICHE FRAGEN

1. Wie heisst deine Stadt oder dein Dorf?

   _____

2. Was gibt es alles in deiner Stadt, in deinem Dorf oder in deinem Stadtteil oder in deiner Nachbarschaft? Gibt es zum Beispiel einen Bahnhof? eine Post? Schreib eine Liste!

   _____

   _____

   _____

   _____

3. Wie heissen einige Geschäfte? In welcher Strasse findest du die Geschäfte?

   _____

   _____

   _____

   _____

4. Was für Sehenswürdigkeiten (places of interest) gibt es? Gibt es zum Beispiel ein interessantes Museum, ein historisches Gebäude oder einen schönen Park?

   _____

   _____

   _____

   _____

ÜBUNG P

Aufsatz. Write a paragraph describing your route to school. Do you walk, ride your bike, or do you take a bus? Tell what streets you travel on and mention some of the things you see along the way.

Mein Schulweg

_____

_____

_____

_____

_____

_____

_____

_____

_____

KLASSENPROJEKT

1. In groups or as a whole class project, make a map of your town, of a section of your city, — or design a town.

2. List what's in your town and tell where each thing is located, for example, **in der ...strasse, am ...platz**.

3. Explain your map to the class. Point out where various things are located. Your classmates may also ask questions, for example, **Gibt es ein Sportgeschäft? Wie heisst es? Wo ist es?**

4. Your classmates take turns playing the role of a visitor to your city or town. The visitor asks you for information or directions to various places. Use your imagination to create humorous exchanges to present to the class.

WORTSCHATZ A-Z

die Ampel, -n *traffic light*
der Blumenladen, ⸚ *flower shop*
die Brücke, -n *bridge*
der Brunnen *fountain*
das Einkaufszentrum, -zentren
　　shopping center
der Fluss, ⸚e *river*
das Fotogeschäft, -e *camera store*
der Jeans-Shop, -s *jeans shop*
der Kinderspielplatz, ⸚e *children's
　　playground*
die Kreuzung, -en *intersection*
der Marktplatz, ⸚e *market place*
das Musikgeschäft, -e *music store*
der Park, -s *park*

der Parkplatz, ⸚e *parking lot*
das Rathaus, ⸚er *town or city hall*
der See, -n *lake*
die Sehenswürdigkeit, -en *place
　　of interest, landmark*
der Sportplatz, ⸚e *athletic field*
die Umgebung, -en *surroundings*
das Verkehrsamt, ⸚e *tourist offiice*
der Wald, ⸚er *forest*
glauben (glaubt, hat geglaubt)
　　to think, believe
Entschuldigung! *excuse me!*
Moment mal! *just a minute!*
zu Hause *(at) home*
zu Fuss *on foot, walking*

Diese Wörter kennst du schon
(also review the list you made on page 392)

das Geschäft, -e *store, business*
der Laden, ⸚ *store*
die Fabrik, -en *factory*
der Flughafen, ⸚ *airport*
das Stadion, Stadien *stadium*
der Tunnel *tunnel*
die Ecke, -n *corner*
der Platz, ⸚e *plaza, square*
die Strasse, -n *street*

der Bus, -se *bus*
das Flugzeug, -e *airplane*
die U-Bahn, -en *subway*
der Wagen *car*
der Zug, ⸚e *train*
mit dem Bus *by bus*
nach Hause *(to) home*
weit *far*

Und so sagst du das... *Here's how to . . .*

ask where something is located

Wo ist der Bahnhof bitte? *Where is the railroad station, please?*
Wo ist hier ein... ? *Is there a . . . around here?*

say where something is located

am ...platz *on the square*
in der ...strasse *on . . . Street*
an der Ecke *on the corner*

gleich um die Ecke *right around
　　the corner*
direkt neben *right next to*

ask for directions

Wie komme ich zum… ? *How do I get to . . .?*

give directions

geradeaus *straight ahead*
bis zur/zum *up to, until you get to*
diese Strasse entlang *down this street*
an (der Schule) vorbei *past (the school)*
über (den Marktplatz) *across the (market place)*

an			at		
vor	} der Kreuzung		before	} the intersection	
nach			after		

to say you don't know

Ich weiss es nicht. *I don't know.*
Tut mir leid. *Sorry.*
Ich kenne mich nicht aus. *I don't know my way around.*
Ich bin nicht von hier. *I'm not from around here.*

Building your vocabulary

Write the compound words you can form. What do they mean in English?

Musik   Foto
Sport —(-geschäft)— Hobby
Schuh   Kleider

Sport   Spiel
Park —(-platz)— Kirch
Schloss   Markt

_____   _____

_____   _____

_____   _____

_____   _____

_____   _____

What do you think the following compound words mean?

das Lebensmittelgeschäft

_____

das Haushaltsgeschäft

_____

das Juweliergeschäft

_____

das Schreibwarengeschäft

_____

das Möbelgeschäft

_____

das Elektrogeschäft

_____

The words **das Geschäft, der Laden**, and **die Handlung** all refer to stores. What do you think these stores sell?

der Blumenladen _____   die Tierhandlung _____

der Gemüseladen _____   die Buchhandlung _____

der Geschenkladen _____

der Spielzeugladen _____

ÜBUNG Q

Spiel 1: Wo ist... ?   Wie komme ich hin?

Write the names of various places, buildings, and landmarks in your area on individual cards. Form two teams. Members from each team alternate picking a card and asking an opposing team member where the place written on the card is located and how you would probably get there — **zu Fuss, mit dem Bus, mit dem Wagen, usw**. Team members may collaborate on answers. If the team answers correctly, it gets a point. To earn an additional point, the team may also give directions to that place. The team with the most points wins.

Spiel 2: In meiner Stadt gibt es...

How long can you and your classmates keep this game going?

In meiner Stadt gibt es einen Supermarkt.
In meiner Stadt gibt es einen Supermarkt und ein Kino.
In meiner Stadt gibt es einen Supermarkt, ein Kino und...

KULTURECKE

Germany has over seventy-nine million inhabitants. Nearly one third of them live in large cities, that is, in cities with over 100,000 inhabitants. The rest of the population lives in villages and towns. Listed below are sixteen federal states (**Bundesländer**) in the Federal Republic. Look up the states on a map of Germany and locate the capital city of each one. Then match each state listed below with its capital city. There are three city states. Can you name them?

BUNDESLAND	LANDESHAUPTSTADT
Baden-Württemberg	Berlin
Bayern	Bremen
Berlin	Dresden
Brandenburg	Düsseldorf
Bremen	Erfurt
Hamburg	Hamburg
Hessen	Hannover
Mecklenburg-Vorpommern	Kiel
Niedersachsen	Magdenburg
Nordrhein-Westfalen	Mainz
Rheinland-Pfalz	München
Saarland	Potsdam
Sachsen	Saarbrücken
Sachsen-Anhalt	Schwerin
Schleswig-Holstein	Stuttgart
Thüringen	Wiesbaden

Wiederholung III
(Lektion 11-15)

Lektion 11

a. Numbers used in counting are referred to as cardinal numbers: **eins** (one), **zwei** (two), **drei** (three) and so on. Cardinal numbers have no endings in German.

Numbers used to express dates or to indicate place in a series are referred to as ordinal numbers: **erste** (first), **zweite** (second), **dritte** (third). Ordinal numbers through 19 add **-te** to the cardinal number. Note the exceptions: **erste**, **dritte**, **siebte**, and **achte**.

erste	**fünfte**	**neunte**	**dreizehnte**	**siebzehnte**
zweite	**sechste**	**zehnte**	**vierzehnte**	**achtzehnte**
dritte	**siebte**	**elfte**	**fünfzehnte**	**neunzehnte**
vierte	**achte**	**zwölfte**	**sechzehnte**	

Ordinal numbers from 20 on add **-ste** to the cardinal number.

zwanzigste	**dreissigste**	**sechzigste**	**neunzigste**
einundzwanzigste	**vierzigste**	**siebzigste**	**hundertste**
zweiundzwanzigste	**fünfzigste**	**achtzigste**	

b. The verb **werden** (will be, will become) is irregular.

ich **werde**	wir **werden**
du **wirst**	ihr **werdet**
er \ sie \ es **wird**	sie **werden**

c. The dative case signals the indirect object in a sentence. It expresses the idea of "to someone" or "for someone."

	DEFINITE ARTICLE	THIRD PERSON PRONOUN	INTERROGATIVE
SING.	dem der dem	ihm ihr ihm	wem?
PLURAL	den (+ n)	ihnen	

Lektion 12

a. Here are more dative forms.

	DEFINITE ARTICLE	INDEFINITE ARTICLE
MASC.	dem	einem
FEM.	der	einer
NEUTER	dem	einem
PLURAL	den (+n)	———————

b. The endings on the possessive adjectives are the same as on the definite and indefinite articles

POSSESSIVE ADJECTIVES									
MASC.	meinem	deinem	seinem	ihrem	seinem	unserem	euerem	ihren	Ihren
FEM.	meiner	deiner	seiner	ihrer	seiner	unserer	euerer	ihrer	Ihrer
NEUTER	meinem	deinem	seinem	ihrem	seinem	unserem	euerem	ihrem	Ihrem
PLURAL	meinen	deinen	seinen	ihren	seinen	unseren	eueren	ihren	Ihren

c. There are some verbs that always have an object in the dative case. Here are the ones you have learned so far.

danken *to thank (someone)*
gefallen *to please (someone)*
gehören *to belong to (someone)*

gratulieren *to congratulate (someone)*
wünschen *to wish (someone)*

Ich danke dir.
Die Bluse gefällt mir.
Die Mütze gehört dem
    Jungen.

Wir gratulieren unseren Eltern zum Hochzeitstag.
Ich wünsche dir alles Gute zum Geburtstag!

Lektion 13

a. Demonstratives are used like definite articles. Their endings are the same as **dieser**, so they are often called **dieser**-words.

dieser, diese dieses *this, that*
jeder, jede, jedes *each*

welcher, welche, welches *which*
alle *all*

	MASCULINE	FEMININE	NEUTER	PLURAL
NOMINATIVE	der dieser	die diese	das dieses	die diese
ACCUSATIVE	den diesen	die diese	das dieses	die diese
DATIVE	dem diesem	der dieser	dem diesem	den diesen

Note that **dieser**-words and definite articles can be used alone as pronouns to refer to something already mentioned.

Welchen Anorak kaufst du? —*Diesen.*
Which anorak are you buying? —This one.

Diese Bluse ist schön. —*Ja, die nehme ich.*
This blouse is pretty. —Yes, I'll take it. (or *I'll take that one.*)

Lektion 14

a. Two-way prepositions can be followed by the accusative or dative case. If the situation involves motion toward a place, the object of the preposition is in the accusative case. If the prepositional phrase indicates location, the object of the preposition is in the dative case.

TWO-WAY PREPOSITIONS	
an *at, on*	**über** *over, above*
auf *on (top of)*	**unter** *under*
hinter *behind*	**vor** *before, in front of*
in *in, into*	**zwischen** *between*
neben *beside, next to*	

b. Certain verbs signal motion toward a place or location.

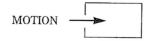

MOTION →	LOCATION ×
legen (legt, hat gelegt) *to lay*	**liegen (liegt, hat gelegen)** *to lie*
stellen (stellt, hat gestellt) *to place, put*	**stehen (steht, hat gestanden)** *to stand, be standing*
setzen (setzt, hat gesetzt) *to set (down)*	**sitzen (sitzt, hat gesessen)** *to sit, be sitting*
sich setzen (setzt sich, hat sich gesetzt) *to sit (down)*	
hängen (hängt, hat gehängt) *to hang*	**hängen (hängt, hat gehangen)** *to hang, be hanging*

Note that the verbs indicating motion are weak — they are regular and their past participles end in -t. Verbs indicating location are strong — they have irregularities and their past participles end in -en.

Lektion 15

Summary of Prepositions

ACCUSATIVE	DATIVE
durch *through* **für** *for* **gegen** *against* **ohne** *without* **um** *around, about; at* (in expressions of time)	**aus** *out of, from* (a place) **ausser** *besides, except for* **bei** *at; near; at the home or place of* **gegenüber** *across from* **mit** *with; by means of* **nach** *after; toward; according to* **seit** *since* **von** *of, from, by* **zu** *to*

ACCUSATIVE AND DATIVE	
an *at, on* **auf** *on, on top of* **hinter** *behind* **in** *in, into* **neben** *beside, next to*	**über** *over, above* **unter** *under* **vor** *before* **zwischen** *between*

CONTRACTIONS	
an + dem = am **an + das = ans** **bei + dem = beim** **in + dem = im**	**in + das = ins** **von + dem = vom** **zu + der = zur** **zu + dem = zum**

ÜBUNG A

In English and in German you will find certain words seem to go together. When you think of one, you often automatically think of the other. Look at the two groups of words below and write the pairs that come to your mind.

Brot	Fenster	Hemd	
Jean	Kaffee	Katze	Messer
Rock	Schuhe	Tisch	

Bluse	Butter	Gabel	
Hund	Krawatte	Kuchen	Socken
Stuhl	T-Shirt	Tür	

1. Brot und _____

2. _____

3. _____

4. _____

5. _____

6. _____

7. _____

8. _____

9. _____

10. _____

ÜBUNG B

Match each German phrase with its English equivalent.

1. Es tut mir weh.   _____ I like it.

2. Es tut mir leid.   _____ It doesn't fit me.

3. Es steht dir gut.   _____ It's too big for me.

4. Es gefällt mir.   _____ I'm sorry.

5. Es passt mir nicht.   _____ It looks good on you.

6. Es ist mir zu gross.   _____ It hurts.

ÜBUNG C

Cross out the word in each box that doesn't fit.

Ohrring	Pulli	blau	Spiegel
Halskette	Schuhe	gelb	Frosch
Anorak	Hemd	grün	Schlange
Armband	Bluse	kurz	Schildkröte

diese jeder meine welche	Spinne Schreibtisch Bücherregal Kommode	Rathaus Fluss Schule Kirche	Hochzeit Geburtstag Kalender Muttertag

ÜBUNG **D**

Sort out the prepositions and write them in the appropriate column below.

aus	mit	hinter	gegen	seit
durch	auf	vor	bei	um
von	zu	ausser	an	neben
in	unter	ohne	nach	
zwischen	für	über	gegenüber	

ACCUSATIVE	DATIVE	ACCUSATIVE AND DATIVE
_____	_____	_____
_____	_____	_____
_____	_____	_____
_____	_____	_____
_____	_____	_____
	_____	
	_____	
	_____	

ÜBUNG **E**

The Kraft family has just moved into a new house. Benjamin, the 13-year-old son, is moving furniture into his room. The paragraph below describes where he is putting everything. Read the paragraph, supplying words for the pictured items.

Benjamin stellt den [Schreibtisch] vor das [Fenster]. Er stellt das [Bett]

in die [Ecke]. Er stellt den [Nachttisch] neben das [Bett], und dann stellt

er den [Wecker] auf den [Nachttisch]. Er stellt den [Scanner] auf die [Kommode].

Die [Lampe] stellt er auf den [Schreibtisch]. Er hängt das [Bild] an die [Wand]

über das [Bett]. Und er hängt seine [Jacke] in den [Schrank].

Now describe where everything is located in Benjamin's room. Remember to use the dative case after the two-way prepositions when talking about location.

Der Schreibtisch steht _____

_____

_____

_____

_____

_____

_____

_____.

ÜBUNG **F**

Look at the two pet store windows pictured below. Compare them. What differences do you see?

Hamsterkäfig DM 60,--

A

Deluxe Hamsterkäfig
mit Fitness-Rad DM 100,--

B

Tierhandlung A **Tierhandlung B**

_____   _____

_____   _____

_____   _____

_____   _____

_____   _____

_____   _____

Proficiency Activities

Speaking

Practice the following situations with a partner. You take the role of A, your partner takes the role of B.

1. A and B are talking about the upcoming birthday of their friend Laura. Laura will be 14 years old on Saturday and she is having a party. A asks B how old Laura will be and when the party is. B responds to A's questions, then A and B discuss what they will give Laura as a present. They both make suggestions and respond to each other's ideas.

2. A and B are talking about birthdays. A asks B when B's birthday was, what B got as presents, and from whom. B responds and asks A about A's last birthday.

3. A is in a department store and is trying on various articles of clothing and deciding whether to buy something or not. B plays the role of the salesclerk and comments on what A is trying on and persuades A to buy something.

4. A is asking B to describe his or her room. A asks what B has in the room and where the items are located. B responds and then asks A about A's room.

5. A asks B for directions to the library in your town. B gives A directions.

Listening

The catalog company Sauermann has just sent out its winter catalog. You will hear a customer, Karin Bauer, order some articles of clothing over the phone from that catalog. Pretend that you are the catalog clerk taking the order. The catalog page and order form are shown below. As you listen, fill out the information on the order form.

für sie

Bluse
Nr. 0976
in Weiss, Blau,
Beige
Gr. 38-44
DM 55,--

Weste
Nr. 0762
in Schwarz,
Rot, Grün
Gr. S, M, L
DM 80,--

Rock
Nr. 0870
in Schwarz, Grau
Rot, Dunkelblau
Gr. 34-46
DM 120,--

für ihn

Rollkragen-Pullover
Nr. 0076
in Weiss, Schwarz,
Grün, Blau, Rot
Gr. SM, M, L, XL
DM 30,--

Pullover
Nr. 0092
in Blau, Grün, Rot
Gr. 46-58
DM 95,--

Hose
Nr. 0063
in Blau, Braun, Schwarz
Gr. 46-56
DM 70,--

Bestellschein

Name

Strasse und Hausnr.

Postleitzahl   Ortsbezeichnung

Telefonnummer

Bestellnr.	Kleidungsstück	Grösse	Farbe	Preis

Reading

If you have a pet or if you just like animals, the following ads and announcements would probably catch your attention. Read the various clippings below and answer the questions that follow.

Jetzt in Deutschland!
Der grosse Welterfolg

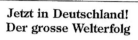
 C A T S

Operettenhaus Hamburg
Karten: 0180 544444

Tiermarkt

2 Meerschweinchen mit Käfig und allem Zubehör zu verschenken
Tel: 07142/77408

Süsse Siam-Katzen zu verkaufen
Tel: 07140/83470

Labrador-Retriever mit Impfung; prämierte Eltern; zu verkaufen
Tel: 07142/66679

Buchtipp

Kleinkopf, Robert
"Das Grosse Buch der Tiere"
Distel Verlag 1996
DM 45,- -
Informationen über alle Tiere der Welt

Hunde-Schule-Pension
Sie verreisen und wissen nicht, wohin mit dem Hund?
Bringen Sie den Hund zu uns!
Hunde-Haus Häberlein
Tel: 0180 74 62 79

TROPENWALD IN GEFAHR!
RETTET DIE TIERE!
Fordern Sie das Informationsblatt an!
Deutsche Umwelthilfe
Rotebühlstr. 8
71342 Stuttgart

Wilhelma
in Stuttgart
Deutschlands einziger zoologisch-botantischer Garten
8000 Tiere und herrliche Pflanzen aus aller Welt
täglich geöffnet
Stuttgart-Bad Canstatt, Neckartalstrasse

1. How much does a book with information about all kinds of animals cost?

_____

2. What is the name of a famous zoo in Stuttgart?

_____

3. Where is the musical "Cats" playing?

_____

4. Where could you board your dog for a few days?

_____

5. What number would you call to find out about some guinea pigs someone wants to give away?

_____

Writing

1. You have just bought a birthday card for your best friend. What would you write on it? Include the date, the salutation, your good wishes, and your signature.

_____

_____

_____

_____

_____

2. List five pieces of furniture or other items you have in your room and describe where each one is located.

_____

_____

_____

_____

_____

3. You have invited a classmate to come over. Write out the directions for getting from the school to your house.

_____

_____

_____

_____

_____

4. Make a list of five people you give a present to on various occasions. Write the names, the occasions, and something you might give to him or her as a present.

_____

_____

_____

_____

_____

5. You just received a beautiful sweater for your birthday from your aunt. It fits you well and you really like the color. Write a thank you note to your aunt.

_____

_____

_____

_____

_____

_____

_____

4
Vierter Teil

16

Gross, grösser, am grössten

Comparison of Adjectives and Adverbs

1 Wortschatz

Aus einem Kinder-Lexikon

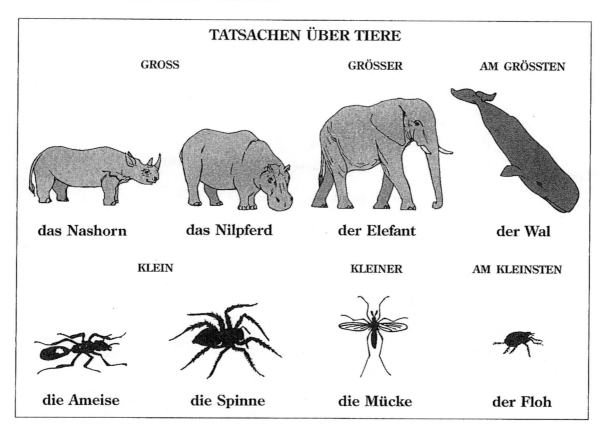

TATSACHEN ÜBER TIERE

GROSS	GRÖSSER	AM GRÖSSTEN
das Nashorn	das Nilpferd	der Elefant

der Wal

KLEIN	KLEINER	AM KLEINSTEN
die Ameise	die Spinne	die Mücke

der Floh

SCHNELL   SCHNELLER   AM SCHNELLSTEN

der Wolf   der Hase   der Löwe   der Gepard

KLUG   KLÜGER   AM KLÜGSTEN

der Hund   die Katze   der Schimpanse   der Delphin

Hast du gewusst?

- **Das Nashorn ist ungefähr so gross wie das Nilpferd.**

- **Der Elefant ist grösser als das Nilpferd.**

- **Der Blauwal ist grösser als der Elefant und das Nilpferd.**
- **Der Blauwal ist am grössten.**

ÜBUNG A

The preceding page is taken from a book of facts for children. Look at the information and answer the following questions.

1. Welches Tier ist grösser, der Elefant oder das Nashorn?

_____

2. Ist eine Ameise so klein wie ein Floh?

_____

3. Welches Tier läuft schneller, der Gepard oder der Löwe?

_____

4. Ist der Delphin klüger als der Schimpanse?

_____

2 The opening page of this lesson compares different animals. Notice how the comparisons are expressed in German. What do you think the following phrases mean in English?

so gross wie _____

grösser als _____

am grössten _____

To make comparisons, you use different forms of adjectives and adverbs. In English, for example, you say big, bigger, biggest. Expressing comparisons in German is much the same. Here are some examples.

POSITIVE	COMPARATIVE	SUPERLATIVE
gross	grösser	am grössten
klein	kleiner	am kleinsten
lang	länger	am längsten
kurz	kürzer	am kürzesten
schnell	schneller	am schnellsten
langsam	langsamer	am langsamsten
alt	älter	am ältesten
jung	jünger	am jüngsten

What observations can you make?

1. What ending is added in the comparative form? _____

2. What ending is added in the superlative form? _____ What word is added in the superative form? _____

3. Which words add umlauts? _____

_____

Here are some rules:

1. In German, all comparative forms end in **-er**.

2. Superlative forms end in **-(e)sten** and are used in a phrase beginning with **am**.

3. Most one-syllable adjectives and adverbs add an umlaut in the comparative and superlative forms. (Remember, only the vowels **a**, **o**, and **u** can take an umlaut.)

4. There are certain exceptions and they must be learned as you go along.

—Some one-syllable words don't take an umlaut.

blond	**blonder**	**am blondesten**
laut	**lauter**	**am lautesten**
toll	**toller**	**am tollsten**

—Some words have slightly different spellings.

dunkel	**dunkler**	**am dunkelsten**
teuer	**teurer**	**am teuersten**

—Some words change completely.

viel	**mehr**	**am meisten**
gut	**besser**	**am besten**
gern	**lieber**	**am liebsten**
hoch	**höher**	**am höchsten**

ÜBUNG B

Review some of the adjectives and adverbs you have already learned. Match the words that are opposite in meaning.

1. alt	_____ arm
2. dick	_____ billig
3. eng	_____ dünn
4. glücklich	_____ falsch
5. gross	_____ hässlich
6. gut	_____ klein
7. hübsch	_____ lang
8. interessant	_____ langweilig
9. kurz	_____ leicht
10. reich	_____ neu
11. richtig	_____ schlecht
12. schwer	_____ traurig
13. teuer	_____ weit

ÜBUNG C

Complete the following chart. Remember, if a word has an umlaut in the positive form, it keeps it in the comparative and in the superlative. If an umlaut is added in the comparative form, it is also added in the superlative form.

POSITIVE	COMPARATIVE	SUPERLATIVE	ENGLISH
	kälter		
		am wärmsten	
		am neuesten	
	lauter		
schön			
	dümmer		
		am stärksten	
schwer			
		am besten	
interessant			

ÜBUNG D

Compare the three pictures in each set. Write the positive, comparative, and superlative forms under the corresponding picture.

lang

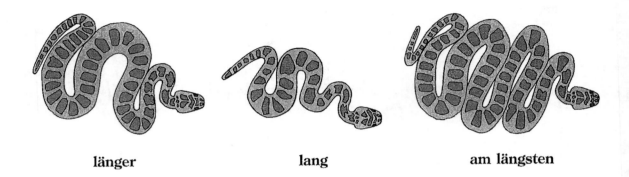

| länger | lang | am längsten |

1. jung

_____   _____   _____

2. stark

_____   _____   _____

3. schnell

_____   _____   _____

4. teuer

_____   _____   _____

5. weit

_____   _____   _____

3 When comparing things, you can make equal comparisons or unequal ones.

EQUAL COMPARISONS:	**Er läuft _so schnell wie_ ich (laufe).** _He runs as fast as I (run)._
UNEQUAL COMPARISONS:	**Sie läuft _schneller als_ ich (laufe).** _She runs faster than I (run)._

ÜBUNG E

Look at the chart that lists how fast various animals run. Write ten statements comparing the speeds of different animals. Use the phrases **so schnell wie, nicht so schnell wie, schneller als.**

der Gepard	96 km/h	der Hase	55 km/h
der Löwe	80 km/h	die Hauskatze	50 km/h
das Rennpferd	67 km/h	der Grizzly-Bär	50 km/h
der Windhund*	60 km/h	der Mensch	49 km/h
der Wolf	55 km/h	der Elefant	40 km/h

*der Windhund *greyhound*

The above speeds are approximate. The designation **km/h** means **Kilometer pro Strunde.** Can you figure out how many miles per hour each speed is equivalent to? *(1 mile = 1.6 kilometers; 1 kilometer = 0.62 miles)*

1. _____

2. _____

3. _____

4. _____

5. _____

6. _____

7. _____

8. _____

9. _____

10. _____

4 The phrases you have been using to make comparisons can also be used to express preference.

> **Ich spiele Volleyball *lieber als* Basketball.**
> *I like to play volleyball better than basketball.*
>
> **Ich spiele Tennis *am liebsten*.**
> *I like to play tennis most of all.*

ÜBUNG F

What do you prefer? Read the choices and write your preference.

BEISPIEL: **Wo wohnst du lieber: in der Stadt oder auf dem Land?**
Ich wohne lieber auf dem Land als in der Stadt.

1. Was für ein Haus gefällt dir besser: ein altes Haus oder ein modernes Haus?

   _____

2. Was isst du lieber: Pizza oder Kuchen?

   _____

3. Was trinkst du lieber: Apfelsaft oder Milch?

   _____

4. Welches Instrument gefällt dir besser: Gitarre oder Klavier?

   _____

5. Welches Fach findest du interessanter: Englisch oder Mathe?

   _____

6. Was liest du lieber: Zeitungen oder Comic-Hefte?

   _____

7. Was spielst du lieber: Monopoly oder Karten?

   _____

ÜBUNG G

Nico and Claudia have a "mutual admiration society." Nico compliments Claudia and Claudia returns the compliment. Write what Claudia says.

BEISPIEL: NICO: **Du bist so intelligent!**
CLAUDIA: **Ja, aber du bist intelligenter als ich!**

NICO: Du siehst so gut aus!

CLAUDIA: _____

NICO: Du bist so lustig!

CLAUDIA: _____

NICO: Du bist gut in Mathe!

CLAUDIA: _____

NICO: Du hast viele Freunde!

CLAUDIA: _____

NICO: Du kannst schnell laufen!

CLAUDIA: _____

NICO: Du bist sehr sportlich!

CLAUDIA: _____

NICO: Du bist sehr musikalisch!

CLAUDIA: _____

NICO: Du bist so nett!

CLAUDIA: _____

ÜBUNG H

Work with a partner and continue the preceding activity orally. Here are some more descriptive words to choose from.

höflich *polite*	**klug** *smart*	**witzig** *witty*
schick *stylish, chic*	**bescheiden** *modest*	**grosszügig** *generous*
mutig *brave*	**freundlich** *friendly*	**fit** *fit, in shape*
fleissig *industrious*	**vernünftig** *sensible*	**ordentlich** *neat*

ÜBUNG I

Sometimes children, especially brothers and sisters, get mad at each other and trade insults instead of compliments. Write what this brother and sister might say to each other!

doof *stupid*	**faul** *lazy*	**blöd** *silly, dumb*
eingebildet *conceited*	**dumm** *dumb*	**dickköpfig** *stubborn, thick-headed*
frech *fresh*	**schlampig** *sloppy*	

BEISPIEL: BRUDER: **Du bist doof!**
SCHWESTER: **Aber nicht so doof wie du!**

BRUDER: _____

SCHWESTER: _____

BRUDER: _____

SCHWESTER: _____

BRUDER: _____

SCHWESTER: _____

BRUDER: _____

SCHWESTER: _____

BRUDER: _____

SCHWESTER: _____

BRUDER: _____

SCHWESTER: _____

ÜBUNG J

Hör gut zu! The following chart gives the average life span of different animals. You will hear a number of statements. Look at the chart as you listen and determine whether each statement is true or false, according to the information on the chart. Place a check mark in the appropriate box.

	1	2	3	4	5	6	7	8
STIMMT								
STIMMT NICHT								

Durchschnittliche Lebensdauer einiger Tiere (in Jahren)

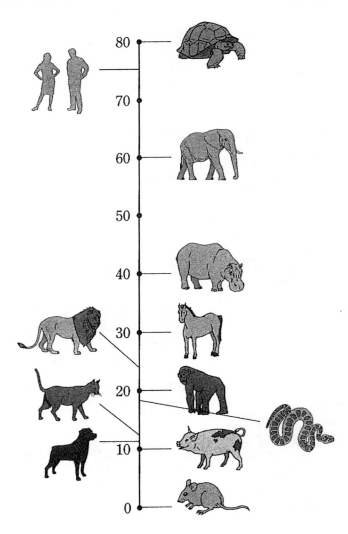

5 Zwei Fabeln

Fables are short tales that often have a moral. Many fables feature animals that talk and behave like humans. Which animals are featured in the following tales? What are they able to do that animals really can't do?

Der König der Tiere

Eines Tages möchte der Löwe die Tiere einladen. «Kommt alle in meine Höhle», sagt er ganz freundlich. Der Löwe ist sehr stolz auf sein zu Hause und fragt ein Tier nach dem andern: «So, wie gefällt es dir bei mir? Ist meine Höhle nicht so schön wie ein Schloss?»

Zuerst fragt der Löwe den Wolf. Der Wolf sagt: «Hm, es stinkt noch mehr als in einem Pferdestall!»

«Was?!» brüllt der Löwe. «Wie kannst du das nur sagen?» Er gibt dem Wolf einen heftigen Schlag ins Gesicht!

Dann fragt der Löwe den Esel: «Wie gefällt es dir bei mir?» Der Esel will ein bisschen vorsichtiger sein als der Wolf. «Ach, Herr Löwe, hier riecht es süsser als in einem Rosengarten!» «Du Heuchler! Du lügst!» schreit der Löwe, und er beisst den Esel in den Schwanz!

Jetzt ist der Fuchs dran. «Nun und du, Fuchs, wie gefällt es dir bei mir?» fragt der Löwe höflich. Der Fuchs ist schlauer als der Wolf und der Esel.

«Leider habe ich heute eine furchtbare Erkältung», antwortet er.

die Höhle *cave*
vorsichtig *careful*
riechen *to smell*
lügen *to lie*

Answer the questions to check your comprehension.

1. Wer ist am schlauesten?

_____

2. Wer ist am dümmsten?

_____

3. Was bedeutet «stolz?»

_____

4. Was bedeutet «schlau?»

_____

Der Fuchs und der Rabe

Der Rabe sitzt auf einem Baum. Im Schnabel hat er ein dickes Stück Käse. Da kommt der Fuchs und denkt: «Der Käse sieht ganz lecker aus!» Der Fuchs begrüsst den Raben: «Guten Tag, lieber Rabe! Ich habe gehört, dass Sie so schön wie die Nachtigall singen können. Bitte, singen Sie mir etwas vor!»

Der Rabe kann das nicht glauben. Der Fuchs meint, er kann schön singen. Der Rabe ist sehr eitel. Er freut sich sehr über dieses Kompliment und merkt nicht, wie der Fuchs ihn schmeichelt.

Der eitle Rabe macht ganz weit den Mund auf und will singen. Dabei fällt der Käse aus seinem Schnabel. Der Fuchs schnappt den Käse vom Boden auf, frisst ihn gierig auf und läuft lachend weg. Der Rabe sitzt traurig auf dem Baum und träumt von dem schönen Stück Käse.

der Rabe *crow*
die Nachtigall *nightingale*
schmeicheln *to flatter*

Answer the questions to check your comprehension.

1. Wer ist klüger, der Fuchs oder der Rabe?

_____

2. Wer ist am Ende hungrig?

_____

3. Was bedeutet «eitel?»

_____

4. Was bedeutet «gierig?»

_____

PERSÖNLICHE FRAGEN ❓

1. Welches Schulfach gefällt dir am besten?

_____

2. Welches Haustier möchtest du am liebsten haben?

_____

3. Was isst du am liebsten?

_____

4. Was für Musik hörst du am liebsten?

_____

5. Hast du Geschwister? Wenn ja, sind sie älter oder jünger als du?

_____

ÜBUNG K

Aufsatz. Write a paragraph about yourself, describing your likes, dislikes, and preferences. Use the questions in the preceding activity as a guide.

_____

_____

_____

_____

_____

_____

_____

_____

KLASSENPROJEKT

1. Working with a partner or in a team, use a ruler that has centimeters to measure various school supplies and items in your classroom and then compare them.

   BEISPIEL: **Der Bleistift ist... Zentimeter lang.**
   Der Kuli ist... Zentimeter lang.
   Der Bleistift ist länger als der Kuli. OR
   Der Kuli ist nicht so lang wie der Bleistift. OR
   Der Kuli ist kürzer als der Bleistift.

   > 1 cm (ZENTIMETER) = 0,39 inches (read: **null Komma neununddreissig**)
   > OR 1 inch   = 2,54 cm (read: **zwei Komma vierundfünfzig**)

2. Measure the height in centimeters of each classmate in the class. Make a chart and go around the room, having each one make one observation.

   BEISPIEL: **Robert is am grössten.**
   Jessica ist grösser als Cindy.
   Cindy ist so gross wie Daniel.

   > **1 Meter hat 100 Zentimeter**
   > OR **100 cm   sind   1 m**
   >
   > **1 m hat** ⎰ 39,37 Inches
   >   ⎱ 3,28 Fuss
   >   1,09 Yard

3. Make a chart showing heights in feet and inches and the equivalent meters and centimeters.

WORTSCHATZ

Tatsachen über Tiere *Facts About Animals*

die Ameise, -n *ant*	der Gepard, -e *cheetah*	der Rabe, -n* *crow*
der Bär, -en* *bear*	die Mücke, -n *mosquito*	der Schimpanse, -n *chimpanzee*
der Delphin, -e *dolphin*	das Nashorn, ̈e *rhinoceros*	der Wal, -e *whale*
der Floh, ̈e *flea*	das Nilpferd, -e *hippopotamus*	

Diese Wörter kennst du schon

der Elefant, -en * *elephant*	der Fuchs, ̈e *fox*	die Schildkröte, -n *turtle*
der Hase, -n* *rabbit (wild)*	der Hund, -e *dog*	die Spinne, -n *spider*
der Löwe, -n* *lion*	die Katze, -n *cat*	der Wolf, ̈e *wolf*
der Mensch, -en* *human being*	das Pferd, -e *horse*	

*The starred nouns belong to a group of nouns that add **-n** or **-en** in the accusative and dative case: **der Bär, den Bären, dem Bären.**

Adjektive und Adverbien

bescheiden *modest*

blöd *silly, dumb*

dumm (dümmer, am dümmsten) *dumb*

dunkel (dunkler, am dunkelsten) *dark*

eingebildet *conceited*

eitel *vain*

faul (fauler, am faulsten) *lazy*

frech *fresh*

freundlich *friendly*

gierig *greedy*

grosszügig *generous*

höflich *polite*

klug (klüger, am klügsten) *smart*

langsam *slow*

ordentlich *neat*

schlampig *sloppy*

schlau (schlauer, am schlau(e)sten) *sly, clever*

stolz *proud*

vernünftig *sensible, reasonable*

witzig *witty*

gern (haben) (lieber, am liebsten) *to like (like better, like best)*

gut (besser, am besten) *good (better, best)*

hoch (höher, am höchsten) *high (higher, highest)*

viel (mehr, am meisten) *a lot (more, most)*

so (gross) wie *as (big) as*

(grösser) als *(bigger) than*

ungefähr *about, approximately*

Und so sagst du das *Here's how to . . .*

make comparisons

Der Gepard läuft schneller als der Löwe. *The cheetah runs faster than the lion.*

Der Wolf ist nicht so schlau wie der Fuchs. *The wolf is not as clever as the fox.*

Der Delphin ist am klügsten. *The dolphin is the smartest (of all).*

express preferences

Ich spiele Volleyball lieber als Basketball. *I like to play volleyball rather than basketball.*

Ich spiele Tennis am liebsten. *I like to play tennis best of all.*

Building your vocabulary

Certain characteristics are often associated with specific animals. What do the following phrases mean? Are the same associations made in English?

1. So eingebildet wie ein Affe. _____
2. So langsam wie eine Schnecke. _____
3. So falsch wie eine Katze. _____
4. So fleissig wie eine Biene. _____
5. So dumm wie eine Kuh. _____
6. So ängstlich wie ein Hase. _____
7. So hungrig wie ein Löwe. _____
8. So dickköpfig wie ein Esel. _____
9. So blöd wie eine Gans. _____
10. So schlau wie ein Fuchs. _____

ÜBUNG L

Spiel: Trio. Make sets of adjective and adverb cards. For each set, write the positive form (**gross**) on the first card; the comparative form (**grösser**) on the second card; and the superlative form (**am grössten**) on the third card. Play *"Trio"* as you would play "Go Fish." Shuffle the cards and deal them to all players. Each player checks his or her hand for a set of three adjectives or adverbs and puts any complete set aside. The dealer then begins by asking for a card he or she needs to make a set. If the person asked has the card, it must be handed over. The dealer may continue asking that person until he or she doesn't have a card to hand over. Then it is the next person's turn. Whoever has the most sets at the end of the game wins.

KULTURECKE

Here are some facts about Germany. Look at the charts and check out where everything is located on a map of Germany. Ask your classmates questions using forms you have learned in this chapter. For example:

1. Wie hoch ist die Zugspitze?
2. Ist die Elbe länger als der Rhein?
3. Welche Stadt hat mehr Einwohner, Frankfurt oder Hamburg?

BERGE	HÖHE
Zugspitze (Nördliche Alpen)	2962 m*
Watzmann (Nördliche Alpen)	2713 m
Feldberg (Schwarzwald)	1493 m
Grosser Arber (Bayrischer Wald)	1456 m
Fichtelberg (Erzgebirge)	1214 m
Brocken (Harz)	1142 m

*Read: zweitausendneunhundertzweiundsechzig Meter hoch.

FLÜSSE INNERHALB DEUTSCHLANDS	LÄNGE
der Rhein	865 km*
die Elbe	700 km
der Main	524 km
die Weser	440 km
die Spree	382 km

*Read: achthundertfünfundsechzig Kilometer lang.

STÄDTE	EINWOHNER (Inhabitants)
Berlin	3 400 000*
Hamburg	1 600 000
München	1 200 000
Köln	1 000 000
Frankfurt am Main	635 000
Essen	624 000
Dortmund	594 000
Düsseldorf	574 000
Stuttgart	570 000
Bremen	544 000
Duisburg	532 000
Leipzig	530 000
Hannover	506 000
Dresden	501 000

*Read: drei Millionen vierhunderttausend Einwohner.

17
Eine Winterreise

Adjective Endings after Definite Articles and *dieser*-Words

1 Wortschatz

Kommen Sie im Winter nach *Puerto Rico!*

der weisse Strand

der blaue Himmel

die warme Luft

das herrliche Wasser

das gute Essen

das frische Obst

die exotischen Blumen

die netten Leute

Kommen Sie im Winter nach Österreich!

die hohen Berge

die gesunde Luft

die herrliche Landschaft

der weisse Schnee

das tolle Skilaufen

der gute Kuchen

die kleinen Dorfer

die alten Schlösser

ÜBUNG A

Read the two brochures advertising places to spend a winter vacation. What features does each place have? Write sentences describing first Puerto Rico, then Austria. Follow the pattern.

In Puerto Rico:
Der Strand ist weiss.

Der Himmel _____

_____

_____

_____

_____

_____

In Österreich:
Die Berge sind hoch.*

Die Luft _____

_____

_____

_____

_____

_____

* Notice that before nouns the adjective **hoch** drops the **c**.

ÜBUNG B

What is different about the adjective when it appears before the noun, as in the brochures, and when it stands alone, as in the sentences you just wrote? — The adjectives appearing before the nouns have endings. Underline the endings.

 2 Now read the following conversation in German.

—Ich möchte nach Puerto Rico reisen.

—Ich möchte lieber nach Österreich reisen.

—Die Landschaft mit dem weissen Strand, dem blauen Himmel und den exotischen Blumen ist sehr schön.

—Ja, aber die Landschaft in Österreich mit den hohen Bergen, den kleinen Dörfern und dem weissen Schnee ist auch schön.

—Ich liebe die warme Luft und das herrliche Wasser, und ich esse das frische Obst so gern.

—Ich liebe die kalte Luft und das tolle Skilaufen, und ich esse den guten Kuchen.

ÜBUNG C

Reread the conversation, write down the adjectives and circling the adjective endings.

ÜBUNG D

Now write all the noun phrases with adjectives that are in the conversation.

Puerto Rico	**Österreich**
dem weissen Strand	**den hohen Bergen**

1. _____   1. _____

2. _____   2. _____

3. _____   3. _____

4. _____   4. _____

5. _____   5. _____

What case is each noun-phrase in? After each one you have written, write D for dative or A for accusative case.

3 Adjectives following definite articles and **dieser**-words (**dieser, jeder, welcher**) have the ending **-e** or **-en**.

	NOMINATIVE	ACCUSATIVE	DATIVE
MASC.	der weisse Strand	den weissen Strand	dem weissen Strand
FEM.	die warme Luft	die warme Luft	der warmen Luft
NEU.	das gute Essen	das gute Essen	dem guten Essen
PL.	die hohen Berge	die hohen Berge	den hohen Bergen*

*Remember that a plural noun in the dative case adds an **-n**.

ÜBUNG E

Express what you like about Puerto Rico in two ways. First use the verb **gefallen,** then use the phrase **gern haben**. Follow the example.

der Strand / weiss   das Essen / gut
der Himmel / blau   das Obst / frisch
die Luft / warm   die Blumen / exotisch
das Wasser / herrlich   die Leute / nett

BEISPIEL: **Der weisse Strand gefällt mir.**
Ich habe den weissen Strand gern.

1. _____

_____

2. _____

_____

3. _____

_____

4. _____

_____

5. _____

_____

6. _____

_____

7. _____

_____

ÜBUNG F

Pretend that you are in Austria and are amazed at how nice everything is. Complete the exclamations below. Use **dieser**.

der Schnee / weiss	**die Luft / gesund**
der Kuchen / gut	**das Dorf / klein**
die Landschaft / herrlich	**die Berge / hoch**
das Skilaufen / toll	**die Schlösser / alt**

1. Dieser _____ Schnee!

2. Diese _____ Luft!

3. Dieses _____ Skilaufen!

4. _____ _____ Landschaft! Hast du diese _____ Landschaft gesehen?

5. _____ _____ Kuchen! Hast du _____ _____ Kuchen probiert?

6. Dieses _____ Dorf! Hast du in diesem _____ Dorf fotografiert?

7. _____ _____ Schlösser! Hast du diese _____ Schlösser gesehen?

8. _____ _____ Berge! Bist du schon in diesen _____ Bergen Skilaufen gegangen?

ÜBUNG G

During the winter vacation, Robert is going to Puerto Rico, Sarah is going to Austria. Look at the pictures and write sentences telling what each one will take along.

der Anorak / schick

die Badehose / grün

die Skier / neu

der Sonnenhut / gross

die Socken / dick

die Skimütze / lustig

das Surfbrett / teuer

die Shorts / rot

das Hemd / modisch

die Sandalen / schwarz

die Stiefel / bequem

der Pullover / warm

BEISPIEL: **Was nimmt Robert mit?**
Robert nimmt das teure Surfbrett mit.*

1. Er nimmt _____.

2. _____

3. _____

4. _____

5. _____

* Note the spelling of **teuer** when an ending is added: the -e before the final -**r** is dropped.

Was nimmt Sarah mit?

1. Sarah nimmt _____ mit.

2. Sie nimmt _____.

3. _____

4. _____

5. _____

6. _____

ÜBUNG **H**

Was meinst du? Was gehört wem? Look at the pictures in each group and write sentences describing what belongs to whom.

das Schloss / alt

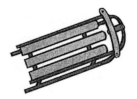

der Sclitten / toll

der Tennisschläger / teuer

der Wagen / schick

die Skimütze / warm

das Geschenk / gross

der Ohrring / hübsch

der Junge / klein

die Skiläuferin / nett

die Prinzessin / schön

das Mädchen / sportlich

die Frau / elegant

der Mann / reich

das Geburtstagskind / glücklich

BEISPIEL: **Das alte Schloss gehört der schönen Prinzessin.**

1. _____

2. _____

3. _____

4. _____

5. _____

6. _____

7. _____

ÜBUNG I

Read the paragraph and fill in the missing adjective endings.

In den Ferien sind wir nach Deutschland gereist. Wir haben die alt_____ Verwandten

besucht. Wir sind mit dem Zug von dem gross_____ Flughafen in Frankfurt nach Stuttgart

gefahren. Der lang_____, bequem_____ Zug war sehr schnell. Die alt_____ Verwandten

wohnen nicht weit von der schön_____ Stadt Stuttgart. Das klein_____ Dorf heisst

Bissingen. Die viel_____ Vettern und Kusinen waren am Bahnhof. Der 90-jährig_____

Bruder von dem alt_____ Grossvater in Amerika war auch da.

4 Read the following vacation ads from a German magazine for young people. Which vacation appeals to you most?

COMPUTER-CAMP

Für Computer-Freaks und auch andere! Einfach computern, soviel du willst, oder du kannst dir auch einen interessanten Computerkurs aussuchen! Aber Compu-Camp bietet auch Actionferien: Skateboarding, Tennis und American Sports! 750 DM

Toller Abenteuer-Urlaub!

Absolute Spitze ist das neue Multi-Activity-Programm: neun Tage Kanu- und Höhlencamp am wildromantischen Fluss Ardeche in Frankreich! 1400 DM

FRANZÖSISCH IN PARIS!

Du machst zwei Wochen lang einen Sprachkurs in Nizza mit, dazu auch viel Sport, dann eine Woche in Paris — Sightseeing, Theater, Konzert! 2650 DM!

Mallorca—Beachlife

Zwei superheisse Wochen im neuen Jugendhotel auf der Mittelmeerinsel Mallorca! 1500 DM!

AUF IN DIE USA!

Ein tolles Programm! Zwei Wochen bei einer Familie in Kalifornien und zwei Wochen auf einer echten Western-Ranch in Colorado! 2800 DM!

Im Trend: Spanien

Zwei Wochen im Jugendhotel. Weisse Strände, tolle In-Discos, Shops und flippige Leute. Diesen Sommer sollst du in der Trend-Stadt Barcelona Spanisch lernen – nicht schlecht! Nur 900 DM!

SURFEN AUF RHODOS

Happy Holidays im sonnigen Griechenland! Eine Woche lang Surfen lernen. Wohnen in 2-3-Bett-Zimmern in Appartements mit Dusche und WC. 1400 DM!

SONNE, PALMEN UND MICKEY!

Disney World in Orlando, Florida: Sieben phantastische
Tage! Ein Rendezvous mit Mickey, King Kong up close.
Shamu, der Killerwal und seine Welt!
Unvergesslich für 3000 DM!

Jugend-Camping-Club

Ein tolles Sportprogramm gibt's im Jugend-Camping-Club
Korsika — Mountainbikes, Surfbretter, Volleyballplatz,
super Strände! Im Zelt schlafen und auch mit anderen
Jugendlichen zusammen im grossen Kochzelt etwas
kochen! Zwei Wochen
für 1200 DM!

1. Which vacations are in the USA?

2. Which one is in Greece?

3. On which vacations would you expect to speak Spanish?

4. On which ones would you expect to speak French?

5. On what river in France can you go canoeing?

6. What do you think the word **Mittelmeerinsel** means?

7. Which vacation would you like to go on?

5 Where would you like to go on a vacation? Pretend you and your classmates have just won a contest and the prize is a trip for the whole class to anywhere in the world.

Wohin sollen wir reisen?

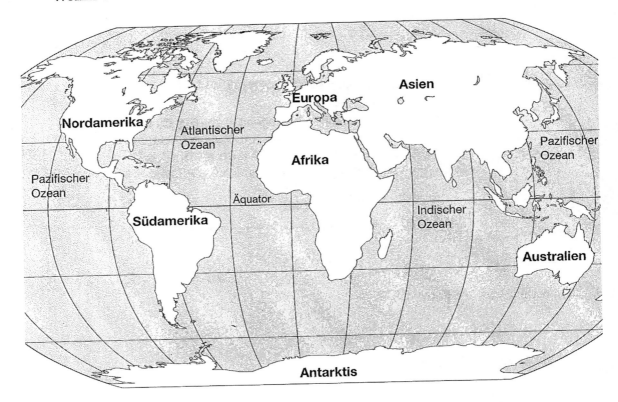

Here are some places you might want to visit. Using a dictionary, add places that you are interested in and are not listed. Tell the continent each country is located in. For example: **China ist in Asien**.

Ich möchte nach...		Ich möchte in... fahren.
Deutschland	China	die Schweiz
Mexiko	Japan	die Türkei
Irland	Südafrika	die Niederlande
Indien	Thailand	die USA
Brasilien	Ägypten	die Philippinen

Note that the preposition **nach** is used with names of cities, states, countries, continents, and islands. With names preceded by an article, the preposition **in** is used.

Warum möchtest du nach... ?
    Es ist dort...
        billig
        interessant
        schön
        sonnig
        warm

Warum möchest du nicht nach... ?
    Es ist dort...
        zu heiss
        zu kalt
        zu langweilig
        zu teuer
        zu wolkig

Es gibt dort...
    viel zu tun
    viel zu sehen
    viel Sonne
    viel Schnee

In... ist es...
    billiger
    interessanter
    kühler
    schöner

ÜBUNG J

Several students make a large outline map of the world to hang on the bulletin board. Each student in the class then writes on the map the name of a country he or she would like to visit — in German, of course! Look up names you don't know in the dictionary.

ÜBUNG K

Go around the room. Each student tells where he or she would like to go and why.

BEISPIEL: **Es ist dort warm. Ich habe das warme Wetter gern.**
                  Es ist dort schön. Mir gefallen die hohen Berge.
                  Es gibt dort viel zu sehen. Ich möchte die alten Schlösser sehen.

ÜBUNG L

Now let's get back to the vacation trip your class won. Work in groups or as a whole class and have a discussion about where to go. One student could write the suggestions on the board along with the reasons for and against going to that place. Here are some ways to make suggestions:

Wir können nach...   *We can go to . . .*
Fahren wir doch nach...   *Let's go to . . .*
Wie wär's mit...   *How about . . . ?*
Warum fahren wir nicht nach...   *Why don't we go to . . . ?*
... wäre schön!   *. . . would be nice!*
Ich möchte lieber nach...   *I would rather go to . . .*

ÜBUNG **M**

Hör gut zu! You will hear some students talking about where they would like to spend their vacations. The first student makes a statement and the second student responds with a suggestion about where he or she might go. Listen to the exchanges and decide whether the first student will take the suggestion or not. Mark the appropriate box.

	1	2	3	4	5	6
JA						
NEIN						

PERSÖNLICHE FRAGEN ?

1. Wohin möchtest du reisen?

   _____

2. Warum? Was gefällt dir dort? Hast du dort Verwandte?

   _____

3. Welche Sprache spricht man dort?

   _____

4. Kannst du diese Sprache verstehen?

   _____

5. Kannst du sie sprechen?

   _____

6. Willst du die Sprache lernen? Wie?

   _____

GESPRÄCH

Two friends, Jens and Susanne, are discussing places they would like to go someday. They mention places and give reasons to go there. They also respond to each other's comments, agreeing or disagreeing and giving reasons. Write the conversation.

_____

_____

_____

_____

_____

_____

_____

_____

_____

KLASSENPROJEKT

Make travel posters for the various places your class would like to visit. Use the posters pictured on the opening page of this lesson as examples.

WORTSCHATZ A-Z

das Abenteuer *adventure*
das Dorf, ¨er *village*
der Himmel *sky*
die Insel, -n *island*
die Landschaft, -en *landscape*
das Mittelmeer *Mediterranean Sea*
der Schnee *snow*
das Surfbrett, -er *surfboard*
der Urlaub, -e *vacation**

der Kontinent, -e *continent*
  Afrika *Africa*
die Antarktis *Antartica*
  Asien *Asia*
  Australien *Australia*
  Europa *Europe*
  Nordamerika *North America*
  Südamerika *South America*
(Learn also the countries listed on p. 356)

exotisch *exotic*
sonnig *sunny*
unvergesslich *unforgettable*
wolkig *cloudy*

Diese Wörter kennst du schon

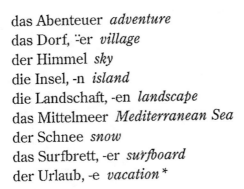

die Luft, ¨e *air*   der Strand, ¨e *beach*   dick *thick*   schnell *fast*
das Schloss, ¨er *castle*   das Wasser *water*   frisch *fresh*

Und so sagst du das...   *Here's how to . . .*

make suggestions

Wir können nach... *We can go to . . .*
Fahren wir doch nach... *Let's go to . . .*
Wie wär's mit... *How about . . . ?*
Warum fahren wir nicht nach . . . *Why don't we go to . . .*
...wäre schön! *. . . would be nice!*

*The word **Ferien** refers to vacation from school; the word **Urlaub** refers to vacation from work.

Building your vocabulary

If you recognize the names of countries in German, you will be able to recognize the corresponding adjectives. The adjectives usually end in **-isch** and some follow a regular pattern, for example:

Ich möchte nach *Japan*, aber zuerst möchte ich die *japanische* Sprache lernen. Ich war im Sommer in *Italien*. Ich mag das *italienische* Essen!

Many adjectives, however, have spelling changes, for example:

Mexiko   mexikanisch   **China   chinesisch**
Deutschand   deutsch   **die Niederlande   niederländisch**
Irland   irisch   **Brasilien   brasilianisch**

Make a list in German of ten countries and write the corresponding adjective next to the name of each country. Look up the adjectives in the dictionary. You will find the adjective in the entry for the country.

1. _____   6. _____

2. _____   7. _____

3. _____   8. _____

4. _____   9. _____

5. _____   10. _____

ÜBUNG N

Geographie-Spiel. Make two sets of cards. Write the names of countries — in German, of course — on one set; write the names of the continents on the other. Shuffle the two sets of cards together. Divide the class into two teams. Team A picks a card from the top of the deck. If it is a country, the team must give the name of the continent it is located on. If it is a continent, the team must give the name of a country located on that continent. Then it's Team B's turn. The team with the most right answers wins.

KULTURECKE

In Europe, motor vehicles have oval emblems with letters that indicate nationality. During vacation times, many cars and campers are on the road. Because Germany is located in the middle of Europe, many of them come to Germany to spend their vacations there, or they drive through Germany to get to another country. See if you can recognize what countries the emblems on the map stand for. Write the letters in front of the corresponding country listed on the next page.

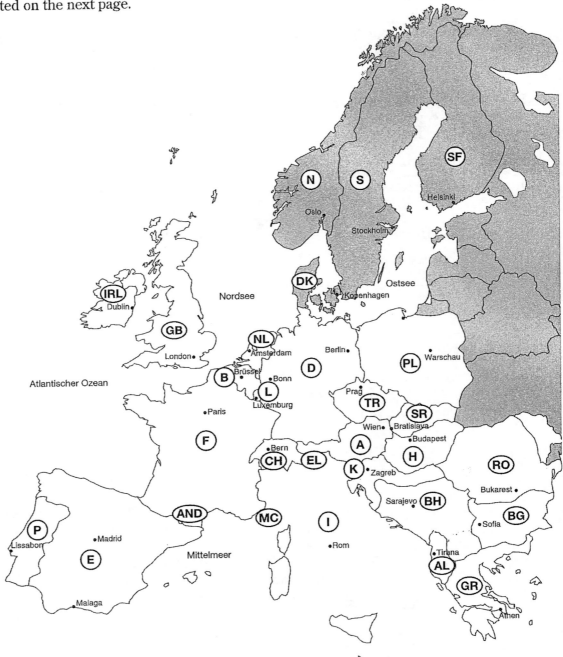

_____ Albanien

_____ Andorra

_____ Belgien

_____ Bosnien-
Herzegowina

_____ Bulgarien

_____ Kroatien

_____ Dänemark

_____ Deutschland

_____ Finland

_____ Frankreich

_____ Griechenland

_____ Grossbritannien

_____ Irland

_____ Italien

_____ Liechtenstein

_____ Luxemburg

_____ Monaco

_____ Niederlande

_____ Norwegen

_____ Österreich

_____ Poland

_____ Portugal

_____ Rumänien

_____ Schweden

_____ Schweiz

_____ Spanien

_____ Tschechische
Republik

_____ Ungarn

18
Ein Mini-Krimi

Adjective Endings After
Indefinite Articles and *ein*-Words

1 Wortschatz

Diebstahl im Vogelhaus

Die Personen

**Inspektor August Klinker
von der Polizei**

**Herr Fritz Fridolin,
der Zoowärter**

Ein grosser Mann mit einem kleinen
Schnurrbart. Trägt immer einen langen,
grauen Trenchcoat und einen schwarzen
Hut.

Ein netter, etwas zerstreuter Mann mit
einem runden, freundlichen Gesicht und
lockigen, dunklen Haaren. Trägt immer
seine weisse Zoowärter-Mütze. Liebt
Tiere, besonders Vögel.

Helmut Holzhacker
der neue Assistent im Zoo

Ein dünner, nervöser Mann mit einer Glatze.
Hat eine lange Narbe auf der linken Backe.
Sehr ungeduldig und unfreundlich, sieht
auch immer böse und schlecht gelaunt aus.

Frau Mathilde Meier

Eine kleine, zierliche, alte Frau mit schönen,
weissen Haaren. Trägt eine kleine, runde
Brille. Sehr gutherzig und grosszügig. Bäckt
gern und lädt immer Leute zum Kaffee und
Kuchen ein.

Der Zoowärter, Herr Fridolin, macht die Tür zum
Vogelhaus auf. «Sehen Sie, Herr Inspektor, hier
wohnen unsere exotischen Vögel. Es ist sehr seltsam.
In den letzten vier Wochen sind vier Vögel spurlos
verschwunden. Letzte Woche war es ein wunderbarer
Kakadu und gestern war es ein Papagei, unser lustiger
Oskar. Er ist ein afrikanischer Graupapagei. Diese
Papageien können besonders gut sprechen.»

    Inspektor Klinker schaut sich um. Das ist ein
schwieriger Fall. Wo sind die Vögel? Nur Herr Fridolin
hat einen Schlüssel für die Käfige — das heisst, nur
Herr Fridolin und der neue Wärter, Helmut
Holzhacker. Herr Holzhacker arbeitet seit fünf Wochen
im Zoo. Er macht die Käfige sauber. Er weiss auch
nicht, was mit den Vögeln passiert ist.

    Der Inspektor geht zurück zur Polizeiwache. «Herr
Inspektor, da war gerade ein komischer Telefonanruf.
Eine alte Frau in der Gärtnerstrasse. Sie sagt, sie hört
den ganzen Tag Vögel. Vielleicht hat sie selbst einen
kleinen Vogel!* Ha, ha!»

    «Hm, den ganzen Tag hört sie Vögel. Wie ist der
Name und die Adresse, bitte?»

seltsam *strange*
spurlos verschwunden
   disappeared without a trace
der Papagei *parrot*

sich umschauen *to look around*
ein schwieriger Fall *a difficult case*
der Schlüssel *key*
der Käfig *cage*

saubermachen *to clean*

---

*The expression **einen Vogel haben** means *to be a little cuckoo*.
It is roughly equivalent to the English expression *to have bats in
your belfry*.

«Frau Mathilde Meier in der Gärtnerstrasse 10.»
«Vielen Dank! Ich geh jetzt.»
«In Ordnung, Herr Inspektor.»

Der Inspektor fährt in die Gärtnerstrasse und findet direkt vor Nummer 10 einen schönen Parkplatz. Nummer 10 ist ein Reihenhaus. Er geht zur Tür und klingelt. Frau Meier macht die Tür auf.

«Guten Tag. Ich bin Inspektor Klinker von der Polizei. Sie sind Frau Mathilde Meier?»

«Ach, ja! Guten Tag, Herr Inspektor! Kommen Sie herein! Wollen Sie eine Tasse Kaffee und ein Stück Kuchen? Ich habe einen frischen Apfelkuchen. Ich habe ihn gerade gebacken.»

«Das ist sehr nett von Ihnen, aber nein, danke. Sie haben bei der Polizei angerufen?»

«Heute Nachmittag. Wissen Sie, Herr Inspektor, ich kann das nicht mehr aushalten!»

«Was halten Sie nicht mehr aus, Frau Meier?»

«Hören Sie das nicht? Es pfeift, es singt, es zwitschert, es schreit, und manchmal spricht auch eine kratzige Stimme.»

eine kratzige Stimme *a scratchy voice*

«Was sagt die Stimme?»

«Manchmal schreit sie 'Hallo, Helmut!' und manchmal höre ich nur 'Fridolin! Fridolin!'. Es macht mich verrückt! Ich habe keine Ruhe mehr! Immer diese Vögel und dann auch die kratzige Stimme!»

die Ruhe *peace and quiet*

«Hm, ärgerlich. Wer wohnt nebenan? Kennen Sie die Leute?»

«Nein, eigentlich nicht. Es sind zwei Brüder. Sie wohnen nicht lange dort. Ein Bruder arbeitet im Zoo.»

«Im Zoo. Soso. Und wissen Sie, wie er heisst?»

«Ich habe mal den Namen am Briefkasten gesehen. Holzhacker, glaube ich, ist der Name.»

«Holzhacker. Interessant.»

Der Inspektor stellt noch ein paar Fragen und verabschiedet sich von Frau Meier. In den nächsten Tagen beobachtet er das Haus von den Gebrüdern Holzhacker. Er sieht,wie Helmut Holzhacker morgens das Haus verlässt und abends wieder zurückkommt. Er sieht, wie der Bruder einkaufen geht und grosse Säcke mit Vogelfutter ins Haus schleppt. Sehr verdächtig. Er sieht, wie ein grosser, teurer Wagen vor das Haus fährt, wie der Fahrer ins Haus geht und nach kurzer Zeit mit einem gedeckten Vogelkäfig wieder herauskommt. Sehr verdächtig.

verdächtig *suspicious*

gedeckt *covered*

Nach ein paar Tagen hat Inspektor Klinker genug gesehen. Er geht zur Tür und klingelt. Helmut Holzhacker macht ganz vorsichtig die Tür ein bisschen auf. Der Inspektor schiebt ihn beiseite und marschiert ins Haus. Dort findet er überall ganz viele Vögel. Was für ein lautes Durcheinander! Die Vögel pfeifen, singen, zwitschern und schreien. Aus einer Ecke ruft ein Papagei laut «Fridolin! Fridolin!» Das sind die verschwundenen Vögel vom Zoo und noch mehr! Es sind Vögel aus Tierhandlungen und aus Privatbesitz. Helmut Holzhacker und sein Bruder sind ganz schlaue Diebe! Sie stehlen exotische Vögel und verkaufen sie an einen reichen, exzentrischen Sammler in Berlin! Fall erledigt!

der Dieb *thief*

Fall erledigt! *case closed!*

ÜBUNG A

Complete each sentence with an appropriate name from the list.

Fridolin   Oskar   Klinker
Meier   Holzhacker

1. Der Inspektor heisst _____.

2. Der Zoowärter heisst _____.

3. Der neue Assistent heisst _____.

4. Die nette alte Frau in der Gärtnerstrasse heisst _____.

5. Der verschwundene Graupapagei heisst _____.

ÜBUNG B

Read each statement and determine whether it is true or false. Write **ja** or **nein**.

_____ 1. Helmut Holzhacker arbeitet schon sehr lange im Zoo.

_____ 2. Frau Meier hat viele Vögel.

_____ 3. Helmut Holzhacker und sein Bruder wohnen zusammen in einem Reinhenhaus.

_____ 4. Der Inspektor kauft Vogelfutter.

_____ 5. Der Mann in Berlin sammelt exotische Vögel.

ÜBUNG C

Here is a list of adjectives. Which ones would you use to describe the people below? You can use some adjectives for more than one person.

gross	**dünn**	**böse**	**freundlich**	**gutherzig**
klein	**nervös**	**unfreundlich**	**nett**	**grosszügig**
zierlich	**zerstreut**	**ungeduldig**	**tierlieb**	**klug**

1. Inspektor Klinker

_____

2. Herr Fridolin

_____

3. Helmut Holzhacker

_____

4. Frau Meier

_____

ÜBUNG D

Answer the following questions in English.

1. What disappeared from the zoo?

_____

2. Why does Frau Meier call the police?

_____

3. What does Inspektor Klinker find suspicious?

_____

4. What are the brothers doing with the birds?

_____

2 Reread the story and underline all the adjectives. Notice if the adjectives follow a definite article or a **dieser**-word or if it follows an indefinite article or an **ein**-word. Circle the adjective endings.

In Lesson 17 you learned the endings on adjectives following the definite article and **dieser**-words. There are only two endings: **-e** or **-en**. Here are the endings for adjectives following the indefinite article and **ein**-words (**kein** and the possessives **mein, dein, sein, ihr,** etc.)

	NOMINATIVE	ACCUSATIVE	DATIVE
MASC. FEM. NEUT.	Das ist... ein **blauer** Mantel eine **weisse** Bluse ein **gelbes** Hemd	Ich habe... einen **blauen** Mantel eine **weisse** Bluse ein **gelbes** Hemd	Das passt zu... einem **blauen** Mantel einer **weissen** Bluse einem **gelben** Hemd
PL.	Das sind... **braune** Schuhe meine **braunen** Schuhe keine **braunen** Schuhe	Ich habe... **braune** Schuhe meine **braunen** Schuhe keine **braunen** Schuhe	Das passt zu... **braunen** Schuhen meinen **braunen** Schuhen keinen **braunen** Schuhen

Note that when there are two adjectives, they both have the same ending.

BEISPIEL: **Ich habe schöne, braune Schuhe.**
Das ist ein alter, billiger Mantel.

ÜBUNG E

Rewrite the sentences, placing the adjective before the noun.

Der Trenchcoat ist grau.
Das ist ein grauer Trenchcoat.

1. Der Mann ist ungeduldig.

_____

2. Die Frau ist nett.

_____

3. Der Inspektor ist klug.

_____

4. Die Zoo-Mütze ist weiss.

_____

5. Die Brille ist rund.

_____

6. Der Papagei ist nervös.

_____

7. Das Gesicht ist freundlich.

_____

8. Der Hut ist schwarz.

_____

9. Die Haare sind lockig.

_____

10. Das Reihenhaus ist hübsch.

_____

ÜBUNG **F**

You are going on a trip. Here's a list of things to take with you. (The list on the left is for girls, the one on the right is for boys.)

Hier ist die Liste:

ein warmer Pullover (rot)	ein warmer Pullover (rot)
eine leichte Jacke (blau)	eine leichte Jacke (blau)
ein langer Rock (schwarz)	eine gute Hose (grau)
eine sportliche Bluse (weiss)	ein sportliches Hemd (weiss)
ein schönes Kleid (grün)	ein schöner Anzug (dunkel)
bequeme Schuhe (braun)	bequeme Schuhe (braun)

BEISPIEL: **Has du einen warmen Pullover?**
Ja, der rote Pullover ist warm.

1. _____

2. _____

3. _____

4. _____

5. _____

ÜBUNG G

Use the clothing wheel you made to practice vocabulary in Lesson 13, page 260. Work with a partner, asking and responding to each other's questions and statements.

BEISPIEL: **Hast du eine weisse Bluse?**
Nein, ich habe keine weisse Bluse.
Ich brauche blaue Schuhe.
Du hast keine blauen Schuhe?
Gefällt dir mein gelbes Hemd?
Ja, dein gelbes Hemd gefällt mir gut.

ÜBUNG H

Read the following picture story, substituting the correct word for the picture.

Ein kleiner und eine kleine wohnen in einem kleinen

in einem kleinen . Sie haben einen kleinen und eine kleine .

In ihrem kleinen sind kleine und kleine .

Sie essen ihr kleines in ihrer kleinen . Abends sitzen sie in

ihrem kleinen vor ihrem kleinen .

1. Read the story aloud as a class. Each student reads a sentence.

2. Rewrite the story using the adjective **gross** instead of **klein**. Write the correct word for each picture.

_____

_____

_____

_____

_____

_____

_____

3. Read the rewritten story aloud as a class. Then read it again, substituting another adjective such as **alt, lustig, toll, blöd**.

3 The verb **tragen**, _to wear_, has a stem vowel change in the second- and third-person singular. What is that vowel change?

tragen _to wear_			
ich	trage	wir	tragen
du	trägst	ihr	tragt
er/sie	trägt	sie/Sie	tragen

What other verbs have you learned that take an umlaut in the second- and third-persons

singular? _____

ÜBUNG I

Write what you are wearing today and what the student sitting next to you is wearing. Include colors.

Ich trage heute _____

_____

_____.

_____ trägt heute _____

_____

_____.

Now different students come to the front of the class. Take turns describing what that person is wearing.

4 When describing a person, you can mention what the person is wearing, but you might also talk about physical characteristics and personality traits.

Wie sieht er aus? Wie sieht sie aus? — **Er sieht gut aus. Sie ist schön.**

der Körper

gross	**klein**	**dick**	**schlank**

die Haare (das Haar)*

kurze Haare   **lange Haare**   **lockige Haare**   **glatte Haare**

dunkle Haare   **helle Haare**   **keine Haare (eine Glatze)**

*You can say **Haar** or **Haare**: **Er hat *kurze Haare*** or **Er hat *kurzes Haar*.**

blonde
braune
schwarze   } Haare
rote

das Gesicht

freundlich

böse

eine grosse
Nase

eine kleine
Nase

ein grosser
Mund

ein kleiner
Mund

braune
blaue
grüne
graue

Augen

andere Merkmale:

trägt eine
Brille

hat eine
Narbe

hat eine
Tätowierung

hat einen
Schnurrbart

Was kannst du auch sagen?

alt	laut	schlampig
bescheiden	lebhaft	schüchtern
eingebildet	lustig	schwach
faul	musikalisch	sportlich
fleissig	mutig	stark
freundlich	ordentlich	unfreundlich
intelligent	ruhig	verrückt
jung		

ÜBUNG J

Write a description of each of the people pictured.

Ferdinand   **Gerlinde**

_____   _____

_____   _____

_____   _____

_____   _____

_____   _____

_____   _____

_____   _____

ÜBUNG K

Write descriptions of three people in your class. Do not write the names.

Exchange descriptions with a classmate and see if you can guess the people each of you has described. Take turns reading the descriptions to the class and see if they can guess who is being described.

Then write a description of a celebrity. Read it to the class and see if your classmates can guess who the person is.

ÜBUNG L

Hör gut zu!

Part 1: You will hear a description of each person pictured. Look at the pictures

Part 2: Now you will hear the description of an unusual being who has just landed from the planet Mars. As you listen, draw this being according to the description you hear.

Der Mensch von Mars

PERSÖNLICHE FRAGEN ?

1. Wie siehst du aus? Bist du gross oder klein — oder vielleicht mittelgross?

_____

2. Was für eine Augenfarbe hast du?

_____

3. Was für Haare hast du? Lang? Kurz? Glatt? Lockig?

_____

Welche Haarfarbe hast du?

_____

4. Trägst du eine Brille? Hast du Kontaktlinsen?

_____

5. Hast du eine Zahnspange (*braces*)? Wenn ja, wie lange musst du die Zahnspange noch tragen?

_____

6. Bist du ordentlich oder schlampig?

_____

7. Bist du sportlich? Bist du musikalisch?

_____

8. Wie ziehst du dich an? Wild? Ein bisschen verrückt? Normal? Konservativ?

_____

9. Was für Adjektive beschreiben dich?

_____

ÜBUNG M

Aufsatz. Write a paragraph describing yourself. Mention physical characteristics and personality traits. Describe what you like to wear, tell your favorite color, and tell some of the things you like to do.

So bin ich!

_____

_____

_____

_____

_____

_____

_____

_____

_____

KLASSENPROJEKT

1. Make a scrapbook or a bulletin board display with the descriptions each student has written. Include a picture — it could be a photograph or a funny caricature students have drawn.

2. Make a book of funny characters, aliens, or monsters. Each student creates a character, writes a description, and draws an accompanying picture.

3. Write a story with some or all of the characters the class has created.

WORTSCHATZ A-Z

die Backe, -n *cheek*
der Briefkasten, ⸚ *mailbox*
der Dieb, -e *thief*
der Diebstahl, ⸚e *theft*
das Durcheinander *chaos, mess*
der Fall, ⸚e *case*; ein schwieriger Fall
  a difficult case; Fall erledigt! *case
  closed!*
die Glatze, -n *bald head*
der Inspektor, -en *inspector*
der Käfig, -e *cage*
der Krimi, -s *detective story, mystery*
die Narbe, -n *scar*
der Papagei, -en *parrot*
die Person, -en *person; characters
  (in a story, etc.)*
die Polizei *police*
die Polizeiwache, -n *police station*

das Reihenhaus, ⸚er *row house*
der Sack, ⸚e *sack*
der Sammler *collector*
der Schlüssel *key*
der Schnurrbart, ⸚e *mustache*
die Stimme, -n *voice*
der Telefonanruf, -e *telephone call*
der Trenchcoat, -s *trenchcoat*
das Vogelfutter *bird food*
der Zoowärter *zoo keeper*

backen (bäckt, hat gebacken)
  to bake
beobachten (beobachtet, hat
  beobachtet) *to observe*
sauber • machen (macht sauber, hat
  saubergemacht) *to clean*

schreien (schreit, hat geschrien)
  to scream, cry
stehlen (stiehlt, hat gestohlen)
  to steal
tragen (trägt, hat getragen) *to wear*
s. um • schauen (schaut sich um, hat
  sich umgeschaut) *to look around*
verkaufen an A (verkauft, hat
  verkauft) *to sell to*
glatt *straight*
gutherzig *kindhearted*
komisch *funny*
lockig *curly*
nervös *nervous*
rund *round*

schlank *slim*
schlecht gelaunt *in a bad mood*
schwierig *difficult*
seltsam *strange*
ungeduldig *impatient*
verdächtig *suspicious*
zerstreut *absent-minded*
zierlich *delicate*
besonders *especially*
Fragen stellen *to ask questions*
nebenan *next door*
in Ordnung *okay*
spurlos verschwunden *disappeared*
  without a trace
überall *everywhere*

Und so sagst du das... *Here's how to . . .*

say how long something has been going on

Er arbeitet seit fünf Wochen im Zoo. *He has been working in the zoo for five weeks.*

ask about someone's appearance

Wie sieht der Inspektor aus? *What does the inspector look like?*

talk about someone's appearance

Er sieht gut aus. *He is handsome.*
Sie ist ein schönes Mädchen. *She is a pretty girl.*

Taking a closer look

1. Locate all the cognates on the above list.
2. Which verbs have a separable prefix? Write a sentence with each verb in the present tense and in the conversational past.
3. Which verbs have a stem vowel change? What is the change? Where does it occur?

ÜBUNG **M**

Ratespiel. One student goes out of the room. The rest of the class chooses another person. The student in the hall returns and asks questions of the class to determine which student they have chosen.

KULTURECKE

Redewendungen: So sagt man das!

Colorful sayings and expressions such as the one you read in this lesson (**einen Vogel haben**) are found in all languages, many of them in German. Some are the same as in English, others are different. What do the expressions below mean? Is the expression the same in English? If not, what is an equivalent expression?

- Sie hat einen Vogel.
- Er hat nicht alle Tassen im Schrank.
- Er ist ganz Ohr.
- Sie ist das fünfte Rad am Wagen.
- Er sieht die Welt durch eine rosa Brille.
- Sie wirft das Kind mit dem Badewasser aus.
- Sie kann das Gras wachsen hören.
- Lieber einen Spatz in der Hand als eine Taube auf dem Dach.
- Er macht aus einer Mücke immer einen Elefanten.
- Bei ihm ist eine Schraube locker.
- Sie hat die Katze im Sack gekauft.
- Er hat die Katze aus dem Sack gelassen.

19

Zeitungen und Zeitschriften

Unpreceded Adjectives;
The Simple Past

1 Wortschatz

Schlagzeilen

Neuer Look für den Frühling:
Die 70iger Jahre kommen wieder!

1

Grosser Sturm über
dem Atlantik

2

JUNGES EHEPAAR GEWINNT
2 MILLIONEN MARK!

3

Tragischer Unfall am Marktplatz

4

Snowboarder und
Bungeejumper—
moderne Eltern machen alles
mit ihren Kindern mit!

5

Deutsche Fussballmannschaft:
Weltcup in Aussicht?

6

Spannender Krimi jetzt im
Royal Film-Palast

7

Amerikanischer Präsident trifft
sich mit deutschem Bundeskanzler

8

Neues Restaurant bietet
vietnamesisches Essen

9

DEUTSCHE TECHNO-GRUPPE
GROSSER ERFOLG IN JAPAN

10

ÜBUNG A

Read the headlines and see if you can place them in the appropriate category. Write the number of the headline under the corresponding category title.

Politik	Wetter	Unterhaltung (*Entertainment*)	Sport	Mode	Eltern und Kinder	Sonstiges (*Misc.*)

2 Underline the adjectives in the headlines. What do you notice about them? —They are not preceded by a determiner (definite or indefinite article or **der**-word or **ein**-word). Circle the ending on each adjective. What do the endings remind you of? —They remind you of the definite articles. Adjectives not preceded by determiners have endings that show gender.

	NOMINATIVE	ACCUSATIVE	DATIVE
MASC.	der grosse Sturm ein grosser Sturm grosser Sturm	den grossen Sturm einen grossen Sturm grossen Sturm	dem grossen Sturm einem grossen Sturm grossem Sturm
FEMI.	die deutsche Schule eine deutsche Schule deutsche Schule	die deutsche Schule eine deutsche Schule deutsche Schule	der deutschen Schule einer deutschen Schule deutscher Schule
NEUT.	das gute Essen ein gutes Essen gutes Essen	das gute Essen ein gutes Essen gutes Essen	dem guten Essen einem guten Essen gutem Essen
PLUR.	die kleinen Kinder kleine Kinder	die kleinen Kinder kleine Kinder	den kleinen Kindern kleinen Kindern

When adjectives are derived from names of cities, the ending is always **-er**.

Das *Münchner* Oktoberfest ist eigentlich im September.
Die *Frankfurter* Zeitung ist sehr gut.

There are a few names of countries and regions that also follow this rule.

***Schweizer* Käse und *Schweizer* Schokolade sind weltbekannt.**
Das ist eine *Schwarzwälder* Kirchtorte.

ÜBUNG B

Rewrite the phrases as they might appear in each headline. Follow the example.

BEISPIEL: **das junge Mädchen**   **Junges Mädchen ins Wasser gefallen.**

1. der alte Mann   _____ gewinnt Senioren-Olympiade!

2. das kleine Kind   _____ vermisst!

3. das schöne Wetter   _____ für morgen angesagt!

4. der teure Wagen   _____ gestohlen!

5. die neue Mode   _____: Inlineskating!

6. die deutschen Kinder   _____ sehen zu viel fern!

ÜBUNG C

You and a friend are looking at restaurant ads in the newspaper and deciding where to go. What kind of food do you like? Say you like each kind of food listed and suggest going to that kind of an ethnic restaurant. (If there are some you don't like, substitute others!)

chinesisch	**mexikanisch**	**französisch**
griechisch	**italienisch**	**thailändisch**

BEISPIEL: **Ich mag _chinesisches_ Essen. Gehen wir in ein _chinesisches_ Restaurant!**

1. _____

_____

2. _____

_____

3. _____

_____

4. _____

_____

5. _____

_____

ÜBUNG D

With a partner, discuss where to go to get something to eat. Consider different kinds of ethnic foods.

BEISPIEL: Du: **Gehen wir in *ein chinesisches* Restaurant.**
Partner: ***Chinesisches* Essen mag ich nicht. Gehen wir lieber in ein...**

ÜBUNG E

You and your partner have decided on a restaurant. In the restaurant, you are both pleased with the food. Your partner makes a comment, you respond. Write your response, using an unpreceded adjective. Follow the example.

BEISPIEL: Partner: **Die Kartoffeln sind *neu*.**
Du: **Prima! Ich mag *neue* Kartoffeln!**

1. Partner: Der Kuchen ist warm.

   Du: _____

2. Partner: Die Brötchen sind frisch.

   Du: _____

3. Partner Der Kaffee ist stark.

   Du: _____

4. Partner: Die Suppe ist kalt.

   Du: _____

5. Partner: Das Essen ist vegetarisch.

   Du: _____

ÜBUNG F

Here are some ads from newspapers. Fill in the missing adjective endings.

Kaufhaus Knüller

Ultraleicht____ Boots aus Leder,
Leinen und Nylon
All____ Grössen
Toll____ Preise!

Schön____ Sommerkleid
für heiss____ Tage!

Bunt____ T-Shirts
in lustig____ Farben!

Schick____ Jeansrock!
nur DM 35,00

Lang____ Regenmantel
für sie und Für ihn!

Internationaler Supermarkt am Rathausplatz

Exquisit___ Spezialitäten aus all___ Welt

Wir haben
dänisch_____ Butter
spanisch_____ Oliven
argentinisch_____ Fleisch
Schweiz_____ Schokolade

französisch_____ Käse
holländisch_____ Tomaten
brasilianisch_____ Kaffee
Münchn_____ Weisswürste

italienisch_____ Eis
norwegisch_____ Fisch
chinesisch_____ Tee
Schwarzwäld_____
Schinken

3 Read the following excerpts from newspaper articles. Can you tell what each one is about?

Mit gestohlenem Auto zum Banküberfall

Ein unbekannter Mann ging heimlich in die Umkleidekabinen vom Kornwestheimer Hallenbad und stahl einen Autoschlüssel. Er benutzte dann das Auto eines Badegastes, um eine Bank zu überfallen.

der Banküberfall *bank robbery*

das Hallenbad *indoor swimming pool*
der Badegast *pool patron*

Fahrradhelme mit lustigem Design

Neue Fahrradhelme sollen Kinderköpfe schützen. Bei Fahrradunfällen haben mehr als 60 Prozent der verunglückten Radler Kopfverletzungen, aber bis jetzt wollten Jugendliche keine Fahrradhelme tragen. «Fahrradhelme sehen doof aus», meinten sie, «und sie sind unbequem.» Der neue «Mercedes-Helm» gibt es jetzt in sechs lustigen Designs und ist «sehr bequem.»

der Fahrradhelm *bicycle helmet*

schützen *to protect*
der Fahrradunfalle *bicycle accident*
verunglückten Radler *bicycle riders injured in an accident*

Guter Rat im Frühling

Der Winter war sehr lang. Sie sassen sehr viel im warmen Zimmer und bewegten sich nicht! Es war zu kalt zum Spazierengehen, und der Aerobics-Kurs war zu weit weg! Aber jetzt wollen Sie fit und schön in den Sommer hinein! Fangen Sie heute mit unserem Fitness-Programm an!

der Rat *advice*

MASSENKARAMBOLAGE IM NEBEL

In dichtem Nebel gab es am Freitagmorgen eine Massen-karambolage auf der Autobahn südlich von München. Achtzig Personenautos und Lastwagen stiessen zusam-men. Es gab vier Tote und vierzig Verletzte.

der Nebel *fog*

die Autobahn *superhighway*

der Tote *dead (person), fatality*

Junge Ohren in Gefahr — Laute Musik führt zu Schwerhörigkeit

Forscher an der Universität Giessen stellten neulich fest, dass 80 Prozent aller 20-jährigen in Deutschland Hörschaden hat. Ursache Nummer eins: viel zu laute Musik in Diskotheken, bei Rockkonzerten und aus dem Walkman.

in Gefahr *in danger*
die Schwerhörigkeit *difficulty hearing*

der Hörschaden *hearing loss*

ÜBUNG G

Answer the questions in English to check your comprehension.

1. Which article has a solution for reducing head injuries suffered in bicycle accidents?

2. Why did the man in Kornwestheim steal a car?

3. Why should people start with a fitness program in the spring?

4. What was discovered by researchers at the University of Giessen?

5. What happened on the **Autobahn** south of Munich?

6. What do you think the word **Massenkarambolage** means?

4 The articles you just read mentioned things that have already happened. You have learned to talk about the past using a form of the verb called the conversational past. This form is used in conversation and in informal writing. There is another verb form that is mainly used in more formal writing such as newspaper articles. It is called the simple past or the narrative past.

The simple past is used to tell a story or relate a sequence of events. It is sometimes used for this purpose in conversation also to avoid having too many verbs in succession. Using the simple past in such instances results in a clearer, more understandable style.

Read the following paragraph and pay attention to the verb forms. They are in the simple past.

> Am Samstag *hatte* ich eine Party. Die Party *fing* um 7 Uhr *an*. Meine Freunde *kamen*, und jeder *brachte* etwas zu essen *mit*. Wir *assen* und *tranken*, wir *tanzten* und *lachten*. Es *war* sehr lustig! Die Zeit *ging* schnell *vorbei*. Wir *wussten* nicht, dass es so spät *war*! Wir *mussten* noch alles aufräumen. Stefan und Julia *sollten* um 11 Uhr wieder zu Hause sein. Sie *konnten* nicht bleiben, aber sie *kamen* am nächsten Tag *zurück* und *halfen mit*.

You remember learning about weak and strong verbs in Lesson 6. Weak verbs follow a regular pattern. In the conversational past, the past participle ends in **-t: sagen, sagt, hat gesagt**. Strong verbs show irregularity. In the conversational past, the past participle ends in **-en: sehen, sieht, hat gesehen**.

The simple past of weak verbs is also regular. The past tense marker **-te** is added to the verb stem. The first and third persons singular do not have additional endings.

sagen	VERB STEM	PAST TENSE MARKER	ENDING	
ich	sag-	te	—	ich *sagte*
du	sag-	te	st	du *sagtest*
er/sie/es	sag-	te	—	er/sie/es *sagte*
wir	sag-	te	n	wir *sagten*
ihr	sag-	te	t	ihr *sagtet*
sie/Sie	sag-	te	n	sie/Sie *sagten*

Verbs with stems ending in **-d** or **-t** add an additional **-e** to the past tense marker.

reden	red-	ete	--	ich *redete*
arbeiten	arbeit-	ete	st	du *arbeitetest*

ÜBUNG H

Write the simple past for each of the following verbs. Do you remember what these verbs mean?

BEISPIEL: **ich wohne**   ich *wohnte*

1. er lernt _____

2. du räumst auf _____

3. sie macht _____

4. ich telefoniere _____

5. er beeilt sich _____

6. wir hören _____

7. wir amüsieren uns _____

8. es regnet _____

9. wir spielen _____

10. du kaufst ein _____

11. ich setze mich _____

12. es bedeutet _____

ÜBUNG I

Write the present tense for each of the following verbs. Can you give the meaning of each verb?

BEISPIEL: **ich wartete**   ich *warte*

1. er brauchte _____

2. ich machte mit _____

3. du arbeitetest _____

4. wir holten _____

5. Sie bestellten _____

6. ich kämmte mich _____

7. wir gratulierten _____

8. sie sammelte _____

9. er übte _____

10. ich besuchte _____

11. er bereitete vor _____

12. wir frühstückten _____

5 In the simple past, strong verbs have a stem vowel change: **sehen** to **sah, trinken** to **trank**. The irregularities in strong verbs are not predictable. You have to learn them as you learn each verb. The parts of the verb that you learn are called the principal parts. For example, for the verb **sehen**, *to see*, you learn: **sieht, sah, hat gesehen**.

The first and third persons singular of strong verbs do not have an ending in the simple past. Here are the forms.

ich	sah		wir	sahen
du	sahst		ihr	saht
er/sie/es	sah		Sie/sie	sahen

Complete this chart showing the principal parts of several common verbs.

INFINITIVE	PRESENT	SIMPLE PAST	CONVERSATIONAL PAST
bleiben *to stay*	er/sie bleibt	blieb	ist geblieben
essen _____	_____	ass	hat gegessen
fahren _____	_____	fuhr	_____
finden _____	_____	fand	_____
geben _____	_____	gab	_____
gehen _____	_____	ging	_____
lesen _____	_____	las	_____
kommen _____	_____	kam	_____
nehmen _____	_____	nahm	_____
sehen _____	_____	sah	_____
sitzen _____	_____	sass	_____
stehen _____	_____	stand	_____
tun _____	_____	tat	_____

The simple past is used mostly in writing. At this stage in your learning, it is only necessary for you to recognize the simple past. There are a few simple past forms, however, that are very commonly used in speaking and in writing, and you should learn them.

	HABEN (to have)	SEIN (to be)	WERDEN (to become)
ich	hatte	war	wurde
du	hattest	warst	wurdest
er/sie/es	hatte	war	wurde
wir	hatten	waren	wurden
ihr	hattet	wart	wurdet
sie, sie	hatten	waren	wurden

ÜBUNG J

Complete each sentence with the simple past of **haben**.

1. Ich _____ keine Zeit.
2. Wir _____ die Zeitung.
3. Robert _____ einen Unfall.
4. Ihr _____ eine Party.
5. Meine Mutter _____ Geburtstag.
6. Die Kinder _____ Fahrräder.

ÜBUNG K

Complete each sentence with the simple past of **sein**.

1. Wo _____ du?
2. Ihr _____ nicht in der Schule.
3. Die Lehrerin _____ krank.
4. Ich _____ müde.
5. Meine Eltern _____ zu Hause.
6. Wir _____ in der Stadt.

ÜBUNG L

Complete each sentence with the simple past of **werden**.

1. Ich _____ im Mai 14.
2. Wann _____ du krank?
3. Wir _____ nicht müde.
4. Ihr _____ erst im Juli 14?
5. Julia und Benjamin _____ lustig.
6. Der Lehrer _____ ungeduldig.

ÜBUNG **M**

Hör gut zu! You will hear a number of statements. Determine whether each one is in the present tense or in the simple past. Mark the corresponding box.

	1	2	3	4	5	6	7	8	9	10
PRESENT										
SIMPLE PAST										

PERSÖNLICHE FRAGEN ?

1. Welche Zeitung lest ihr zu Hause?

   _____

2. Welche Zeitschriften lesen deine Eltern?

   _____

3. Welche Zeitschriften liest du?

   _____

4. Was ist deine Lieblingszeitschrift?

   _____

5. Habt ihr eine Schülerzeitung in eurer Schule? Wenn ja, wie heisst sie?

   _____

6. Machst du bei der Zeitung mit? Wenn ja, was machst du?

   _____

ÜBUNG N

Here is a picture story about an accident. The following sentences describing the accident are out of order. Rearrange the story by putting the number next to the correct sentence.

Eine traurige Geschichte

1

2

3

4

5

6

7

8

9

10   11   12

_____ Sie erzählten Witze und lachten.

_____ Fritz sah den Lastwagen nicht. Er fuhr zu weit nach links und fuhr gegen den Lastwagen.

_____ Fritz hatte eine Kopfverletzung. Er hatte sich auch den Arm und das Bein gebrochen.

_____ Fritz lag auf der Strasse. Er hatte am Bein furchtbare Schmerzen.

_____ Am Freitag nach der Schule fuhren sie mit dem Rad die Strasse entlang.

_____ Franz ging schnell und holte einen Polizisten. Viele Leute standen herum und wollten helfen.

_____ Sie machten Dummheiten. Sie passten nicht auf den Verkehr auf.

_____ Es war ein schöner, sonniger Tag.

_____ Fritz und Franz waren gute Freunde.

_____ Da kam ein kleiner Lastwagen.

_____ Der Krankenwagen kam und fuhr Fritz ins Krankenhaus.

_____ Moral: Pass auf im Verkehr und mach keine Dummheiten!

KLASSENPROJEKT

Make a German class newspaper. Include reports on events, announcements, interviews, funny ads, and comics.

WORTSCHATZ A-Z

die Autobahn, -en *superhighway*

der Banküberfall, ¨e *bank robbery*

der Bundeskanzler *Chancellor of Germany*

das Ehepaar, -e *married couple*

der Erfolg, -e *success*

der Fahrradhelm, -e *bicycle helmet*

die Gefahr, -en *danger*

das Hallenbad, ¨er *indoor swimming pool*

der Hörschaden *hearing loss*

der Jugendliche, -n* *young person*

die Karambolage, -n *huge crash or collision*

der Lastwagen *truck*

die Mannschaft, -en *team*

der Rat *advice*

die Schlagzeile, -n *headline*

der Sturm, ¨e *storm*

der Tote, -n* *fatality, dead (person)*

der Unfall, ¨e *accident*

die Ursache, -n *cause*

der Verletzte, -n* *injured (person)*

die Verletzung, -en *injury*

die Zeitschrift, -en *magazine*

die Zeitung, -en *newspaper*

benutzen *to use*

bieten (bietet, bot, hat geboten) *to offer*

fest•stellen *to find out, determine*

führen zu *to lead to*

gewinnen (gewinnt, gewann, hat gewonnen) *to win*

schützen *to protect*

s. treffen mit (triff, traf, hat getroffen) *to meet with*

überfallen (überfällt, überfiel, hat überfallen) *to rob*

zusammen•stossen (stösst zusammen, stiess zusammen, ist zusammengestossen) *to collide*

neulich *recently*

spannend *thrilling*

südlich von *south of*

tragisch *tragic*

in Aussicht *in sight*

Schwarzwälderkirschtorte *Black Forest cherry cake*

Schweizer Schokolade *Swiss chocolate*

Taking a closer look

1. Which verbs are strong and which are weak? How can you tell?
2. Write the principal parts of the weak verbs.

* These nouns add an -n in the accusative and dative case: **der Jugendliche, den Jugendlichen, dem Jugendlichen; der Tote, den Toten, dem Toten; der Verletzte, den Verletzten, dem Verletzten.**

ÜBUNG O

Lustige Schlagzeilen. Write the following categories on the board and brainstorm some suggestions for each one: **wer?, was?, wo?, mit wem?** Form groups of four and give each group a piece of paper. The first person answers the question **wer?** and folds over the paper so what has been written can't be seen. The next person answers the question **was?** and folds over the paper. The third answers **wo?** and the fourth **mit wem?** Then, each group reads its headline to the class.

KULTURECKE

Germany has many newspapers. Local and regional ones provide international and national news as well as local news, advertisements for local stores and businesses, announcements, and information about local events. There are also numerous influential national newspapers, such as *Die Frankfurter Allgemeine*, *Die Weit*, and *Die Süddeutsche Zeitung*.

There are more than 20,000 periodicals published in Germany. Here are some popular titles.

News magazines: *Spiegel*, *Focus*

Illustrated magazines: *Stern*, *Bunte*, *Quick*

Women's magazines: *Brigitte*, *Freundin*

Youth's magazines: *Bravo*, *Bravo Girl*, *Mädchen*, *Popcorn*, *Pop Rocky*

Radio and TV magazines with programming schedules: *Hör zu*, *Hören und Sehen*

A recent magazine survey provided some information on the reading habits of young people today—how much they read and what they read.

Was machen Jugendliche am liebsten an einem normalen Wochentag?	
Fernsehen	51%
Lesen	30%
Musikhören	24%
Freunden	18%
Sport	15%

Was lesen Jugendliche am liebsten?	
Zeitschriften	47%
Bücher	32%
Comics	20%
Zeitungen	12%

20

Was kommt im Fernsehen?

The Future

1 Wortschatz

Aus einem Fernsehprogramm

1. PROGRAMM

6.00 **ML-Mona Lisa** Frauenjournal
6.45 **Sportschau** Resultate und Berichte
7.00 **Bonn direkt** Berichte, Kommentare, Analysen und Diskussion
8.00 **Du und dein Haustier** Tips und Ratschläge
8.30 **Gesund und gut** Gesund kochen und essen
9.00 **Mord ist ihr Hobby** Krimiserie mit Angela Lansbury
10.00 **Bärbel Schäfer** Talkshow
11.00 **Cartoons** Asterix in Spanien, Wickie, Scooby Doo, Tom und Jerry, die Schlümpfe
12.00 **Info: Arbeit und Beruf**
13.00 **Nachrichten und Wetter**
13.15 **Die deutsche Hitparade**
14.00 **Kinderquatsch mit Michael** Spiele, Lieder, lustige Geschichten mit Michael Schanze
15.00 **Batman** Comicserie: «Fünf vor zwölf» Batman und Robin versuchen, den Uhrenkönig zu überwältigen.
16.00 **Kidz** Nadine, Melanie, Remo und Mario servieren euch ein tolles Programm
16.30 **Melrose Place** Jugendserie
17.00 **Gute Zeiten, schlechte Zeiten** Unterhaltungsserie: Claudius will noch mehr Geld von Tina
17.45 **Die Sportreportage** mit Magdalena Müller: Fussball und Eishockey—Bundesliga Play-off

2. PROGRAMM

6.00 **Morgenmagazin**
8.00 **Bananas in Pyjamas** Die hilfsbereiten Zwillingsbananen B1 und B2 versuchen, Gutes zu tun.

8.30 **Sesamstrasse**
9.15 **Aerobic** mit Tanya Taros
10.00 **Traumurlaub** Reisebilder aus Griechenland
11.00 **Der Preis ist heiss** Spielshow
11.30 **Familienduell** Spiel, Spass und grosse Gewinne
12.00 **Vera am Mittag** Talkshow
13.00 **Mittagsmagazin**
13.15 **Zeit für Musik** Kurt Masur dirigiert das Leipziger Gewandhaus Orchester
14.00 **Sport Aktuell** Eiskunstlauf-Weltmeisterschaft für Damen
15.00 **Das Recht zu lieben** Unterhaltungsserie
15.30 **Reich und schön** Unterhaltungsserie

18.30 Eine schrecklich nette Familie Komödie
19.00 Musik Revue Die Junior-Jazzband und Eva Dostalova singen und spielen heisse Rhythmen
19.30 Glücksrad Die grosse Gewinnshow aus Berlin
20.00 Tagesschau
20.15 Der Bergdoktor Arztserie: «Tropenfieber». Christl arbeitet seit Jahren als Krankenschwester in Äthiopien. Heute kommt sie zu Besuch, aber es geht nicht alles wie geplant.
21.00 Akte X - Die unheimlichen Fälle des FBI Krimiserie: «Der Zirkus» Scully und Mulder untersuchen in Florida einen Mord im Zirkus.
22.00 Gottschalks Hausparty Gäste, Gespräche und Spiele mit Superquassler Thomas Gottschalk
23.00 Die Harald Schmidt-Show Late-Night-Talk

16.00 Spiderman (Der Spinnenmensch) Phantasiefilm (USA, 1977)
17.00 Zurück in die Vergangenheit Science-fiction-Serie
17.30 Musikszene Internationale Musikvideos
18.00 Mensch, bleib gesund Gymnastik für die ganze Familie
18.30 Explosiv — Das Starmagazin
19.00 Heute Journal
19.15 Weltspiegel Auslandskorrespondenten berichten
20.00 Olympiade der Tiere Höher, schneller, stärker — Mensch und Tier im Vergleich
21.00 Derrick Krimiserie: «Mord um Mitternacht» Das Detektiv-Team Horst Tappert und Fritz Wepper entdecken einen Mörder
22.00 Tagesthemen
22.30 Videodrome Horrorfilm (USA 1982) James Woods und Deborah Harry. Ein Schocker

ÜBUNG

Refer to the TV program to answer the questions.

1. Wann kommt das «Morgenmagazin»? Um wieviel Uhr?

2. Wie heisst ein Krimi, der um 21.00 kommt?

3. Was für eine Sendung ist «Eine schrecklich nette Familie»?

4. In welcher Sendung siehst du Magdalena Müller?

5. Wie heisst eine Talkshow Moderatorin?

6. Wer sind die Stars in der Sendung «Kidz»?

7. Wie heisst eine Sendung, die aus den USA kommt?

8. Welche Sendungen siehst du dir an, wenn du Tiere gern hast?

ÜBUNG B

Here is a list of different categories of shows. For each one, write the name of a show that is on the TV program that fits that category.

1. Nachrichten _____

2. Sport _____

3. Politik _____

4. Reisen _____

5. Film _____

6. Krimi _____

7. Komödie _____

8. Cartoon _____

9. Spielshow _____

10. Talkshow _____

11. Unterhaltungsserie _____

12. Musik _____

13. Gesundheit _____

14. Kindersendung _____

15. Jugendsendung _____

2 Toni and Stefan are talking about what they're going to watch on TV tonight. Read their conversation. Notice the verb they use to express what they're going to watch.

TONI: Was siehst du dir heute abend im Fernsehen an?

STEFAN: Ich sehe mir «Akte X» an. Du auch?

TONI: Na, klar! Mein Bruder und ich, wir sehen uns die «Akte X» immer an! Mein Vater sieht sich die Sendung auch an.

STEFAN: Seht ihr euch um 20 Uhr die «Olympiade der Tiere» an?

TONI: Meine Schwester und mein Bruder sehen sich das an. Ich muss meine Hausaufgaben machen, damit ich mir um 21 Uhr die «Akte X» ansehen kann.

STEFAN: Ich sehe mir Tiersendungen sehr gern an. Ich mache am Nachmittag meine Hausaufgaben.

3 The verb **sich etwas ansehen** (to look at, to watch something) has a number of characteristics. It is a _____ verb with a _____ prefix. The reflexive pronoun is in the _____ case. This verb, like the related verb **sehen,** which you already know, has a stem vowel change: **e** changes to _____ in the **du** and **er/sie**-form. Underline the forms of the verb **sich etwas ansehen** in the conversation above, then complete the following sentences with the correct forms of that verb.

Ich _____ _____ die Sportschau an.

Du _____ _____ einen Film an.

Toni (Er) _____ _____ die «Akte X» an.

Julia (Sie) _____ _____ «Derrick» an.

Wir _____ _____ die Nachrichten an.

Ihr _____ _____ ein Spielshow an.

Die Kinder (Sie) _____ _____ «Kinderquatsch mit Michael» an.

Now complete the same sentences again, this time in the conversational past. The conversational past of **sehen** is **hat gesehen**. What do you think the conversational past of **sich etwas ansehen** is? _____

Ich_____ _____ die Sportschau _____.

Du _____ _____ einen Film _____.

Toni (Er) _____ _____ die «Akte X» _____.

Julia (Sie) _____ _____ «Derrick» _____.

Wir _____ _____ die Nachrichten _____.

Ihr _____ _____ ein Spielshow _____.

Die Kinder (Sie) _____ _____ «Kinderquatsch mit Michael»

_____.

ÜBUNG C

Practice using the verb **sich etwas ansehen** by answering the following questions with a complete sentence. Refer to the preceding dialogue.

1. Was sieht sich Toni heute abend an?

   _____

2. Was sieht sich Stefan heute abend an?

   _____

3. Was sieht sich Tonis Vater an?

   _____

4. Was sehen sich Tonis Schwester und Bruder an?

   _____

ÜBUNG D

From the TV schedule on pages 398 and 399, pick five programs that you would like to see.

Was möchtest du dir ansehen?

Ich möchte mir _____

_____

_____ **ansehen.**

ÜBUNG **E**

Write what you actually watched on TV yesterday.

Was hast du dir gestern im Fernsehen angesehen?

Ich habe mir _____

_____

_____ **angesehen.**

ÜBUNG **F**

Partnerarbeit. Ask your partner what he or she would like to see and why. Then your partner asks you. Do you agree with each other? Here are some words you can use to describe why you like or don't like particular shows.

gut!   schlecht!

spannend _thrilling, exciting_	**langweilig** _boring_
interessant _interesting_	**uninteressant** _uninteresting_
lustig _funny_	**zu traurig** _too sad_
unterhaltend _entertaining_	**zu brutal** _too violent_
lehrreich _educational_	**grausam** _cruel_
fantasievoll _imaginative_	**zu schmalzig** _too corny_

You have been using the present tense to express what is going to happen at some future time.

Ich mache meine Hausaufgaben.
I'm going to do my homework. *

When the present tense is used to express future time, a word is often used that indicates the future time.

Ich sehe mir heute abend die «Akte X» an.
I'm going to watch "The X-Files" tonight. *

A third way to express future time is to use the verb **werden** plus an infinitive. The conjugated verb **werden** is in second position in the clause or sentence; the infinitive is in last position.

Er *wird* den Lehrer *fragen*.
He will ask the teacher.

Ich *werde* das Buch *lesen*.
I will read the book.

You learned the forms of **werden** in Lesson 11. Here they are again.

ich *werde* fragen	wir *werden* fragen
du *wirst* fragen	ihr *werdet* fragen
er/sie *wird* fragen	sie/Sie *werden* fragen

In Lesson 5 you learned the modal verbs (**wollen, sollen, müssen, können, dürfen,** and **mögen**). With the modals, as with the future tense, the conjugated verb is in second position and the infinitive is at the end of the clause or sentence.

Ich *werde* mir den Krimi *ansehen*. *I'm going to watch the mystery.*
Ich *will* mir den Krimi *ansehen*. *I want to watch the mystery.*

Be sure not to confuse **werden** + *infinitive* and **wollen** + *infinitive*.

Ich *werde gehen*. *I will go.*
Ich *will gehen*. *I want to go.*

ÜBUNG **G**

Your little brother wants to do everything you do. You make a statement, he says he will do the same thing. Write what he says, using the future tense — **werden** + *infinitive*. Follow the example.

BEISPIEL: Du: **Ich gehe ins Kino.**
Dein Bruder: **Ich werde auch ins Kino gehen.**

*Note that the phrase "going to" is used in English but is not literally translated into German.

1. Ich spiele Basketball.

   _____

2. Ich sehe mir den Krimi an.

   _____

3. Ich esse einen Apfel.

   _____

4. Ich lese die Zeitung.

   _____

5. Ich fahre in die Stadt.

   _____

ÜBUNG **H**

Write sentences in the future, using an element from each box.

er Anna wir ich du Beni und Max ihr	werden wird werdet wirst werde	heute später nächste Woche morgen bald am Samstag am Wochenende	eine Radtour machen einkaufen gehen Karten spielen eine Party haben Pizza essen in die Stadt fahren nach Hause kommen

1. _____

2. _____

3. _____

4. _____

5. _____

6. _____

7. _____

ÜBUNG I

What's in the future for you? Complete the following survey.

Wie sieht deine Zukunft aus? Was wirst du tun?

Ich werde...

zur Universität gehen
zum Militär gehen
einen interessanten Job finden
einen guten Beruf erlernen
reisen

Ich interessiere mich für...

Sport
Musik
Wissenschaft
Politik
Computer

Ich werde (vielleicht)... studieren.

Medizin	Jura	Biologie	Informatik
Sprachen	Geschichte	Literatur	Psychologie

Ich werde (vielleicht)... werden.*

Arzt/Ärztin	Informatiker/in	Ingenieur/in	Polizist/in
Lehrer/in	Krankenpfleger/in	Schauspieler/in	Architekt/in
Künstler/in	Astronaut/in	Journalist/in	Rechtsanwalt/ Rechtsanwältin

---

ÜBUNG J

Interview a classmate using the following questions as a guide. Then your classmate will interview you. Use the following questions as a guide.

1. Wofür interessierst du dich? Ich interessiere mich für...

2. Was wirst du nach der Schule machen? Ich werde...

3. Was wirst du studieren? Ich werde...

4. Was wirst du werden? Ich werde (vielleicht)...

---

*Note that in German there is no indefinite article before the profession as in English.

Ich werde Arzt. *I am going to be a doctor.*

ÜBUNG K

Report what your partner says to the class. Then, as each student reports, jot down the information. Using the notes you have taken, write a few sentences about three students in the class.

1. _____

_____

_____

_____

2. _____

_____

_____

_____

3. _____

_____

_____

_____

Now write a few sentences about yourself.

Meine Zukunft

_____

_____

_____

_____

ÜBUNG L

Hör gut zu! Listen to the following comments and determine if each one refers to something that happened in the past, something that is happening now, or something that will happen in the future.

	1	2	3	4	5	6	7	8
PAST								
PRESENT								
FUTURE								

5 Through cable TV (**Kabelfernsehen**) and video rentals (**Leihvideos**), there are many opportunities to see films in Germany just as there are in the United States. Here is a page from a TV magazine that gives information about movies that are going to be shown this week.

Fernsehwoche-Magazin gibt Filmtips

Benji: sein grösstes Abenteuer
Tierfilm (USA, 1987)

Der Hund Benji fällt aus dem Boot und strandet in der Wildnis. Er findet dort eine Gruppe von Puma-Babies.

Silverado
Western (USA, 1985)

Kevin Costner spielt die Rolle von dem Revolverhelden Jake. Das war der Beginn von Costners Super-Karriere.

Star Trek III: Auf der Suche nach Mr. Spock
Science-fiction-Film von Leonard Nimroy mit William Shatner. Spocks Vater Savik will die Leiche seines Sohnes zu dem Heimatplaneten Vulkan zurückbringen.

Das Piano
Liebesfilm von Jane Campion mit Holly Hunter
(Australien/Frankreich, 1994)

Um 1850 kommt die stumme Ada mit ihrer kleinen Tochter Flora von Schottland nach Neuseeland. Sie soll dort einen Mann heiraten, den sie überhaupt nicht kennt.

Der Chef
Kriminalfilm (Frankreich, 1972)

Das Kino Traumpaar von Frankreich, Catherine Deneuve und Alain Delon, spielen in diesem spannenden Krimi von Jean-Pierre Melville.

Bills und Teds verrückte Reise durch die Zeit
Komödie mit Keanu Reeves (USA, 1988)

Bill und Ted lernen Geschichte.

Edgar Wallace: Der Blinde
Kriminalfilm mit Joachim Kemmer (Deutschland, 1995)

In London verschwinden auf mysteriöse Weise junge Mädchen auf offener Strasse. Jedes Mal steht ein Blinder in der Nähe.

James Bond 007: Goldfinger
Actionfilm (England, 1964)

Sean Connery ist der einmalige Agent James Bond.

Godzilla — Die Rückkehr des Monsters
Horrorfilm (Japan, 1984)

Das Monster Godzilla terrorisiert die Küste Japans.

Projekt B — Jackie Chans gnadenloser Kampf
Karatefilm (Hongkong, 1987)

Jackie Chan als Inspektor Dragon Ma ist voll Action. Tolle Kampf-Akrobatik und viel Humor.

Wolfsblut
Abenteuerfilm mit Ethan Hawke (USA ,1990)

Der junge Jack kommt zur Zeit des grossen Goldrausches nach Alaska. Mit dem erfahrenen Goldgräber Alex trifft er auf einen Mischling zwischen Hund und Wolf.

Der grosse Diktator
Komödie (USA, 1940)

Der unvergessliche Filmklassiker mit Charlie Chaplin.

Erdbeben
Katastrophenfilm mit Charlton Heston (USA, 1974)

Einstürzende Wolkenkratzer und eine tödliche Flutwelle.

Asterix: Operation Hinkelstein
Zeichentrickfilm (Deutschland, 1989)

Die neuesten Abenteuer der weltberühmten Zeichentrickhelden. Super-Comic-Spass für die ganze Familie.

ÜBUNG M

Answer the questions based on the film descriptions from the TV magazine.

1. Was für Filme siehst du gern (Actionfilme, Komödien, usw.)?

_____

_____

2. Welche Filme hast du schon gesehen?

_____

_____

3. Welche Filme möchtest du sehen? Warum? Magst du zum Beispiel Komödien oder hast du vielleicht den Schauspieler oder die Schauspielerin gern?

_____

_____

4. Welche Filme interessieren dich nicht? Warum nicht?

_____

_____

ÜBUNG N

Bring in pictures of movie and television stars and ask your classmates questions. For example: **Wer ist das? Wie heissen seine oder ihre Filme? In welcher Fernseh sendung spielt er oder sie? Wie findest du den Film? Wie findest du die Sendung?**

ÜBUNG O

Bring in a movie ad from your newspaper. Tell the class what kind of a movie it is, whether you've seen it, and why you like it or don't like it.

PERSÖNLICHE FRAGEN

1. Wann siehst du fern? Am Nachmittag? Am Abend?

   _____

2. Wie viele Stunden am Tag siehst du gewöhnlich fern?

   _____

3. Welche Sendungen findest du gut?

   _____

   _____

4. Welche Sendungen findest du nicht so gut?

   _____

   _____

5. Wie heisst deine Lieblingssendung?

   _____

6. Welche Fernsehschauspieler und Schauspielerinnen hast du gern?

   _____

7. Habt ihr Kabelfernsehen?

   _____

8. Gibt es Sendungen, die du nicht sehen darfst? Wie heissen sie? _____

   _____

9. Leihst du oft Videofilme aus?

   _____

10. Was für Filme siehst du gern?

   _____

11. Wer sind deine Lieblingsschauspieler?

   _____

ÜBUNG P

Aufsatz. Write a short composition about your TV and film viewing habits. Use the questions on the preceding page as a guide.

_____

_____

_____

_____

_____

_____

_____

_____

_____

_____

_____

_____

_____

KLASSENPROJEKT

1. Design a TV guide. List various programs and movies. Make up names in German for familiar shows. Note that many English words are used in German listings. Use the TV program on the first two pages of this lesson as a modal.

2. Design ads in German for movies you have seen or would like to see.

WORTSCHATZ A-Z

das Abenteuer *adventure*
der Bericht, -e *report*
der Beruf, -e *trade, occupation*
das Fernsehprogramm, -e *TV
    programming schedule*
der Held, -en (den Helden, dem Helden)
    hero
der Job, -s *job*
die Jugend *youth, young people*
der Kampf, ¨e *fight, struggle*
der Mord, -e *murder*
der Mörder *murderer*
die Nachricht, -en *news report*
das Programm, -e *TV channel, station*
die Sendung, -en *TV program*
die Serie, -n *series*
die Spielshow, -s *game show*
die Sportschau *sports report*
die Tagesschau *news*
die Unterhaltungsserie, -n *drama series*
die Vergangenheit, -en *past*
die Zukunft *future*

Was für ein Film ist das? *What kind of a
    movie is that?*
der Abenteuerfilm, -e *adventure film*
der Actionfilm, -e *action film*
der Katastrophenfilm, -e *disaster film*
die Komödie, -n *comedy*
der Kriminalfilm, -e *crime movie*
der Liebesfilm, -e *love story, romantic
    movie*

der Science-fiction-Film, -e *science
    fiction film*
der Zeichentrickfilm, -e *animated film,
    cartoon*
das Fach, ¨er *subject area*
Informatik *computer science*
Jura *law*
Medizin *medicine*
Wissenschaft *science*
s. etwas an•sehen (sieht sich etwas an,
    sah sich etwas an, hat sich etwas ange
        sehen) *to look at, watch something*
s. interessieren für (interessiert sich für,
    hat sich für etwas interessiert) *to be
    interested in*
studieren (studiert, hat studiert) *to study
    (at a college or university)*
versuchen (versucht, hat versucht) *to try*
einen Beruf erlernen *to learn a trade
    or occupation*
im Fernsehen kommen *to be on TV*
zur Universität gehen *to go to a university*
zum Militär gehen *to join the military*
brutal *violent*
fantasievoll *imaginative*
grausam *cruel*
lehrreich *educational*
spannend *thrilling, exciting*
schmalzig *corny, mushy*
uninteressant *uninteresting*
unterhaltend *entertaining*

Und so sagst du das... *Here's how to . . .*

express future time

Ich sehe mir (heute abend) einen Film an. *I'm watching a movie tonight.*
Ich werde mir heute abend die Nachrichten ansehen. *I'm going to watch the news tonight.*

ask what someone is interested in and tell what you are interested in

Wofür interessierst du dich?   *What are you interested in?*
Ich interessiere mich für Musik.   *I'm interested in music.*

Buiding your vocabulary

1. You can modify and qualify what you want to say by using such words as **zu, sehr, ganz, ziemlich**. For example: **Der Film war...**

   zu schmalzig   *too corny*
   sehr lehrreich   *very educational*

   ziemlich brutal   *rather violent*
   ganz interessant   *quite interesting*

2. Many compounds are formed with the words **Film, Sendung, Schau** or **Show**, and **Serie**. How many can you form?

   _____

   _____

   _____

3. There are many cognates in German in entertainment and media. Find all the ones on this list. What false cognate do you recognize?

   _____

   _____

   _____

Ratespiel: Wie heisst...

Form two teams. Each team makes a list of movies, TV programs, actors, and actresses. Then each team takes a turn asking the other team a question.

Kennt ihr den Film...?
Was für ein Film ist das?
Kennt ihr den Schauspieler...?
Wie heisst ein Film (eine Fernsehsendung) mit diesem Schauspieler?

KULTURECKE

In Germany, there are both public and commercial broadcasting systems. ZDF and ARD are the two nationally transmitted broadcasting networks. A third network, das dritte Programm, provides regional and educational programming.

Since 1985 commercial broadcasting companies have been operating in Germany. They are transmitted by satellite and cable. Some of the most popular ones are RTL and SAT 1, which broadcast mainly sports, entertainment, and feature films, as well as a number of political programs. Other popular companies are Pro 7, offering mainly films, and Tele 5, which specializes in game shows.

American shows and films are extremely popular in Germany. German TV production companies are producing more and more shows and films, however, and they are becoming increasingly popular.

DEUTSCHE SERIEN
Derrick
Tatort
Ein Fall für zwei
Freunde fürs Leben
Die Autobahnpolizei
Verbotene Liebe
Marienhof

US SERIEN
Rosanne
Alf
Eine schrecklich nette Familie
Beverly Hills 90210
Die Simpsons
Baywatch
Der Klient

Wiederholung IV

(Lektion 16-20)

Lektion 16

Using adjectives and adverbs to express comparisons is similar in German and English.

POSITIVE	COMPARATIVE	SUPERLATIVE
gross *big* klein *small*	grösser *bigger* kleiner *smaller*	am grössten *biggest* am kleinsten *smallest*

1. In German, all comparative forms ends in **-er**.

2. Superlative forms end in **-(e)sten** and are used in a phrase beginning with **am**.

3. Most one-syllable adjectives and adverbs add an umlaut in the comparative and superlative forms.

4. Here are some exceptions:

   —Some one-syllable words don't take an umlaut

   blond, blonder, am blondesten
   laut, lauter, am lautesten
   toll, toller, am tollsten

   —Some words have slightly different spellings

   dunkel, dunkler, am dunkelsten
   teuer, teurer, am teuersten

   —Some words change completely

   viel, mehr, am meisten   **gern, lieber, am liebsten**
   gut, besser, am besten   **hoch, höher, am höchsten**

5. When comparing things, you can make equal or unequal comparisons.

   Er läuft *so schnell wie* ich (laufe).   *He runs as fast as I (run).*
   Sie läuft *schneller als* ich (laufe).   *She runs faster than I (run).*

Lektion 17

Adjective Endings after Definite Articles and **dieser**-words

	NOMINATIVE	ACCUSATIVE	DATIVE
MASC. FEM. NEU. PLU.	Wie schön... der weisse Strand die warme Luft das gute Essen die hohen Berge	Ich liebe... den weissen Strand die warme Luft das gute Essen die hohen Berge	Ich bin von... begeistert! dem weissen Strand der warmen Luft dem guten Essen den hohen Bergen

Lektion 18

Adjective Endings after Indefinite Articles and **ein**-words

	NOMINATIVE	ACCUSATIVE	DATIVE
MASC. FEM. NEU.	Das ist... ein blauer Mantel eine weisse Bluse ein gelbes Hemd	Ich habe... einen blauen Mantel eine weisse Bluse ein gelbes Hemd	Das passt zu... einem blauen Mantel einer weissen Bluse einem gelben Hemd
PLU.	Das sind... braune Schuhe meine braunen Schuhe keine braunen Schuhe	Ich habe... braune Schuhe meine braunen Schuhe keine braunen Schuhe	Das passt zu... braunen Schuhen meinen braunen Schuhen keinen braunen Schuhen

Lektion 19

a.   Endings on Unpreceded Adjectives

	NOMINATIVE	ACCUSATIVE	DATIVE
MASC. FEM. NEU. PLU.	grosser Sturm deutsche Schule gutes Essen kleine Kinder	grossen Sturm deutsche Schule gutes Essen kleine Kinder	grossem Sturm deutscher Schule gutem Essen kleinen Kindern

—Adjectives derived from names of cities always end in **-er**.

das Münchner Oktoberfest
die Frankfurter Zeitung

—The names of certain countries and regions also follow this rule.

Schweizer Schokolade
eine Schwarzwälder Kirschtorte

b. The simple past tense is used to tell a story or relate a sequence of events.

—The simple past of weak verbs has the past tense marker **-te**. Verbs with stems ending in **-d** or **-t** add an additional **-e-** to the past tense marker.

	SAGEN	REDEN	ARBEITEN
ich	sagte	redete	arbeitete
du	sagtest	redetest	arbeitetest
er/sie/es	sagte	redete	arbeitete
wir	sagten	redeten	arbeiteten
ihr	sagtet	redetet	arbeitetet
sie/Sie	sagten	redeten	arbeiteten

—The simple past of strong verbs has a stem vowel change. There is no regular pattern, so the forms must be learned as you learn each new strong verb. At this point, however, you just have to able to recognize these forms.

SEHEN	
ich *sah*	wir *sahen*
du *sahst*	ihr *saht*
er/sie/es *sah*	sie/Sie *sahen*

—The simple past tense forms of **haben**, **sein**, and **werden** are very commonly used in both speaking and writing, so you should learn them.

	HABEN	SEIN	WERDEN
ich	hatte	war	wurde
du	hattest	warst	wurdest
er/sie/es	hatte	war	wurde
wir	hatten	waren	wurden
ihr	hattet	wart	wurdet
sie, Sie	hatten	waren	wurden

Lektion 20

There are three ways to express future time in German.

1. You may use the present tense.

   Wir *fahren* in die Stadt.   *We're going to go into the city.*

2. You may use the present tense with a word or phrase that indicates future time.

   Wir *fahren morgen* in die Stadt.   *We're going to go into the city tomorrow.*

3. You may use the future tense: the verb werden plus an infinitive.

   Wir *werden* in die Stadt *fahren*.   *We will go into the city.*

ÜBUNG **A**

Fill in the names of the animals pictured.

ÜBUNG B

With the help of the sentences below, complete the puzzle with verbs ending in **-ieren**.

						I	E	R	E	N
1						I	E	R	E	N
2						I	E	R	E	N
3						I	E	R	E	N
4						I	E	R	E	N
5						I	E	R	E	N
6						I	E	R	E	N
7						I	E	R	E	N
8						I	E	R	E	N

1. Wir machen einen Spaziergang. = Wir gehen _____.

2. *to happen*

3. Ich möchte auf einer Universität _____.

4. Du sollst die Hose _____, bevor du sie kaufst.

5. Dieses Hemd kannst du mit einem Rock oder mit Jeans _____.

6. Wir wollen dir zum Geburtstag ganz herzlich _____.

7. Wir _____ uns nicht für Politik.

8. Ich habe eine neue Kamera, und ich möchte jetzt ganz viel _____.

ÜBUNG C

Identify the verb in each sentence. Then determine if the verb in each sentence is in the present tense, the conversational past, or the future. Write the verbs in the appropriate columns below.

1. Ich werde einen Kuchen backen.
2. Meine Schwester hat ihre Freunde zu einer Party eingeladen.
3. Du trägst heute ein schickes Hemd.
4. Der Zoowärter macht die Käfige sauber.
5. Wo werden wir uns morgen treffen?
6. Der Inspektor hat sich langsam umgeschaut.

7. Das Kind hat laut geschrien.
8. Mein Vater gewinnt immer beim Kartenspielen.
9. Ich interessiere mich für Sport und Musik.
10. Die Lehrerin wird die neuen Bücher morgen benützen.
11. Wer hat das Geld gestohlen?
12. Die zwei Wagen werden gleich zusammenstossen.

Conversational Past	Present	Future

ÜBUNG D

These verbs all have a stem vowel change. Write the verb and the **er/sie**-form in the appropriate column.

backen	geben	sehen	unterhalten
einladen	laufen	stehlen	waschen
essen	lesen	tragen	werden
fahren	nehmen	treffen	zusammenstossen

a → ä	e → i	e → ie
backen er/sie bäckt		
		au → äu
		o → ö

ÜBUNG E

Fill in the forms of the adjectives that are missing, positive, comparative, and superlative.

1. gross		
2.	höher	
3. gut		
4.		am schnellsten
5.		am meisten
6.	klüger	
7. klein		
8. lang		

ÜBUNG F

You are taking a trip. Make a list of things to take along by combining each item below with an appropriate adjective. Write your list using unpreceded adjectives (nominative case).

die Jacke	warm	bunt
der Pullover	blau	schick
die Hose	bequem	rot
das Hemd	schön	dunkel
die Schuhe	leicht	

BEISPIEL: **leichte Jacke**

_____   _____

_____   _____

Now you have everything spread out on the bed. Describe the items using a definite article (nominative case).

BEISPIEL: **Auf dem Bett liegt (liegen) _die_ leichte Jacke.**

_____   _____

_____   _____

Your mother asks you what you are taking. Tell her the items, using an indefinite article (accusative case).

BEISPIEL: **Ich nehme _eine_ leichte Jacke.**

_____   _____

_____   _____

ÜBUNG G

The computer service TREFF matches up penpals. Fill out the following form with information about yourself.

TREFF

Name _____

Adresse _____

Telefonnr. _____

Alter _____

Schule _____

Interessen:

    Musik _____

    Sport _____

    Hobbys _____

    Klubs _____

Lieblingsfächer _____

Lieblingsessen _____

Lieblingsfernsehsendung _____

Lieblingsmusikgruppe _____

Lieblingssänger/in _____

Lieblingsschauspieler/in _____

Proficiency Activities

Speaking

Practice the following situations with a partner. You take the role of A, your partner takes the role of B.

1. A and B are talking about their likes and preferences in things such as music, films, and food. A asks B what kind of music he or she likes and prefers, what kinds of films he or she likes and prefers, and what kinds of food he or she likes most of all. B responds.

2. A and B are discussing where they like to go and what they like to do on their vacation. A mentions a place where he or she would like to go and explains why. B agrees and mentions some things he or she would like to do at that vacation spot, or disagrees and tells where he or she would like to go and why.

3. A and B are penpals and they are arranging to meet for the first time. A suggests a place to meet and describes himself or herself to B so B will recognize A. B agrees to A's suggestion on where to meet and describes herself or himself.

4. A and B are discussing where to go to eat. A says what kind of food he or she likes and makes a suggestion. B doesn't like the kind of food A suggests. B tells what he or she prefers and makes another suggestion. A responds.

5. A and B are talking about their future plans. They ask each other about their interests and what they plan to do after high school.

Listening

You will hear a number of radio advertisements. What is each one an ad for? Listen carefully and write the number of what you hear next to the type of business it is advertising.

restaurant	
movie theater	
clothing store	
pet store	
travel agency	

Reading

Read the jokes below and pick an appropriate punch line for each one from the list.

Write the number of the punch line in front of the joke it goes with.

1. «Wollen Sie einen Sänger oder einen Tänzer?»
2. «Ja, und mit viel Kuchen!»
3. «Ja, er hat Bauchschmerzen, und heute ist gar keine Schule.»
4. «Das kann nicht sein. Mücken können nicht schwimmen.»
5. «Ja, das finde ich auch seltsam. Das Buch hat ihm überhaupt nicht gefallen.»
6. «Nein, essen.»
7. «Gehen wir zu Fuss oder nehmen wir uns einen Hund?»
8. «Ich habe schon ein Kaninchen.»
9. «Das Ohr.»
10 «Weisst du. ich war ziemlich lange krank.»

_____ Zwei Flöhe kommen aus dem Kino. Es regnet. «Hm», fragt der eine Floh, «was meinst du?»

_____ Ein Mann sitzt mit seinem Dachshund im Kino. Der Dachshund lacht und lacht. Da dreht sich die Dame vor ihm um und sagt: «Ihr Hund findet den Film ganz lustig. Ist das nicht ein bisschen seltsam?»

_____ Eine Frau kommt in die Tierhandlung. Sie möchte gern einen Kanarienvogel kaufen, der schön singen kann. «Nehmen Sie den hier. Er kann ja gut singen», sagt der Verkäufer. «Aber er hat nur ein Bein», sagt die Frau. «Na und?» antwortet der Verkäufer.

_____ Ein Elefant und eine Maus gehen spazieren. Nach einer Weile fragt der Elefant: «Warum bist du eigentlich so klein?» Die Maus wird rot und sagt ganz leise:

_____ Die Kinder haben Mathe. Der Lehrer sagt zu einem Schüler: «Florian, ich schenke dir heute zwei Kaninchen, und morgen schenke ich dir drei Kaninchen. Wie viele Kaninchen hast du dann?» «Ich habe dann sechs», sagt Florian. «Falsch», sagt der Lehrer, «das sind nur fünf.» «Nein, das sind wirklich sechs», meint Florian. «Wieso?» möchte der Lehrer wissen. Florian antwortet:

_____ «Susi, wie möchtest du den Kaffee? Mit viel Milch und Zucker?»

_____ Frau Schmidt sagt zu Herrn Schmidt: «Unser Robert ist heute wirklich krank.» «Meinst du?»

_____ Gabi erzählt ihrer Freundin ganz stolz: «Ich kann französisch, italienisch, spanisch . . .» «Sprechen?» fragt Monika. Da antwortet Gabi:

_____ «Was hört alles und sagt nichts?»

_____ Herr Liebermann sitzt im Restaurant. Der Kellner bringt ihm eine Suppe. «Moment mal», schreit Herr Liebermann. «Da schwimmt in der Suppe eine Mücke!» Der Kellner kommt zurück und sagt:

Writing

1. Choose three people in your family or circle of friends and write sentences comparing them in age, height, and abilities in areas such as sports or music. Tell, for example, who is the oldest, who is the youngest, who is taller or shorter, who plays a particular sport or instrument better. Write at least five sentences.

_____

_____

_____

_____

_____

_____

2. Write a postcard to a friend from your winter vacation. Tell where you are and mention why you like the spot and some of the things you are doing. Don't forget the date, the greeting, and the closing.

3. You are writing a short story. Create three characters for your story and describe them, telling about physical characteristics, dress, and personality traits.

_____

_____

_____

_____

_____

_____

_____

_____

4. Write a list of things you like and dislike — for example, Chinese food, loud music, and so on. Write at least three things on each list.

Ich mag...	**Ich mag... nicht**
_____	_____
_____	_____
_____	_____
_____	_____
_____	_____

5. You are applying for a summer job. On the application you are requested to write a short paragraph about yourself. Include information about your strong points, your interests, and your plans for the future.

_____

_____

_____

_____

_____

Vocabularies

Almost all German words in this textbook are included in this vocabulary. Noun plurals are identified as follows: *der* **Anhänger** = *der* **Anhänger**, *die* **Anhänger**: *der* **Abend**, **-e** = *der* **Abend**, *die* **Abende**; *der* **Apfelsaft**, **ˮe** = *der* **Apfelsaft**, *die* **Apfelsäfte**, and so on. The principal parts of strong verbs are also given.

German-English Vocabulary

A

ab: ab und zu now and then
ab•drehen to twist off, break off
der **Abend, -e** evening; **am Abend** in the evening
das **Abendessen** supper
der **Abendlauf** evening skating
abends in the evening; evenings
das **Abenteuer** adventure
der **Abenteuerfilm, -e** adventure film
ab•fahren (fährt ab, fuhr ab, ist abgefahren) to drive, ride away; to depart
ab•geben (gibt ab, gab ab, hat abgegeben) to check, hand in
der **Abschied** farewell
das **Acryl** acrylic
der **Actionfilm, -e** action film
der **Affe, -n (den …-n, dem, …-n)** monkey
das **Afrika** Africa
alle all
alles everything
alles Gute best wishes
als: als (grösser) als… (bigger) than . . .
alt old
die **Ameise, -n** ant
die **Ampel, -n** traffic light

an on
an: an (der Schule) vorbei D past (the school)
an•fangen (fängt an, fing an, hat angefangen) to start
an•kommen (kommt an, kam an, ist angekommen) to arrive
an•kreuzen to mark
an•probieren to try on
an•rufen (ruft an, rief an, hat angerufen) to call up
an•sagen to announce
der **Anfänger** beginner
das **Angebot** special; **im Angebot** on sale
angeln to fish
der **Anhänger** pendant
die **Anmeldung, -en** registration
der **Anorak, -s** anorak, parka
die **Antarktis** Antarctica
die **Antwort, -en** answer
antworten to answer
der **Anzug, ˮe** (man's) suit
der **Apfelkuchen** apple cake
der **Apfelsaft, ˮe** apple juice
die **Apotheke, -n** pharmacy
das **Aquarium, -rien** aquarium
arbeiten to work
ärgerlich annoying

arm poor
der **Arm, -e** arm
das **Armband, ˮer** bracelet
der **Arzt, ˮe** doctor
das **Asien** Asia
auch also, too
auch: ich auch me too
auf on (top of)
auf•füllen to fill up
auf•machen to open
auf•passen to pay attention, watch out
auf•passen auf A to watch out for, pay attention to
auf•räumen to clean up
auf•schreiben (schreibt auf, schrieb auf, hat aufgeschrieben) to write down
auf•setzen: s. die Mütze
auf•setzen to put on one's cap
auf•stehen (steht auf, stand auf, ist aufgestanden) to get up
der **Aufsatz, ˮe** composition
der **Augenarzt, ˮe** eye doctor
aus out, out of; from (a place), made of
aus•leihen (leiht aus, lieh aus, hat ausgeliehen) to rent, borrow
aus•sehen (sieht aus, sah aus, hat ausgesehen) to look, appear

aus•suchen to select, choose

aus•tragen (trägt aus, trug aus, hat ausge- tragen) to deliver

der Ausflug,¨e excursion, outing

der Auslandskorrespondent, -en (den ...-en, dem ...-en) foreign correspondent

ausser besides, except for

die Aussicht, -en view; in Aussicht in sight

Australien Australia

die Autobahn, -en super- highway

der Autoschlüssel car key

B

die Backe, -n cheek

backen (bäckt, backte, hat gebacken) to bake

der Bäcker baker

die Bäckerei, -en bakery

der Badeanzug, ¨e (woman's) bathing suit

die Badehose, -n swim trunks

baden to bathe, swim

der Bahnhof, ¨e train station

bald soon

die Band, -s band

die Bank, -en bank

der Banküberfall, ¨e bank robbery

der Bär, -en (den ...-en, dem ...-en) bear

der Bass, ¨e bass

das Bastelbuch, ¨er crafts book

basteln to do crafts

der Bauch, ¨e stomach

das Bauchweh stomachache

der Bauernhof, ¨e farm

der Baum, ¨e tree

die Baumwolle cotton

beantworten to answer

bedeuten to mean

begeistert enthusiastic

beginnen (beginnt, begann, hat begonnen) to start, begin

begrüssen to greet

bei by; near at (some one's house)

beim: beim (Skilaufen) while (skiing)

das Bein, -e leg

beiseite aside

das Beispiel, -e example; zum Beispiel for example

beissen (beisst, biss, hat gebissen) to bite

bekommen (bekommt, bekam, hat bekommen) to get, receive

bellen to bark

benutzen to use

beobachten to observe

bequem comfortable

der Berg, -e mountain

der Bericht, -e report

berichten to report

der Beruf, -e trade, occupation

bescheiden modest

besonder- special

besonders especially

Besserung: gute Besserung! get well soon!

bestellen to order

besuchen to visit

beträufeln to sprinkle

das Bett, -en bed

die Bewegung, -en move- ment, exercise

die Bibliothek, -en library

bieten (bietet, bot, hat geboten) to offer

das Bild, -er picture

das Bilderrätsel picture puzzle

billig cheap

bis until

bis: bis zur/zum up to, until you get to

bisschen: ein bisschen a little

bitte please; you're welcome; bitte schön you're welcome; wie bitte? how's that again?, what did you say?

bitten (bittet, bat, hat gebeten) to ask, request

blau blue

bleiben (bleibt, blieb, ist geblieben) to stay, remain

der Bleistift, -e pencil

blöd silly, dumb

die Blume, -n flower

der Blumenladen, ¨ flower shop

der Blumentopf, ¨e flowerpot

die Blumenvase, -n flower vase

die Bluse, -n blouse

das Blut blood

der Boden, ¨ floor

der Braten roast

die Bratwurst, ¨e fried sausage

brauchen to need

braun brown

brechen: s. etwas brechen (bricht s. etwas, brach s. etwas, hat s. etwas gebrochen) to break something

die Brezel, -n pretzel

der Brief, -e letter

der Briefkasten, ¨ mailbox

die Briefmarke, -n stamp

das Brot, -e bread

das Brötchen roll

die Brücke, -n bridge

der Bruder, ¨ brother

brüllen to roar

der Brunnen fountain

brutal violent

das Bücherregal, -e bookcase

die Buchhandlung, -en book store

der Bundeskanzler Chancellor of Germany

das Bundesland, ¨er federal state

der Bus, -se bus

die Busfahrt, -en bus trip

Bushaltestelle, -n bus stop

C

die CD, -s CD (compact disc)

der CD-Spieler CD player

das **Chanukahfest, -e**
Hanukkah

der **Chef, -s** boss

die **Clique, -n** group of
friends, clique

die **Cola, -s** cola

das **Comic-Heft, -e** comic
book

der **Computer** computer

das **Computerspiel, -e**
computer game

die **Currywurst, ¨e**
sausage with spicy
curry sauce

D

das **Dach, ¨er** roof

die **Dame, -n** lady

damit so that

der **Dank: vielen Dank!**
thank you!, many thanks!

danken D to thank;
danke thanks; **danke
schön** thank you

darüber over it

darum therefore

das the

der **Dauerlauf, ¨e** long
distance running

dein your (sing.)

die **Delphine, -n** dolphin

das **Deutsch** German
(language); **deutsch**
German (adj.)

das **Deutschland** Germany

dicht thick

dick fat; thick

der **Dieb, -e** thief

der **Diebstahl, ¨e** theft

der **Dienstag** Tuesday

dieser (diese, dieses)
this

direkt: direkt neben
right next to

doch: geh doch spazieren!
why don't you go for a
walk?

der **Donnerstag** Thursday

doof stupid

das **Dorf, ¨er** village

dort there **dort
drüben** over there

dran: er ist dran
it's his turn

**dumm (dümmer, am
dümmsten)** dumb

die **Dummheit, -en** stupid,
silly thing

**dunkel (dunkler, am
dunkelsten)** dark

dunkelblau dark blue

dünn thin

durch through

das **Durcheinander** chaos,
mess

**dürfen (darf, durfte,
hat gedurft)** to be
permitted, allowed to

der **Durst: Durst haben**
to be thirsty

echt really

E

die **Ecke, -n** corner

das **Ehepaar, -e** married
couple

das **Ei, -er** egg

eigen- own

ein•kaufen to shop

**ein•laden (lädt ein, lud
ein, hat eingeladen)**
to invite

**ein•steigen (steigt ein,
stieg ein, ist einge-
stiegen)** to board,
climb in

ein•stürzen to collapse

der **Einführungskurs, -e**
introductory course

eingebildet conceited

einige some; a few

**einkaufen: einkaufen
gehen** to go shopping

die **Einkaufsliste, -n**
shopping list

das **Einkaufszentrum, -zen
tren** shopping center

einmal once

einmal once; someday

einmalig unique, one
of a kind

das **Eis** ice cream

eitel vain

der **Elefant, -en (den ...-en,
dem ...-en)** elephant

der **Ellbogen** elbow

die **Eltern** (pl.) parents

die **Energie** energy

eng tight

der **Enkel** grandson

die **Enkelin, -nen** grand
daughter

entdecken to discover

entlang along; **diese
Strasse entlang A**
down this street

entschuldigen to
excuse

die **Entschuldigung, -en**
excuse; **Entschul-
digung!** excuse me!

der **Entschuldigungsbrief, -e**
letter of excuse, absent
note

enttäuscht
disappointed

die **Entzündung, -en**
infection

das **Erdbeben** earthquake

erfahren experienced

der **Erfolg, -e** success

erhitzen to heat

die **Erkältung, -en** cold

die **Erlaubnis** permission

**erlernen: einen Beruf
erlernen** to learn a
trade or occupation

die **Ernährung** nutrition

der **Ersatzteil, -e**
replacement part

erst- first

erst only

der **Erwachsene, -n
(den -n, dem -n)** adult

erzählen to tell

das **Essen** food

**essen (isst, ass, hat
gegessen)** to eat

das **Esszimmer** dining room

etwas something

euer your (pl.)

das **Europa** Europe

exotisch exotic

F

die **Fabel, -n** fable

die **Fabrik, -en** factory

das **Fach, ¨er** subject area

der **Fachhändler** expert,
specialist

**fahren (fährt, fuhr, ist
gefahren)** to ride,
drive, go by vehicle

das **Fahrrad, ¨er** bicycle

der **Fahrradhelm, -e**
bicycle helmet

die **Fahrschule, -n** driving
school

der Fall, ¨-e case; ein schwieriger Fall a difficult case; **Fall erledigt!** case closed!

fallen (fällt, fiel, ist gefallen) to fall

falsch wrong, false

die Familie, -n family

die Fanta, -s orange-flavored carbonated drink

fantasievoll imaginative

die Farbe, -n color

der Farbstift, -e colored pencil

faul lazy

faul (fauler, am faulsten) lazy

faulenzen to be lazy

feiern to celebrate, party

der Feiertag, -e holiday

das Fenster window

das Fensterbrett, -er windowsill

die Ferien (pl.) vacation

das Ferienlager vacation camp

der Ferientermin, -e vacation date

fern•sehen (sieht fern, sah fern, hat ferngesehen) to watch TV

der Fernseher TV set

das Fernsehprogramm, -e TV schedule

die Fernsehsendung, -en TV program

fest•stellen to find out, determine

das Fieber fever

der Filzstift, -e marker

finden (findet, fand, hat gefunden) to find; **wie findest du (Skifahren)?** how do you like (skiing)? what do you think of . . .?

der Fisch, -e fish

das Fischbrot, -e fish sandwich

fithalten: Sport hält fit sports keep you in shape

die Flasche, -n bottle

das Fleisch meat

die Fleischerei, -n butcher shop

fleissig industrious, hard-working

fliegen (fliegt, flog, ist geflogen) to fly

der Floh, ¨-e flea

die Flöte, -n flute

der Flughafen, ¨ airport

das Flugzeug, -e airplane

der Fluss, ¨-e river

die Flutwelle, -n tidal wave

fördern to promote

der Forscher researcher

der Fortgeschrittene, -n (den -n, dem -n) advanced (person)

die Frage, -n question; Fragen stellen to ask questions

das Frankreich France

französisch French

die Frau, -en wife; woman

frech fresh

der Freitag Friday

die Freizeit leisure time

fressen (frisst, frass, hat gefressen) to eat (of animals)

der Freund, -e friend

die Freundin, -nen girl friend

freundlich friendly

frisch fresh

froh happy, merry, glad

der Frosch, ¨-e frog

früh early

der Frühling, -e spring

das Frühstück, -e breakfast

der Fuchs, ¨-e fox

führen to lead

führen zu to lead to

der Führerschein, -e driver's license

für A for

der Fuss, ¨-e foot; zu Fuss gehen to go on foot, walk

füttern to feed (an animal)

G

die Gabel, -n fork

ganz really, completely; right

gar: gar nicht not at all

die Gardinen (pl.) curtains

der Garten, ¨ garden

der Gast, ¨-e guest

geben (gibt, gab, hat gegeben) to give; **es gibt** there is, there are; **was gibt's?** what's up?

geborene (geb.) maiden name

die Geburt, -en birth

der Geburtstag, -e birthday; **Geburtstag haben: er hat Geburtstag** it is his birthday; **zum Geburtstag** for (your) birthday

die Geburtstagskarte, -n birthday card

der Geburtstagskuchen birthday cake

der Geburtstagstisch, -e table with birthday presents, mail, etc.

geduldig patient

die Gefahr, -en danger

gefährlich dangerous

gefallen (gefällt, gefiel, hat gefallen) D to be pleasing to someone

gegen against

gegenüber across (from)

gehen (geht, ging, ist gegangen) to go; **wie geht es dir?** how are you?; **es geht mir...** I'm feeling . . .; **das geht schon, aber...** it's okay, but . . .; **geht das?** is that okay?

gehören D to belong to

die Geige, -n violin

gelb yellow

das Geld money

die Gemeinde, -n municipality

das Gemüse vegetable

der Gemüseladen, green grocer

die Gemüseplatte, -n vegetable plate

gemütlich cozy, comfortable

genug enough

geöffnet open

der **Gepard, -e** cheetah

geradeaus straight ahead

gern gladly; **gern haben** to like; **gern machen** to like to do; **gern (haben) (lieber, am liebsten)** to like (like better, like best)

das **Geschäft, -e** store, business

das **Geschenk, -e** present

die **Geschichte, -n** story; history

die **Geschwister** *(pl.)* brothers and sisters

das **Gesicht, -er** face

gespannt: ganz gespannt eagerly anticipating

das **Gespräch, -e** conversation

gestern yesterday

gesund healthy

das **Getreide** grain

gewinnen (gewinnt, gewann, hat gewonnen) to win

gewöhnlich usually

gierig greedy

giessen (giesst, goss, hat gegossen) to pour

die **Giftzentrale, -n** center for poison control

die **Gitarre, -n** guitar

das **Glas, ¨er** glass

glatt straight

die **Glatze, -n** bald head

glauben to think, to believe

gleich right; right away, immediately; **gleich um die Ecke** right around the corner

das **Gleitschirmfliegen** glider flying

das **Glück** happiness; good luck; **viel Glück!** good luck; (I wish you) much happiness

glücklich happy

der **Glückwunsch, ¨e** good wishes

gnadenlos merciless

der **Goldgräber** gold digger

das **Gras, ¨er** grass

gratulieren D to congratulate

grau grey

grausam cruel

das **Griechenland** Greece

gross big; tall

grossartig terrific

die **Grösse, -n** size

die **Grosseltern** *(pl.)* grandparents

die **Grossmutter, ¨** grandmother

der **Grossvater, ¨** grandfather

grosszügig generous

grün green

der **Gruss, ¨e** greeting

grüssen to greet, say hello to

die **Gurke, -n** pickle

der **Gürtel** belt

gut good; well; **gut (besser, am besten)** good (better, best)

Gute: alles Gute best wishes

gutherzig kindhearted

das **Gymnasium, Gymnasien** academic secondary school

die **Gymnastik** gymnastics; exercises; **Gymnastik machen** to do exercises

H

das **Haar, -e** hair

haben (hat, hatte, hat gehabt) to have

das **Hähnchen** chicken

das **Hallenbad, ¨er** indoor swimming pool

hallo! hello!

der **Hals, ¨e** neck

die **Halsentzündung, -en** sore throat

die **Halskette, -n** necklace

der **Hamburger** hamburger

der **Hamster** hamster

die **Hand, ¨e** hand

das **Handgelenk, -e** wrist

der **Handschuh, -e** glove

hängen (hängt, hing, hat gehangen) to hang, be hanging

der **Hase, -n (den ...-n, dem ...-n)** rabbit

hässlich ugly

das **Hauptgericht, -e** main dish

die **Hauptstrasse, -n** main street

das **Haus, ¨er** house

die **Hausaufgabe, -n** homework assignment

Hause: nach Hause (to) home; **zu Hause** at home

das **Haustier, -e** pet

das **Heft, -e** notebook

heftig strong, vigorous

die **Heftmaschine, -n** stapler

die **Heimat, -en** home, homeland

heimlich secretly

heiss hot

heissen (heisst, hiess, hat geheissen) to be called; **wie heisst du?** what's your name?; **ich heisse...** my name is...

der **Held, -en (den ...-en, dem ...-en)** hero

helfen (hilft, half, hat geholfen) D to help

hellblau light blue

das **Hemd, -en** shirt

der **Herbst, -e** fall

der **Herr, -en** Mr.; gentleman; master

herrlich wonderful, beautiful

herum•sitzen (sitzt herum, sass herum, hat herumgesessen) to sit around

herzlich heartfelt, cordial; **herzliche Grüsse** best regards

heute today; **heute nachmittag** this afternoon

hier here; around here; **hier ist** this is (on phone)

der **Himmel** sky; heaven

hinter behind

das **Hobby, -s** hobby

hoch (höher, am höchsten) high (higher, highest)

die **Hochzeit, -en** wedding

der **Hochzeitstag, -e**
wedding anniversary
hoffen to hope
hoffentlich hopefully, I
hope
die **Hoffnung, -en** hope
höflich polite
die **Höhle, -n** cave
holen to get, fetch
der **Honig** honey
hören to hear; to listen
to; **hören: hör gut zu!**
listen carefully!
der **Hörschaden** hearing
loss
die **Hose, -n** pants
das **Hotel, -s** hotel
hübsch pretty
der **Hund, -e** dog
der **Hunger: Hunger haben**
to be hungry
der **Husten** cough **husten**
to cough
der **Hustensaft, ̈-e** cough
medicine
der **Hut, ̈-e** hat

I

die **Idee, -n** idea
ihr her; their
im (in dem): im (April)
in (April)
der **Imbiss-Stand, ̈-e**
snack stand
immer always; **immer**
noch still
die **Impfung, -en**
vaccination
in in, into
die **Informatik** computer
science
der **Informatiker** computer
programmer
der **Ingenieur, -e** engineer
innerhalb within
die **Insel, -n** island
der **Inspektor, -en** inspector
das **Instrument, -e**
instrument
das **Italien** Italy

J

die **Jacke, -n** jacket
der **Jäger** hunter
das **Jahr, -e** year

die **Jahreszeit, -en** season
die **Jeans** (*pl.*) jeans
der **Jeans-Shop, -s** jeans
shop
jeder (jede, jedes)
each, every; that
jetzt now
der **Job, -s** job
der **Joghurt** yogurt
die **Jugend** youth, young
people
der **Jugendliche, -n (den -n,**
dem -n) young person
die **Jugendvollversamm-**
lung, -en full-meet-
ing for all young people
jung young
der **Junge, -n (den ...-n,**
dem ...-n) boy
die **Jura** law

K

der **Kaffee, -s** coffee
der **Käfig, -e** cage
der **Kalender,** calendar
kämmen: s. die Haare
kämmen to comb
one's hair
der **Kampf, ̈-e** fight,
struggle
der **Kanarienvogel, ̈**
canary
die **Kanumiete, -n** canoe
rental fee
die **Kapuze, -n** hood
die **Karambolage, -n**
huge crash or collision
die **Karriere, -n** career
die **Kartoffel, -n** potato
das **Kartoffelpüree**
mashed potatoes
der **Käse** cheese
die **Kasse, -n** register,
cashier
der **Katastrophenfilm, -e**
disaster film
die **Katze, -n** cat
kaufen to buy
das **Kaufhaus, ̈-er**
department store
der **Keller** basement
kennen (kennt, kannte,
hat gekannt) to know
(be acquainted with)
die **Kettenübung, -en**
chain activity

das **Keyboard, -s** key
board
das **Kind, -er** child
der **Kinderspielplatz, ̈-e**
children's playground
das **Kino, -s** movie theater
die **Kirche, -n** church
kirchlich: kirchliche
Trauung church
wedding ceremony
die **Klarinette, -n** clarinet
das **Klavier, -e** piano
das **Kleid, -er** dress
die **Kleidung** clothing
klein small; short
klingeln to ring (the
doorbell)
klug (klüger, am
klügsten) smart
knabbern to nibble
das **Knabberzeug** snacks,
nibblies
knallrot bright red
das **Knie, -e** knee
der **Knöchel** ankle
kochen to cook
kolrabenschwarz
jet black
kombinieren to
combine
komisch funny
kommen (kommt,
kam, ist gekommen)
to come; **im Fernse-**
hen kommen to be
on TV; **komm!**
come on!;
kommen aus to come
from; **wie komme**
ich zum...? how do I
get to . . . ?
die **Kommode, -n** dresser
die **Komödie, -n** comedy
der **König, -e** king
können (kann, konnte,
hat gekonnt) to be
able to; can
der **Kontinent, -e** continent
der **Korb, ̈-e** basket
kosten to cost
der **Kram** junk
krank sick
das **Krankenhaus, ̈-er**
hospital
der **Krankenpfleger**
(male) nurse
das **Kraut, ̈-er** herb

die **Krawatte, -n** tie
die **Kreuzung, -en** intersection
der **Krimi, -s** detective story, mystery
der **Kriminalfilm, -e** crime movie
die **Küche, -n** kitchen
der **Kuli, -s** ballpoint pen
der **Künstler** artist
kurz short
die **Kusine, -n** (female) cousin
der **Kuss, ¨e** kiss
die **Küste, -n** coast

L

lächeln to smile
lachen to laugh
der **Laden, ¨** store
das **Lager: auf Lager** in stock
die **Lampe, -n** lamp
die **Landeshauptstadt, ¨e** state capital city
die **Landschaft, -en** landscape
lang long
langsam slow; slowly
langweilig boring
lassen (lässt, liess, hat gelassen) to let
der **Lastwagen** truck
laut loud
der **Lautsprecher** loud-speaker
die **Lebensmittel** *(pl.)* groceries
lebhaft lively
lecker delicious
das **Leder** leather
legen to lay
der **Lehrer** male teacher
die **Lehrerin, -nen** female teacher
lehrreich educational
die **Leiche, -n** body, corpse
leicht light; easy
leid tun D (tut leid, tat leid, hat leid getan) to be sorry; **es tut mir leid** I'm sorry
leider unfortunately
das **Leinen** linen
leise soft
lernen to learn; to study

lesen (liest, las, hat gelesen) to read
letzt- last
letzt-: in letzter Zeit recently
die **Leute (pl.)** people
das **Lexikon, -s** dictionary
lieb- dear
die **Liebe** love
lieben to love
lieber rather; **lieber als** better than
der **Liebesfilm, -e** love story, romantic movie
liebsten: am liebsten most of all
das **Lied, -er** song
liegen (liegt, lag, hat gelegen) to lie
das **Liftticket, -s** lift ticket
lila purple
die **Limonade, -n** carbonated lemon soda
das **Lineal, -e** ruler
links left, on the left
locker loose
lockig curly
der **Löffel** spoon
los: was ist los? what's the matter?
der **Löwe, -n (den ...-n, dem ...-n)** lion
die **Luft, ¨e** air
lustig funny, fun

M

machen to do; to make; to take (a walk, a hike, etc.)
das **Mal, -e** time
manchmal sometimes
der **Mann, ¨er** husband; man
die **Mannschaft, -en** team
der **Mantel, ¨** coat
die **Mark** mark (German monetary unit)
der **Marktplatz, ¨e** market place
die **Massenbewegung, -en** mass movement
der **Matrose, -n (den -n, dem -n)** sailor
die **Maus, ¨e** mouse
die **Mayonnaise** mayonnaise

die **Medizin** medicine
das **Meerschweinchen** guinea pig
mein my
meinen to think, have the opinion; **meinst du?** do you think so?
die **Meisterschaft, -en** championship
der **Mensch, -en (den -en, dem -en)** human being
merken to notice
das **Merkmal, -e** charachteristic
das **Messer** knife
die **Milch** milk
das **Militär: zum Militär gehen** to join the military
das **Mineralwasser, ¨** mineral water
mit D with; by (means of); **mit dem Zug** by train
mit•bringen (bringt mit, brachte mit, hat mitgebracht) to bring along
mit•fahren (fährt mit, fuhr mit, ist mitgefahren) to drive, ride, go along
mit•machen to participate, go along with
das **Mittagessen** lunch
das **Mittelmeer** Mediterranean Sea
die **Mittelschule, -n** middle school
die **Mitternacht** midnight
der **Mittwoch** Wednesday
das **Möbel** furniture
das **Möbelstück, -e** piece of furniture
möchten would like
die **Mode, -n** fashion
modisch fashionable
mögen (mag, mochte, hat gemocht) to like
möglich possible
Moment! just a minute!
der **Monat, -e** month
der **Montag** Monday; **am Montag** on Monday; **montags** Mondays

der **Mord, -e** murder
der **Mörder** murderer
der **Morgen** morning;
  am Morgen in the
    morning (early);
  morgen tomorrow;
  morgens in the morning
    (early); mornings
die **Mücke, -n** mosquito
  müde tired
die **Münze, -n** coin
das **Museum, Museen**
  museum
die **Musik** music
  musikalisch musical
das **Musikgeschäft, -e**
  music store
die **Musikkassette, -n**
  music tape
  **müssen (muss, musste,
  hat gemusst)** to have
    to; must
  mutig brave
die **Mutter, ⁻** mother
der **Muttertag, -e** Mother's
  Day
die **Mütze, -n** cap

N

  nach after; toward, to,
    in the direction of;
    according to
die **Nachbarschaft, -en**
  neighborhood
die **Nachhilfe** extra help
der **Nachmittag, -e**
  afternoon; **am Nach-
  mittag** in the afternoon;
  nachmittags in the
    afternoon; afternoons
die **Nachricht, -en** news
  report
die **Nachspeise, -n** dessert
  nächst- next;
  in nächster Zeit
    in the near future
die **Nacht, ⁻e** night
der **Nachttisch, -e** night
  table
  nagelneu brand new
die **Nähe: ganz in der Nähe**
  right near by
die **Narbe, -n** scar
das **Nashorn, ⁻er**
  rhinoceros

  natürlich naturally, of
    course
  neben next to
  nebenan next door
der **Neffe, -n (den ...-n,
  dem ...-n)** nephew
  **nehmen (nimmt,
  nahm, hat genom-
  men)** to take
der **Neid** envy
  nervös nervous
  nett nice
  neu new
  neulich recently
  nicht not
die **Nichte, -n** niece
  nichts nothing
  nie never
das **Nilpferd, -e**
  hippopotamus
  noch still; **was noch?**
    what else?; **noch ein**
    another; **noch nie**
    never yet
  nochmals again
  Nordamerika North
    America
der **Notruf, -e** emergency
  call
der **Nudelauflauf, ⁻e**
  noodle casserole
  null zero
die **Nummer (Nr.)** number

O

die **Oberschule, -n** high
  school
das **Obst** fruit
  oder or
  offen open; public
  oft often
  ohne A without
  das **Ohr, -en** ear
der **Ohrring, -e** earring
die **Olive, -n** olive
der **Onkel** uncle
das **Orchester** orchestra
  ordentlich neat
die **Ordnung: in Ordnung**
  okay
die **Ortsbezeichnung, -en**
  name of town or city
das **Ortsnetz, -e** area code
  Ostern Easter
das **Österreich** Austria

das **Outfit, -s** outfit
  paar: ein paar a few

P

das **Paket, -e** package
der **Papagei, -en** parrot
der **Papierkorb, ⁻e**
  wastepaper basket
der **Paprika, -s** pepper
  (vegetable)
der **Park, -s** park
der **Parkplatz, ⁻e** parking
  lot
die **Partysachen** (*pl.*)
  party things
  passen D to fit
  **passieren (ist
passiert)**
  to happen
die **Pause, -n** break,
  recess
das **Pech** bad luck; **so
  ein Pech!** what bad
  luck!
die **Person, -en** person;
  a character (in a story,
  etc.)
der **Pfennig, -e** penny
das **Pferd, -e** horse
der **Pferdestall, ⁻e** stable
das **Pfingsten** Whitsunday
  or Pentecost
die **Pflanze, -n** plant
das **Photo, -s** photo
das **Photogeschäft, -e**
  camera store
  photographieren
    to photograph
der **Pilz, -e** mushroom
die **Pizza, -s** pizza
  planen to plan
der **Platz, ⁻e** plaza, square
die **Polizei** police (force)
die **Polizeiwache,** police
  station
der **Polizist, -en (den ...-en,
  dem ...-en)** policeman
das **Polohemd, -en**
  polo shirt
die **Pommes frites** (*pl.*)
  French fries
die **Post** mail
die **Postämter** post office
das **Poster** poster
die **Postleitzahl, -en**
  zip code

die **Praline, -n** fancy chocolate candy

der **Preis, -e** prize

preiswert reasonable (in price)

prima great

probieren to try; **probier doch mal...** why don't you try . .

das **Programm, -e** TV channel, station

der **Pudding, -s** pudding

der **Puderzucker** powder sugar

der **Pulli, -s** (short for **Pullover**) (pullover) sweater

pünktlich on time, punctual

putzen: s. die Zähne putzen to brush one's teeth

Q

der **Quatsch** nonsense

R

der **Rabe, -n (den ...-n, dem ...-n)** crow

das **Rad, ¨er** bicycle; wheel; **Rad fahren** (see **fahren**) to ride on a bike, to bicycle

der **Radiergummi, -s** eraser

die **Radtour, -en** bicycle tour, trip; **eine Radtour machen** to take a bike trip

der **Rasen** lawn, grass

der **Rat** advice

das **Ratespiel, -e** guessing game

das **Rathaus, ¨er** town or city hall

der **Ratschlag, -schläge** advice

rauchen to smoke

das **Recht, -e** right

rechts right, on the right

der **Rechtsanwalt, ¨e** lawyer

reden to talk

der **Regenmantel, ¨** raincoat

regnen to rain

reich rich

das **Reihenhaus, ¨er** row house

die **Reise, -n** trip

reisen (ist gereist) to travel

reiten (reitet, ritt, ist geritten) to ride (a horse)

rennen (rennt, rannte, ist gerannt) to run

das **Restaurant, -s** restaurant

retten to save

die **Rettungsleitstelle** rescue hotline

richten to fix, arrange

richtig correct, right; real

der **Rock, ¨e** skirt

der **Rollkragen-Pullover** turtleneck sweater

der **Rollschuh, -e** roller skate; **Rollschuh laufen** (see **laufen**) to roller skate

rosa pink

rot red

das **Rote Kreuz** Red Cross

der **Rücken** back

der **Rucksack, ¨e** back pack

ruhig quiet

rund round

S

der **Sack, ¨e** sack

der **Salat, -e** lettuce, salad

sammeln to collect

der **Sammler** collector

der **Samstag** Saturday

die **Sandale, -n** sandle

sauber•machen to clean

Schade! too bad!

der **Schal, -s** scarf

der **Schatz** sweetheart

schauen to look

der **Schauspieler** actor

die **Scheibe, -n** slice

der **Schein, -e** bill

schenken to give as a gift

die **Schere, -n** scissors

schick chic, smart

schicken to send

schieben (schiebt, schob, hat geschoben) to push

die **Schildkröte, -n** turtle

Schimpanse, -n chimpanzee

der **Schlafanzug, ¨e** pajamas

schlafen (schläft, schlief, hat geschlafen) to sleep

der **Schlafsack, ¨e** sleeping bag

der **Schlag, ¨e** punch

der **Schläger** racquet

die **Schlagsahne** whipped cream

die **Schlagzeile, -n** headline

das **Schlagzeug, -e** drums

schlampig sloppy

die **Schlange, -n** snake

schlank slim

schlapp wilted, weak, droopy

schlau (schlauer, am schlausten) sly, clever

schlecht bad; awful

schlechtgelaunt in a bad mood

schleppen to drag

schlimm bad

der **Schlitten** sled

der **Schlittschuh, -e** ice skate; **Schlittschuh laufen (see laufen)** to ice skate

das **Schloss, ¨er** castle

schlucken to swallow

die **Schlümpfe** Smurfs

der **Schlüssel** key

schmalzig corny, mushy

schmecken to taste; **es schmeckt nicht gut** it doesn't taste good

der **Schmerz, -en** pain

die **Schmerztablette, -n** pain reliever

der **Schmuck** jewelry

der **Schnabel, ¨** beak

der **Schnee** snow

schneiden (schneidet, schnitt, hat geschnitten)

to cut

schnell fast

der **Schnurrbart, ˝e** mustache

die **Schokolade, -n** chocolate

schon already

schön pretty, beautiful, nice; **etwas Schönes** something nice

der **Schornsteinfeger** chimney sweeper

der **Schrank, ˝e** closet, cupboard

die **Schraube, -n** screw

schreiben to write

der **Schreibtisch, -e** desk

schreien (schreit, schrie, hat geschrien) to scream, cry

schüchtern shy

der **Schuh, -e** shoe

die **Schule, -n** school

das **Schulfach, ˝er** school subject

die **Schulsachen** (*pl.*) school supplies

die **Schultasche, -n** schoolbag

die **Schulter, -n** shoulder

schützen to protect

schwach weak

der **Schwanz, ˝e** tail

schwarz black

der **Schwarzwald** Black Forest

die **Schweiz** Switzerland

der **Schweizer** Swiss

schwer heavy; hard, difficult

die **Schwester, -n** sister

schwierig difficult

das **Schwimmbad, ˝er** swimming pool

schwimmen (schwimmt, -schwamm, ist geschwommen) to swim

der **Science-fiction-Film, -e** science fiction film

der **See, -n** lake

das **Segelbrett, -er** windsurfing board

segeln to sail

die **Sehenswürdigkeit, -en** place of interest, landmark

sehr very; **sehr viel** a lot

sein his; its

sein (ist, war, ist gewesen) to be

seit since; **er ist seit fünf Wochen hier** he has been here for five weeks

seltsam strange

die **Sendung, -en** TV program

der **Senf, -e** mustard

die **Serie, -n** series

der **Sessel, -n** easy chair

setzen to set, put

die **Shorts** (*pl.*) shorts

s. amüsieren to enjoy oneself, have a good time

s. ansehen: s. etwas ansehen (sieht s. etwas an, sah s. etwas an, hat s. etwas angesehen) to watch something

s. an•ziehen (zieht s. an, zog s. an, hat s. angezogen) to get dressed

s. aus•kennen (kennt s. aus, kannte s. aus, hat s. ausgekannt) to know one's way around

s. aus•ziehen (zieht s. aus, zog s. aus, hat s. ausgezogen) to get undressed

s. bedanken to say thank you

s. beeilen to hurry

s. bewegen to get exercise

s. duschen to shower

s. etwas an•sehen (sieht s. etwas an, sah s. etwas an, hat s. etwas angesehen) to look at, watch something

s. fit•halten (hält s. fit, hielt s. fit, hat s. fitgehalten) to keep fit

s. freuen (über A) to be happy (about)

s. freuen über A to be happy about

s. fühlen to feel

s. interessieren für to be interested in

s. kämmen to comb (one's hair)

s. konzentrieren to concentrate

s. setzen to sit (down)

s. setzen to sit down

s. treffen mit (trifft, traf, hat getroffen) to meet with

s. um•drehen to turn around

s. um•schauen to look around

s. um•ziehen (zieht s. um, zog s. um, hat s. umgezogen) to change (clothes)

s. unterhalten (mit D) (unterhält s. unter hielt s., hat s. unter halten) to have a conversation (with)

s. verabschieden to say goodbye

s. verletzen to hurt, injure oneself

s. verloben to get engaged

s. verstecken to hide oneself

s. vor•bereiten: s. etwas zu essen vor bereiten to fix one self something to eat

s. waschen (wäscht s. wusch s., hat s. gewaschen) to wash oneself

s. waschen: s. die Haare waschen to wash one's hair

s. wünschen D to wish for

sicher sure, surely

das **Silber** silver

singen (singt, sang, hat gesungen) to sing

sitzen (sitzt, sass, hat gesessen) to sit, be sitting

Ski laufen (läuft Ski, lief Ski, ist Ski

gelaufen)
to go skiing

der **Ski, -er ski; Ski laufen**
(see **laufen**) to ski

das **Skigebiet, -e** ski area

so: so (gross) wie...
as (big) as . . .

die **Socke, -n** sock

das **Sofa, -s** sofa

sogar even

der **Sohn, ¨e** son

sollen to be supposed
to; ought; should

der **Sommer** summer

sonnig sunny

der **Sonntag** Sunday

die **Sorge: s. Sorgen machen
um A** to worry about

sorgen für to take care of

so so so-so

das **Spanien** Spain

spannend thrilling, exciting

sparen to save

der **Spass: macht Spass** is
fun; **viel Spass!** have fun!

spät late

später: bis später!
see you later!

der **Spatz, -en** sparrow

**spazieren•gehen (geht
spazieren, ging
spazieren, ist
spazierengegangen)**
to take a walk

der **Spaziergang, ¨e** walk;
**einen Spaziergang
machen** to take a
walk

die **Speisekarte, -n** menu

der **Spiegel,** mirror

das **Spiel, -e** game

die **Spielshow, -s** game
show

die **Spinne, -n** spider

spinnen: du spinnst!
you're crazy!

Spitze, -n peak,
pinnacle

der **Spitzer** pencil-
sharpener

der **Sport** sport(s)

das **Sportgeschäft, -e**
sporting goods store

der **Sportler** athlete

sportlich athletic

der **Sportplatz, ¨e** athletic
field

die **Sportschau** sports
report

die **Sprache, -n** language

der **Sprachkurs, -e**
language course

**sprechen (spricht,
sprach, hat gesprochen)**
to speak

der **Sprudel** seltzer

spurlos without a trace

das **Stadion, Stadien**
stadium

die **Stadt, ¨e** city

Stadtbummel stroll
through the city

die **Stadtmitte** center of
the city, downtown

der **Stadtteil, -e** section of
the city

die **Stadtverwaltung, -en**
city administration

der **Stangenzimt** stick
cinnamon

stark strong

**stehen (steht, stand,
hat gestanden)**
to stand; **es steht dir
gut** it suits you, it
looks good on you

**stehlen (stiehlt, stahl,
hat gestohlen)** to steal

stellen to place, put

der **Stiefel** boot

der **Stiel, -e** stem

die **Stimme, -n** voice

stimmen to be right,
correct

stolz proud

der **Strand, ¨e** beach

die **Strasse, -n** street

das **Stück, ¨e** piece

studieren to study (at
a college or university)

der **Stuhl, ¨e** chair

stumm mute

die **Stunde, -n** hour

stundenlang for hours

der **Sturm, ¨e** storm

das **Südamerika** South
America

südlich von south of

die **Suppe, -n** soup

Surfbrett, -er surfboard

die **Süssigkeit, -en** candy,
sweets

das **Sweatshirt, -s** sweatshirt

T

der **Tag, -e** day

die **Tagesschau** news

täglich daily

tagsüber during the day

die **Tankstelle, -n** gas station

die **Tante, -n** aunt

der **Tanz, ¨e** dance

tanzen to dance

der **Taschenrechner** calculator

die **Tasse, -n** cup

die **Tatsache, -n** fact

die **Taube, -n** dove

das **Team, -s** team

der **Tee** tea

das **Telefon, -e** telephone

der **Telefonanruf, -e**
telephone call

telefonieren to
telephone

der **Tennisschuh, -e** sneaker

der **Teppich, -e** carpet, rug

teuer expensive

das **Theater** theater

das **Tier, -e** animal

der **Tisch, -e** table

die **Tochter, ¨** daughter

tödlich fatal, deadly

toll great, terrific

die **Tomate, -n** tomato

das **Top, -s** top (clothing)

die **Torte, -n** torte, fancy cake

tot dead

der **Tote, -n (den -n, dem -n)**
fatality, dead (person)

**tragen (trägt, trug, hat
getragen)** to wear;
to carry

tragisch tragic

der **Traubensaft, ¨e** grape
juice

die **Trauer** grief, mourning

träumen von to dream of

das **Traumzimmer** dream
room

traurig sad

die **Trauung, -en** wedding

der **Trenchcoat, -s** trench
coat

die **Treue** faith, loyalty

**trinken (trinkt, trank,
hat getrunken)** to
drink

die **Trompete, -n** trumpet

der **Tropenwald, ¨er** rain
forest

Tschüs! bye!, so long!

das **T-Shirt, -s** T-shirt

tun (tut, tat, hat getan) to do

der **Tunnel** tunnel

die **Tür, -en** door

turnen to do gymnastics

die **Turnhose, -n** gym shorts

der **Turnschuh, -e** sneaker

typisch typical

U

die **U-Bahn, -en** subway

üben to practice

über above, over; about; **über (den Marktplatz)** across the market place

überall everywhere

überfallen (überfällt, überfiel, hat überfallen) to rob

überhaupt: überhaupt nicht not at all

überstreuen to sprinkle over

überwältigen to overpower, overcome

die **Übung, -en** exercise, activity

die **Uhr, -en** clock; **es ist zwei Uhr** it's two o'clock

um around, about; at (in expressions of time)

die **Umfrage, -n** questionnaire

die **Umgebung, -en** surroundings

umgezogen moved

die **Umkleidekabine, -n** changing room

die **Umwelthilfe** environmental defense fund

unbekannt unknown

der **Unfall, ¨e** accident

ungeduldig impatient

ungefähr about, approximately

uninteressant uninteresting

die **Unschuld** innocence

unser our

unter under

unterhaltend entertaining

die **Unterhaltungsserie, -n** drama series

die **Unterkunft,** lodging

der **Unterricht** instruction

unvergesslich unforgettable

der **Urlaub, -e** vacation

die **Ursache, -n** cause

V

der **Vater, ¨** father

der **Vatertag, -e** Father's Day

der **Vegetarier** vegetarian (male)

die **Vegetarierin, -nen** vegetarian (female)

vegetarisch vegetarian

verbrennen (verbrennt, verbrannt, hat verbrannt) to burn up

verdächtig suspicious

verdienen to earn

der **Verein, -e** club

das **Vereinsheim, -e** clubhouse

die **Vergangenheit,** past

vergessen (vergisst, vergass, hat vergessen) to forget

der **Vergleich, -e** comparison

verkaufen an A to sell to

das **Verkehrsamt, ¨er** tourist office

verlassen (verlässt, verliess, hat verlassen) to leave

der **Verletzte, -n (den -n, dem -n)** injured (person)

die **Verletzung, -en** injury

die **Verlobung, -en** engagement

vernünftig sensible, reasonable

verpassen to miss

die **Verpflegung** food, meals

verpflichtet obligated

verrückt crazy

verschwinden (verschwindet, verschwand, ist verschwunden) to disappear

verschwunden disappeared

die **Versicherung, -en** insurance

verstauchen: s. etwas verstauchen to sprain something

verstehen (versteht, verstand, hat verstanden) to understand

versuchen to try

verteilen auf A to divide among

der **Vertragszwang** pressure to sign a contract

der **Verwandte, -n (den ... -n, dem ...-n)** relative

der **Vetter, -n** (male) cousin

das **Videospiel, -e** video game

viel much; many, a lot; **viel (mehr; am meisten)** a lot (more, most)

vielleicht maybe

der **Vogel, ¨** bird

das **Vogelfutter** bird food

das **Vogelhaus, ¨er** bird house

von D from; by; of

vor in front of; **vor zwei Wochen** two weeks ago

vor•bereiten to prepare

vor•haben (hat vor, hatte vor, hat vorgehabt) to have something on, have plans

vorbei•gehen (geht vorbei, ging vorbei, ist vorbeigegangen) to pass by

vorgestern day before yesterday

der **Vormittag, -e** morning; **am Vormittag** in the morning (before noon); **vormittags** in the morning (before noon); mornings

W

wachsen (wächst, wuchs, ist gewachsen) to grow

der **Wagen** car

wahr true; **nicht wahr?** isn't that so?

der **Wal, -le** whale

der **Wald, ¨er** forest

die **Wand, ¨e** wall

wandern (ist gewandert) to hike

die **Wanderung, -en** hike
wann when
wäre would be;
wie wär's mit... how about . . . ?
warten to wait
warum why
was what; **was für (ein)** what kind of (a)
das **Wasser** water
das **WC, -s** (water closet), toilet
wecken to wake up
der **Wecker** alarm clock
weg away
weh tun (tut weh, tat weh, hat weh getan) D to hurt
die **Weihnachten** Christmas
das **Weihnachtsfest, -e** Christmas
weil because
die **Weise, -n** way, manner
weiss white
weit far; wide; big
welcher (welche, welches) which
die **Welt, -en** world
weltberühmt world-famous
der **Welterfolg, -e** international success
wem to whom, for whom
wen whom
wenn when; if
wer who ; whoever
werden (wird, wurde, ist geworden) will be, will become
die **Weste, -n** vest
wichtig important
wie how; **wie viel** how much;
wie viele how many
wieder again

wiederholen to repeat
Wiederhören: auf Wiederhören! good bye! (on phone)
das **Wiedersehen: auf Wiedersehen! Wiedersehen!** bye!
die **Wildnis** wilderness
der **Winter** winter
wissen (weiss, wusste, hat gewusst) know (information, a fact)
die **Wissenschaft** science
witzig witty
wo where
die **Woche, -n** week
das **Wochenende, -n** weekend
woher where from
wohin where to
wohnen to live
das **Wohnzimmer** living room
der **Wolf, ¨e** wolf
der **Wolkenkratzer** skyscraper
wolkig cloudy
die **Wolle** wool
wollen (will, wollte, hat gewollt) to want to
das **Wort, ¨er** word
das **Wörterbuch, ¨er** dictionary
der **Wortschatz** vocabulary
wünschen D to wish
würde would
die **Wurst, ¨e** sausage

Z

zahlen to pay
die **Zahlung: in Zahlung nehmen** to take as a trade-in
der **Zahn, ¨e** tooth
der **Zahnarzt, ¨e** dentist
das **Zahnweh** toothache

der **Zeichentrickfilm, -e** animated film, cartoon
zeichnen to draw
zeigen to show
die **Zeitschrift, -en** magazine
die **Zeitung, -en** newspaper
das **Zelt, -e** tent
zelten to camp out (in a tent)
zerstreut absent-minded
ziehen lassen to let stand
ziemlich rather, quite
zierlich delicate
das **Zimmer** room
die **Zitrone, -n** lemon
der **Zoo, -s** zoo
der **Zoowärter** zoo keeper
zu to; closed **zu D** to, for, on the occasion of
zu•geben (gibt zu, gab zu, hat zugegeben) to add
zu•giessen (giesst zu, goss zu, hat zugegossen) to pour into
zu•machen to close
das **Zubehör** accessories
der **Zucker** sugar
zuerst first
der **Zug, ¨e** train
zugedeckt covered
die **Zukunft** future
die **Zunge, -n** tongue
zurück back
zurück•laufen (läuft zurück, lief zurück, ist zurückgelaufen) to run back
zusammen together
zusammen•stossen (stösst zusammen, stiess zusammen, ist zusammengestossen) to collide
die **Zwiebel, -n** onion
zwischen between

English-German Vocabulary

Most words needed to do the activities in this textbook are included in this English-German vocabulary. Students may find it necessary to consult a dictionary, however, when doing the freer activities and when answering the personal questions.

A

a, an   ein, eine
above   über
absent-minded   zerstreut
accident   der Unfall, ¨e
across   über;
across from   gegenüber
action film   der Actionfilm, -e
acrylic   das Acryl
adventure   das Abenteuer
adventure film   der Abenteuerfilm, -e
advice   der Rat
after   nach
afternoon   der Nachmittag, -e;
this afternoon   heute nachmittag
ago: (two weeks) ago   vor (zwei Wochen)
air   die Luft, ¨e
airplane   das Flugzeug, -e
airport   der Flughafen, ¨
all   alle
allow: to be allowed to   dürfen
along   entlang
along   mit
already   schon
also   auch
always   immer
ambulance   der Krankenwagen
animal   das Tier, -e
ankle   der Knöchel
anniversary   der Hochzeitstag, -e
another   noch ein
ant   die Ameise, -n
apple   der Apfel; **apple cake**   der Apfelkuchen; **apple juice**   der Apfelsaft, ¨e
approximately   ungefähr
aquarium   das Aquarium, die Aquarien
arm   der Arm, -e
armchair   der Sessel, -n
around   um

arrive   an•kommen
as   wie; **as (big) as**   so (gross) wie
ask   fragen; **to ask for**   bitten um A; **to ask a question**   eine Frage stellen
at (time)   um;
at 6 o'clock   um sechs Uhr
athletic   sportlich
athletic field   der Sportplatz, ¨e
attention: to pay attention   auf•passen
aunt   die Tante, -n
awful   schlecht ; schlimm

B

back   der Rücken
back   zurück
back pack   der Rucksack, ¨e
bad   schlecht; schlimm;
too bad!   Schade!
bake   backen
bakery   die Bäckerei, -en
bald head   die Glatze, -n
ballpoint pen   der Kuli, -s
band   die Band, -s
in the band   in der Band
bank   die Bank, -en
bank robbery   der Banküberfall, -e
basement   der Keller, -
basket   der Korb, ¨e;
wastepaper basket   der Papierkorb, ¨e
bathing suit (women's)   der Badeanzug, ¨e; **(men's)**   die Badehose, -n
be   sein
beach   der Strand, ¨e
bear   der Bär, -en
beautiful   schön, herrlich
bed   das Bett, -en
before   vor
behind   hinter
believe   glauben
belong (to)   gehören D
belt   der Gürtel
best   am besten; best-

better   besser
between   zwischen
beverage   das Getränk, -e
bicycle   das Fahrrad, ¨er;
bicycle   das Rad, ¨er; **to bicycle**   Rad fahren
bicycle helmet   der Fahrradhelm, -e
big   gross
bird   der Vogel, ¨; **bird food**   das Vogelfutter
birdhouse   das Vogelhaus, ¨er
birthday   der Geburtstag, -e;
for (your) birthday   zum Geburtstag; **my birthday is in May**   ich habe im Mai Geburtstag; **it's my birthday**   ich habe Geburtstag; **happy birthday**   alles Gute zum Geburtstag
black   schwarz
blouse   die Bluse, -n
blue   blau
board, get on   ein•steigen
body   der Körper
book   das Buch, ¨er
bookstore   die Buchhandlung, -en
bookcase   das Bücherregal, -e
boot   der Stiefel, -n
boring   langweilig
boy   der Junge, -n
bracelet   das Armband, ¨er
brave   mutig
break   brechen; **to break (a leg)**   s. (das Bein) brechen
breakfast   das Frühstück, -e
bridge   die Brücke, -n
bright: bright red   knallrot
bring along   mit•bringen
brother   der Bruder, ¨
bus   der Bus, -se
but   aber
butcher shop   die Fleischerei, -en
by   von; bei; **mit dem Zug by train**
bye   Tschüs!, Wiedersehen!, auf Wiedersehen!

C

cafe das Cafe, -s
cage der Käfig, -e
cake der Kuchen, -
birthday cake der Geburtstagskuchen
calendar der Kalender
call up an•rufen
calculator der Taschenrechner
camera store das Fotogeschäft, -e
camp das Ferienlager, -
camp out (in a tent) zelten
can können
candy die Süssigkeit, -en
candy fancy chocolate die Praline, -n
cap die Mütze, -n
car der Wagen, - ;das Auto, -s
card die Karte -n;
birthday card die Geburtstagskarte, -n
care: to take care of sorgen für
carry tragen
cartoon der Zeichentrickfilm, -e
case der Fall, ⁻e; **case solved!** Fall erledigt!
cashier die Kasse, -n
casserole der Auflauf, ⁻e
castle das Schloss, ⁻er
cat die Katze, -n
cause die Ursache, -n
CD (compact disc) die CD, -s
CD player der CD-Spieler, -
celebrate feiern
chair der Stuhl, ⁻e
change (clothes) s. um•ziehen
character (in a story, play, etc.) die Person, -en
cheap billig
check ab•geben
cheek die Backe, -n
cheese der Käse, -
cheetah der Gepard, -e
chic schick
chicken das Hähnchen
child das Kind, -er
chimpanzee die Schimpanse, -n
Christmas das Weihnachtsfest, -e
church die Kirche, -n
city die Stadt, ⁻e
city hall das Rathaus, ⁻er
clarinet die Klarinette, -n

clean sauber•machen
clean up auf•räumen
clever schlau
clock die Uhr, -en; **alarm clock** der Wecker, -
close in der Nähe
closet der Schrank, ⁻e
clothing die Kleidung
cloudy wolkig
coat der Mantel, ⁻e
coffee der Kaffee, -s
coin die Münze, -n
cold die Erkältung, -en; **to get a cold** s. erkälten
collect sammeln
collide zusammen•stossen
color die Farbe, -n
colored pencil der Farbstift, -e
comb (one's hair) (s.) die Haare kämmen
combine kombinieren
come kommen; **to come from** kommen aus
comedy die Komödie, -n
comfortable bequem
comic book das Comic-Heft, -e
completely ganz
computer der Computer, **computer game** das Computerspiel, -e **computer science** Informatik
conceited eingebildet
concentrate s. konzentrieren
congratulate gratulieren D
conversation: to have a conversation (with) s. unterhalten (mit D)
corner die Ecke, -n
cost kosten; **how much does that cost?** was kostet das?
cotton die Baumwolle; **made of cotton** aus Baumwolle
cough der Husten; **to cough** husten; **cough medicine** der Hustensaft, ⁻e
cousin (female) die Kusine, -n
cousin (male) der Vetter, -n
cozy gemütlich
crafts: to do crafts basteln
crazy verrückt; **you're crazy!** du spinnst!
cream: whipped cream die Schlagsahne
crime movie der Kriminalfilm, -e
crow der Rabe, -n

cruel grausam
curly lockig
curtains die Gardinen (*pl.*)

D

dance tanzen
danger die Gefahr, -en
dangerous gefährlich
dark dunkel
daughter die Tochter, ⁻e
day der Tag, -e; **day before yesterday** vorgestern
dead tot; **dead person** der Tote, -n
delicate zierlich
delicious lecker
dentist der Zahnarzt, ⁻e
depart ab•fahren
department store das Kaufhaus, ⁻er
desk der Schreibtisch, -e
dessert die Nachspeise, -n
dictionary das Wörterbuch, ⁻er
difficult schwer
difficult schwierig
dining room das Esszimmer
disappeared verschwunden
disappointed enttäuscht
disaster film der Katastrophenfilm, -e
dish das Gericht, -e; **main dish** das Hauptgericht, -e
do tun; machen
doctor der Arzt, ⁻e
dog der Hund, -e
dolphin die Delphine, -n
door die Tür, -en
drama series die Unterhaltungsserie, -n
draw zeichnen
dress das Kleid, -er **to get dressed** (s.) an•ziehen
dresser die Kommode, -n
drink trinken
drive fahren
drums das Schlagzeug, -e
dumb dumm; blöd

E

each jeder (jede, jedes)
ear das Ohr, -en
early früh
earring der Ohrring, -e
easy leicht
eat essen
educational lehrreich
elbow der Ellbogen, -
elephant der Elefant, -en

else: what else? was noch?
energy die Energie
engagement die Verlobung, -en
enjoy: to enjoy oneself
s. amüsieren
enough genug
entertaining unterhaltend
enthusiastic begeistert
eraser der Radiergummi, -s
especially besonders
evening der Abend, -e;
in the evening am Abend
every jeder (jede, jedes)
everything alles
everywhere überall
exciting spannend
excuse die Entschuldigung, -
en; **to excuse** entschuldigen; **excuse me!**
Entschuldigung!
exercise die Bewegung, -en;
to get exercise s. bewegen; **to do exercises**
Gymnastik machen
exotic exotisch
expensive teuer
eye das Auge, -n
eye doctor der Augenarzt, ⁻e

F

face das Gesicht, -er
fact die Tatsache, -n
factory die Fabrik, -en
fall der Herbst; **to fall**
fallen
family die Familie, -n
farm der Bauernhof, ⁻e
fashion die Mode, -n
fashionable modisch
fast schnell
fat dick
father der Vater; **Father's
Day** der Vatertag, -e
feel (s.) fühlen; **I'm feeling. . .** es geht mir . . .
fever das Fieber
few wenig; **a few** ein paar
fight der Kampf, ⁻e
find finden
first erst-
fish der Fisch, -e
to fish, go fishing
angeln; **fish sandwich**
das Fischbrot, -e
fit passen D **to keep fit**
s. fit•halten
flea der Floh, ⁻e
floor der Boden, ⁻e

flower die Blume, -n **flower shop** der Blumenladen
flowerpot der Blumentopf, ⁻e
flute die Flöte, -n
fly fliegen
food das Essen
foot der Fuss, ⁻e
for für; **for your birthday** zum Geburtstag;
for Christmas zu
Weihnachten **he has
been here for two days**
er ist seit zwei Tagen hier
forest der Wald, ⁻er
forget vergessen
fountain der Brunnen
fox der Fuchs, ⁻e
free time die Freizeit
French fries die Pommes
frites (*pl.*)
fresh frech
friend der Freund, -e
friendly freundlich
frog der Frosch, ⁻e
from von
front: in front of vor
fruit das Obst
fun: it's fun es macht
Spass; **have fun!** viel
Spass!
funny lustig
funny komisch
furniture das Möbel
future die Zukunft

G

game das Spiel, -e
game show die Spielshow, -s
garden der Garten, ⁻en
gas station die Tankstelle, -n
generous grosszügig
German deutsch (adj.);
(language) Deutsch
get (receive) bekommen
get up auf•stehen
girlfriend die Freundin, -nen
give geben
glad, gladly gern
glasses die Brille, -n; **to
wear glasses** eine Brille
tragen
glove der Handschuh, -e
go gehen
good gut
goodbye auf Wiedersehen;
(on phone) auf Wiederhören!

granddaughter die Enkelin, -nen
grandfather der Grossvater, ⁻
grandmother die Grossmutter, ⁻
grandparents die
Grosseltern (*pl.*)
grandson der Enkel, -
grape die Traube, -n;
grape juice der Traubensaft, ⁻e
great toll
great prima
green grün
greet begrüssen
guest der Gast, ⁻e
guinea pig das Meer-
schweinchen
guitar die Gitarre, -n
gym shorts die Turnhose, -n
gymnastics die Gymnastik
to do gymnastics turnen

H

hair das Haar, -e; **to wash
one's hair** s. die Haare
waschen; **to comb one's
hair** s. die Haare kämmen
hamburger der Hamburger
hamster der Hamster
hand die Hand, ⁻e
hang hängen
Hanukkah das Chanukahfest, -e
happen passieren; **what
happened?** was ist passiert?
happiness das Glück
happy froh
happy glücklich; **to be
happy (about)** s. freuen
(über A)
hard (difficult) schwer
hat der Hut, ⁻e
have haben
headline die Schlagzeile, -n
healthy gesund
hear hören
here hier
hero der Held, -en
hide verstecken; **to hide
oneself** s. verstecken
high hoch
hike die Wanderung, -en;
to hike wandern
hippopotamus das Nil-
pferd, -e
his sein, seine
hobby das Hobby, -s
holiday der Feiertag, -e
home: (to) home nach
Hause; **(at) home** zu
Hause

homework die Hausaufgabe, -n; **to do homework** die Hausaufgaben machen
honey der Honig
hood die Kapuze, -n
hope hoffen
horse das Pferd, -e
hospital das Krankenhaus, ¨er
hot heiss
hotel das Hotel, -s
hour die Stunde, -n; **for hours** stundenlang
house das Haus, ¨er
how wie
human being der Mensch, -en
hungry: to be hungry Hunger haben
hurry s. beeilen
hurt weh tun D; **it hurts** es tut weh
husband der Mann, ¨er

I

ice cream das Eis
ice skate der Schlittschuh, -e; **to ice skate** Schlittschuh laufen
idea die Idee, -n
if wenn
imaginative fantasievoll
immediately gleich
impatient ungeduldig
in, into in
in: in the evening am Abend
infection die Entzündung, -en
injure: to injure, hurt oneself s. verletzen
injured verletzt; **injured person** der Verletzte, -n
injury die Verletzung, -en
inspector der Inspektor, -en
instrument das Instrument, -e
interest das Interesse, -n; **to be interested in** s. interessieren für **interesting** interessant
intersection die Kreuzung, -en
invitation die Einladung, -en
invite ein•laden
island die Insel, -n

J

jacket die Jacke, -n
jewelry der Schmuck
job der Job, -s
juice der Saft, ¨e
junk der Kram

K

key der Schlüssel, -
keyboard das Keyboard, -s
kind: what kind of (a) was für (ein)
kindhearted gutherzig
kiss der Kuss, ¨e
kitchen die Küche, -n
knee das Knie, -
know (a fact, information) wissen;
know one's way around (a place) s. aus•kennen
know (be acquainted with) kennen; **(a fact, information)** wissen; **(how to do something)** können

L

lake der See, -n
lamp die Lampe, -n
landmark die Sehenswürdigkeit, -en
landscape die Landschaft, -en
last letzt-
later später; **see you later!** bis später!
laugh lachen
law Jura
lay legen
lazy faul **to be lazy, do nothing** faulenzen
lead (to) führen (zu)
learn (a trade or occupation) einen Beruf erlernen
left links
leg das Bein, -e
letter der Brief, -e
lettuce der Salat, -e
library die Bibliothek, -en
lie liegen
light hell
like gefallen D; **I like it** es gefällt mir
like mögen; gern haben; **to like to do** gern machen
lion der Löwe, -n
listen to hören

little klein; **a little** ein bisschen
live wohnen
lively lebhaft
living room das Wohnzimmer
long lang
look schauen
look (appear) aus•sehen **look around** s. um•schauen
loud laut
loudspeaker der Lautsprecher
love die Liebe; **to love** lieben
luck das Glück ; **good luck!** viel Glück!
lunch das Mittagessen

M

mad böse
magazine die Zeitschrift, -en
mail die Post
mailbox der Briefkasten
make machen
man der Mann, ¨er
many viel, viele
map die Karte, -n; **city map** der Stadtplan, ¨e
marker der Filzstift, -e
market place der Marktplatz, ¨e
matter: what's the matter? was ist los?
maybe vielleicht
mayonnaise die Mayonnaise
mean böse
meat das Fleisch
medicine die Medizin
meet treffen; **to meet with** s. treffen mit
menu die Speisekarte, -n
mess das Durcheinander
military das Militär: **to join the military** zum Militär gehen
mirror der Spiegel, -
modest bescheiden
monkey der Affe, -n
month der Monat, -e
mood: in a bad mood schlechtgelaunt
morning der Morgen; der Vormittag, -e
mosquito die Mücke, -n

most   am meisten; am liebsten
mother   die Mutter,-
Mother's Day   der Muttertag
mountain   der Berg, -e
mouse   die Maus, -̈e
mouth   der Mund, -̈er
movement   die Bewegung, -en
movies   das Kino, -s **to go to the movies**   ins Kino gehen
much   viel; **how much** wie viel
murder   der Mord, -e
murderer   der Mörder, -
museum   das Museum, Museen
mushroom   der Pilz, -e
mushy   schmalzig
music   die Musik
music store   das Musikgeschäft, -e
musical   musikalisch
must   müssen
mustache   der Schnurrbart, -̈e
mustard   der Senf
mystery   der Krimi, -s

N

name: what's your name? wie heisst du? **my name is . . .**   ich heisse . . .
neat   ordentlich
neck   der Hals, -̈e
necklace   die Halskette, -n
need   brauchen
nephew   der Neffe, -n
nervous   nervös
never   nie; **never yet;** noch nie
new   neu
news   die Tagesschau
news report   die Nachricht, -en
newspaper   die Zeitung, -en
next   nächst-
next door   nebenan
next to   neben
nice   nett
niece   die Nichte, -n
night table   der Nachttisch, -e
none   kein
noodles   die Nudeln;
noodle casserole   der Nudelauflauf, -̈e
nose   die Nase, -n
not   nicht
notebook   das Heft, -e
nothing   nichts

now   jetzt; **now and then** ab und zu

O

o'clock: it's two o'clock   es ist zwei Uhr
observe   beobachten
occupation   der Beruf, -e
of   von
offer   bieten
often   oft
okay   in Ordnung
old   alt
olive   die Olive, -n
on   an; **on top of**   auf   **on Tuesday**   am Dienstag
once   einmal
onion   die Zwiebel, -n
open   auf•machen
orchestra   das Orchester **in the orchestra**   im Orchester
order   bestellen
outing   der Ausflug, -̈e
over   über

P

package   das Paket, -e
pain   der Schmerz, -en
pain reliever   die Schmerztablette, -n
pants   die Hose, -n
parents   die Eltern *(pl.)*
park   der Park, -s
parka   der Anorak, -s
parking lot   der Parkplatz, -̈e
parrot   der Papagei, -en
participate   mit•machen
party supplies   die Partysachen *(pl.)*
past   die Vergangenheit, -en
past (the school)   an (der Schule) vorbei
pay   zahlen
pencil   der Bleistift, -e
pencil sharpener   der Spitzer
pendant   der Anhänger
people   die Leute *(pl.)*
pepper (green)   der Paprika
permission   die Erlaubnis; **to ask for permission** Erlaubnis bitten
person   die Person, -en
pet   das Haustier, -e
pharmacy   die Apotheke, -n
photo   das Photo, -s

photograph   photografieren
piano   das Klavier, -e
pickle   die Gurke, -n
picture   das Bild, -er; **to take pictures**   photografieren
piece   das Stück, -e; **piece of furniture**   das Möbelstück, -e
pizza   die Pizza, -s
plan   der Plan, -̈e; **to plan** planen; **to have plans** vor•haben
play   spielen
playground   der Kinderspielplatz, -̈e
please   bitte
police   die Polizei
police station   die Polizeiwache, -n
polite   höflich
polo shirt   das Polohemd, -en
poor   arm
post office   die Post, das Postamt
poster   das Poster
potato   die Kartoffel, -n; **mashed potatoes**   das Kartoffelpüree
practice   üben
prepare   vor•bereiten **to make oneself something to eat**   s. etwas zu essen vor•bereiten
present   das Geschenk, -e **to give as a present** schenken
pretty   hübsch, schön
protect   schützen
pudding   der Pudding, -s
put   stellen

Q

question   die Frage, -n ; **to ask questions**   Fragen stellen

R

rabbit (domestic) das Kaninchen **(wild)** der Hase, -n
racquet   der Schläger
raincoat   der Regenmantel, -̈
rather   lieber
read   lesen
really   wirklich; **really nice**   ganz nett

reasonable (in price) preiswert
recently neulich
recess die Pause, -n
red rot
regards: best regards herzliche Grüsse
relative der Verwandte, -n
report der Bericht, -e
request bitten
restaurant das Restaurant, -s
rhinoceros das Nashorn, ⁻er
rich reich
ride (a horse) reiten; **(in a vehicle)** fahren
right rechts; richtig gleich; **right around the corner** gleich um die Ecke
river der Fluss, ⁻e
roast der Braten, -
rob überfallen
roller skate der Rollschuh, -e; **to roller skate** Rollschuh laufen
romantic movie der Liebesfilm, -e
room das Zimmer, -
round rund
row house das Reihenhaus, ⁻er
rug der Teppich, -e
ruler das Lineal, -e
run rennen; laufen

S

sad traurig
sail segeln
salad der Salat, -e
sale das Angebot;
on sale im Angebot
sandal die Sandale, -n
sausage die Wurst, ⁻e
scar die Narbe, -n
scarf der Schal, -s
school die Schule, -n; **to go to school** in die Schule gehen
school supplies die Schulsachen (pl.)
schoolbag die Schultasche, -n
science Wissenschaft
scissors die Schere, -n
scream schreien
season die Jahreszeit, -en
see sehen
sell (to) verkaufen (an A)
sensible vernünftig

series die Serie, -n
set setzen
shirt das Hemd, -en
shoe der Schuh, -e
shop der Laden; **to shop** ein•kaufen; **to go shopping** ein•kaufen gehen
shopping center das Einkaufszentrum, -zentren
shopping list die Einkaufsliste, -n
short kurz; klein
shorts die Shorts (pl.)
should sollen
shoulder die Schulter, -n
shower s. duschen
shy schüchtern
siblings (brothers and sisters) die Geschwister (pl.)
sick krank
silly blöd
since seit
sister die Schwester, -n
sit sitzen; **to sit (down)** sich niedersetzen
size die Grösse, -n
ski Ski fahren
ski area das Skigebiet, -e
skirt der Rock, ⁻e
sky der Himmel, -
sled der Schlitten, -
sleep schlafen
sleeping bag der Schlafsack, ⁻e
slim schlank
sloppy schlampig
slow langsam
small klein
smart klug
smile lächeln
smoke rauchen
snack stand der Imbissstand, ⁻e
snake die Schlange, -n
sneaker der Turnschuh, -e; der Tennisschuh, -e
snow der Schnee
soccer der Fussball
sock der Sock, -en
sofa das Sofa, -s
some einige
sometimes manchmal
son der Sohn, ⁻e
soon bald
sorry: to be sorry leid tun D; **I'm sorry** es tut mir leid
soup die Suppe, -n
speak sprechen
spider die Spinne, -n

sport (s) der Sport
sporting goods store das Sportgeschäft, -e
sports report die Sportschau
sprain: to sprain (one's ankle) s. (den Knöchel) verstauchen
spring der Frühling; das Frühjahr
square der Platz, ⁻e
stadium das Stadion, Stadien
stamp die Briefmarke, -n
stand stehen
stapler die Heftmaschine, -n
station (train) der Bahnhof, ⁻e
stay bleiben
steal stehlen
still noch; immer noch
stomach der Bauch, ⁻e
stomachache das Bauchweh
store das Geschäft, -e
storm der Sturm, ⁻e
straight (hair) glatt
straight ahead geradeaus
strange seltsam
street die Strasse, -n
strong stark
study(at a college or a university) studieren; **(for a test, etc.)** lernen
subject (school) das Fach, ⁻er
subway die U-Bahn, -en
suit (man's) der Anzug, ⁻e; **(woman's)** das Kostüm, -e
suit: it suits you es steht dir
summer der Sommer
sunny sonnig
superhighway die Autobahn, -en
supermarket der Supermarkt, ⁻e
supper das Abendessen
surfboard das Surfbrett, -er
surroundings die Umgebung, -en
suspicious verdächtig
swallow schlucken
sweater der Pullover, der Pulli, -s
sweatshirt das Sweatshirt, -s
swim schwimmen
swimming pool das Schwimmbad, ⁻er

T

table der Tisch, -e
take nehmen; **take: take (a walk, a hike, etc.)** machen

tall gross
tape die Kassette, -n
taste schmecken; **it doesn't taste good** es schmeckt nicht
tea der Tee
teacher (male) der Lehrer; **(female)** die Lehrerin, -nen
team das Team, -s
telephone das Telefon, -e
telephone call der Telefonanruf, -e
television das Fernsehen; **television set** der Fernseher **to watch television** fern•sehen
tent das Zelt, -e
terrific toll; grossartig
than: (bigger) than (grösser) als
thank danken D; **thank you** danke; danke schön **to say thank you** s. bedanken **thanks** der Dank **thank you!** vielen Dank!
that das
the der, die, das
theater das Theater
theft der Diebstahl, ¨e
there dort; **over there** dort drüben
there: there is, there are es gibt
thick dick
thief der Dieb, -e
thin dünn
think denken; **to have an opinion** meinen
thirsty: to be thirsty Durst haben
this dieser (diese, dieses)
thrilling spannend
throat der Hals, ¨e; **sore throat** die Halsentzündung, -en
tie die Krawatte, -n
tight eng
tired müde
to zu
to (a place) nach
to shop ein•kaufen; **to go shopping** einkaufen gehen
today heute
together zusammen
tomato die Tomate, -n
too auch; zu **me too** ich auch

tooth der Zahn, ¨e; **to brush one's teeth** s. die Zähne putzen
toothache das Zahnweh
top (clothing) das Top, -s
tourist office das Verkehrsamt, ¨er
traffic light die Ampel, -n
train der Zug, ¨e
trenchcoat der Trenchcoat, -s
trip die Reise, -n; **bicycle trip** die Radtour, -en
truck der Lastwagen
true wahr
trumpet die Trompete, -n
try probieren, versuchen **try on** an•probieren
T-shirt das T-Shirt, -s
tunnel der Tunnel
turn s. drehen; **to turn around** s. um•drehen
turtle die Schildkröte, -n
TV channel das Programm, -e **TV program** die Fernsehsendung, -en **TV schedule** das Fernsehprogramm, -e

U

ugly hässlich
uncle der Onkel
under unter
undress (s.) aus•ziehen
unfortunately leider
until bis
use benutzen

V

vacation (from school) die Ferien *(pl.)*; **(from work)** der Urlaub
vase die Vase, -n; **flower vase** die Blumenvase, -n
vegetable(s) das Gemüse; **vegetable plate** die Gemüseplatte, -n
vegetarian der Vegetarier, *(m.)*; die Vegetarierin, -nen *(f.)* vegetarisch *(adj)*
very sehr
vest die Weste, -n
video game das Videospiel, -e
view die Aussicht, -en
village das Dorf, ¨er
violent brutal

violin die Geige, -n
visit besuchen
voice die Stimme, -n

W

walk der Spaziergang; **to take a walk** spazieren•gehen, einen Spaziergang machen; **to walk** zu Fuss gehen; laufen
wall die Wand, ¨e
want to wollen
wash (s.)waschen
watch s. etwas an•sehen
watch (something) s. (etwas) an•sehen **to watch TV** fern•sehen
water das Wasser
weak schwach
wear tragen
wedding die Hochzeit, -en
week die Woche, -n
weit far
welcome: you're welcome bitte; bitte schön
well gut
well: get well soon! gute Besserung!
whale der Wal, -le
what was
when wann
when wenn
whenever wenn
where wo; **where to** wohin; **where from** woher
which welcher (welche, welches)
while: while (skiing) beim (Skilaufen)
white weiss
who wer
whoever wer
whom: to whom, for whom wem
why warum
wide weit
wife die Frau, -en
will: will be, will become werden
win gewinnen
window das Fenster
windowsill das Fensterbrett, -er
winter der Winter
wish der Wunsch, ¨e; **to**

wish wünschen D; **to**
wish for s. wünschen D;
with mit D
without ohne A
witty witzig
wolf der Wolf, ¨e
woman die Frau, -en
wool die Wolle
word das Wort, ¨er
work die Arbeit; **to work**
  arbeiten
worry die Sorge, -n; **to**

worry about s. Sorgen
  machen um A
would: would like möchten
wrist das Handgelenk, -e
write schreiben

Y

year das Jahr, -e
yellow gelb
yesterday gestern;
  day before yesterday

  vorgestern
yogurt der Joghurt
young jung **young person**
  der Jugendliche, -n

Z

zoo der Zoo, -s
zoo keeper der Zoowärter

Grammar Index

450

Topical Index

Function Index